Kabul: Final Call

KABUL: FINAL CALL

The inside story of the withdrawal from Afghanistan

August 2021

Laurie Bristow

Whittles Publishing

Published by
Whittles Publishing Ltd.,
Dunbeath,
Caithness, KW6 6EG,
Scotland, UK

www.whittlespublishing.com

© 2024 Laurie Bristow
ISBN 978-184995-581-2

CONTENTS

ACKNOWLEDGEMENTS

Most of the people to whom I owe thanks cannot be named: the civilian staff in the FCDO, the Home Office and the MOD, and the military personnel in Kabul who delivered Operation Pitting. They are the very best of us.

A few of them can be named, and it is an honour to do so: Alex Pinfield, Andy McCoubrey, Katrina Johnson, Martin Longden.

The names of some other people have been changed in this book to protect their identities. That does not diminish their contribution.

In addition, I owe a special thank you to Jason, the security manager at the British Embassy Kabul, and to the close protection teams. They kept us all unharmed: that is their job. But they did so much more than that. They got me, and others, through the darkest of times.

Brigadier Dan Blanchford was the mastermind of Operation Pitting and a privilege to work with. Lt Col Dave Middleton and his team demonstrated what resilient and compassionate leadership looks like. Through them, my thanks to the service personnel under their command. The military at Camp Taipan were a joy to live and work with in such joyless times.

Brigadier Tom is at the heart of the events recounted in this book. Together we tracked the final months of the Islamic Republic of Afghanistan, its collapse and the events that followed. His wise advice, sharp intelligence and quirky humour made all the difference. He read early drafts of this book and helped me make sense of some events which made precious little sense at the time.

Nigel Casey, Leslie Craig, the Afghanistan Directorate in the FCDO and the security team in the FCDO had our backs in London.

Ben Shread and James Langan's photography and filming told the story of Operation Pitting for the wider public. James went to great lengths to help identify suitable images for this book and to secure permissions for their use.

Other photos reproduced in the book were taken by members of Operation Pitting. I am most grateful to colleagues who made their pictures available.

Caroline Petherick made countless improvements to the manuscript and helped me think through what I was trying to say. Others who read the manuscript and suggested improvements included Alex Pinfield, Martin Longden, Iradj Bagherzade, Jeremy Condor and Fiona Bristow. James Bristow came up with the idea on which the cover is based.

Keith Whittles and the team at Whittles Publishing steered the project to completion with tact and good humour.

This book is for Fiona, Thomas, James, Hilary and Stanley. And for the families of all those who went before us.

PRAISE FOR KABUL: FINAL CALL

A gripping and gruelling read. Sir Laurie is a natural raconteur. He brings to life the harrowing personal drama of his months in Kabul as well as giving an unflinching inside account of the politics and machinations that accompanied this foreign policy catastrophe. *Kabul: Final Call* is an extraordinary work of contemporary history and invaluable for all who wish to understand how the summer of 2021 felt to those who lived it. It is also a masterclass in crisis leadership and a lesson in the skills of diplomacy. It should be required reading for aspiring diplomats.

The questions Sir Laurie poses and some of his answers merit serious consideration by policy makers. If we do not learn from our history in Afghanistan over the last twenty years and more, we risk future errors and we dishonour those who sacrificed so much.

Despite my knowing many of the people, places and activities Sir Laurie describes so vividly, I still find it impossible to imagine the stress and trauma experienced by all in the summer of 2021. This book brings me closer to that horror than is comfortable. But above all *Kabul: Final Call* is a human story – a fitting testament to the courage of diplomats, civil servants and military who risked their lives to save thousands. Public servants who made the best of things in the worst of times.

Sir Nicholas Kay, *Ambassador to Afghanistan, 2017–19 and NATO Senior Civilian Representative to the Islamic Republic of Afghanistan*

In this truly extraordinary eyewitness account of an historic tragedy unfolding, Britain's last Ambassador to Afghanistan, Sir Laurie Bristow, displays the qualities that led him to be given this challenging assignment in the first place: courage – moral, intellectual and physical – of a very high order, and clear-sighted but compassionate analysis of the faults and failures that led Britain and America to scuttle out of Afghanistan in such disgraceful disorder. It is also very well written, in beautiful clear prose. A must-read for any student of history, great power politics, and politico-military relations.

Sir Sherard Cowper-Coles, *British Ambassador to Afghanistan and Special Representative for Afghanistan and Pakistan, 2007–10*

A frank and thoughtful firsthand account of the fall of Kabul in 2021 from a senior British diplomat. Sir Laurie Bristow brings historical perspective, acute political knowledge of the Western and regional politics and sharp observations about the state of disarray and illusion among the Afghan political leadership. His heart and compassion is a thread throughout the book: compassion for the Afghan women and men betrayed and devastated once more, regard for the soldiers and civilians on the ground, facing consequences of decisions beyond them, as the rug is pulled from under their feet by the political leadership in capitals far away. It is a hard and necessary read about the failure of Western interventions, Afghanistan and how collective political complacency leads to the victory of violence, tyranny and brutality.

Shaharzad Akbar, Executive Director of Rawadari, an
Afghan human rights organization and former chair of the
Afghanistan Independent Human Rights Commission

This is a brutally frank account, beautifully told – an insider's chronicle of a painful unravelling. It is essential reading in our time.

A must-read diary of fateful days seared in memory and history, this is an honest reckoning which raises uncomfortable and essential questions. These are extraordinary stories of chaos and courage from the coalface of a crisis.

Lyse Doucet, a senior journalist and the BBC's Chief International Correspondent

Arriving en scene two months before the fall of Kabul, Ambassador Laurie Bristow gives a taut firsthand account of the harrowing end of the defining conflict of the post-9/11 era. He provides unique insider insight into the decisions and misjudgments that led to the chaotic departure of the US and NATO, the massive evacuation effort, and the Taliban's victory.

J Alexander Thier, CEO of Lapis and former senior
US official responsible for assistance to Afghanistan

A fair, comprehensive account of the events by a brave, committed, and dedicated first hand observer. Britain was very lucky to have had Laurie Bristow as its ambassador at this critical moment and his dignity, calm and common sense define his account.

Rory Stewart, a British academic, author and broadcaster, and former
diplomat and politician. He is the Brady-Johnson Professor of the Practice
of Grand Strategy at Yale University's Jackson School of Global Affairs

PREFACE

I was the last British Ambassador to Kabul during the violent and chaotic final months of the republic in the summer of 2021. I arrived in Kabul on 14 June 2021, expecting this to be one of my toughest assignments in a 31-year career in the British diplomatic service. It was. Eleven weeks later I was on one of the last Royal Air Force flights out of Kabul, ambassador to an Islamic Republic of Afghanistan that no longer existed.

The 20-year US-led campaign in Afghanistan ended in failure, culminating in the collapse of the republic that we had supported, and the return to power of the Taliban whom we had overthrown after the 9/11 attacks. There followed an extraordinary fortnight in Kabul airport when soldiers and civilians carried out the biggest airlift in living memory, made possible by an uneasy and fragile truce with the Taliban – the same people that we had fought for much of the previous 20 years, who had been ejected from power in 2001 and who had themselves just overthrown the Government of the Islamic Republic of Afghanistan by military force.

In this book I set out the events that led to the fall of Kabul and its immediate consequences, as they looked to me at the time. I draw on the notes I made at the time and on information that has emerged since; there were important parts of the picture that I did not see or only partially understood at the time. In addition, in such a fast-moving and utterly chaotic environment, there were some episodes that only made sense after the event with access to information that was not available to me at the time.

For a long time after returning from Kabul in August 2021, I was reluctant to write this book. Several things have changed that. First, a number of people, including the late Iradj Bagherzade, persuaded me that I should record a first-hand account of what this major historic event looked and felt like on the ground while the memory of it was still fresh. In addition, I wanted to give an honest first-hand account of how the decisions and events that led to the fall of the republic looked to someone at the sharp end. And I wanted to pay tribute to the courage of those who carried out the evacuation from

Kabul. I owe that to the people I worked with in Afghanistan, civilians and military, British and Afghans and others. And to the people who went before us. Too many of them lost their health or their lives trying to build a different future for Afghanistan.

In late 2020 I was offered the job of Ambassador to Afghanistan, with a start date of June 2021. I insisted on taking a week to think it through before agreeing. It was a very different proposition from my previous job as Ambassador to Vladimir Putin's Russia, itself one of the toughest assignments in the Diplomatic Service. Kabul was by 2020 one of the most dangerous cities in the world and getting worse – a country torn apart by a war that the Afghan Government was inexorably losing, accelerated by the decision of two successive US presidents to press ahead with the withdrawal of US and allied forces. It was a diplomatic posting for volunteers only.

It was clear in late 2020 that we were approaching a decisive turning point in the Afghanistan campaign, which had been at the top of Britain's defence and foreign policy for two decades, at times bending it out of shape, consuming lives and soaking up resources and political capital.

On 29 February 2020 President Trump had made an agreement with the Taliban, in Doha, Qatar, that all US and NATO forces would leave Afghanistan by 1 May 2021. This would allow him to go into the 2020 presidential election as the man who had got American troops out of Afghanistan. The Government of Afghanistan was not, however, a party to the Doha Agreement, which put it in a very difficult position. Under the agreement, the Taliban had agreed to engage in peace talks with the Government of Afghanistan. It would turn out, however, that in reality they had intensified their war against the republic, seeking outright military victory while playing for time in the subsequent peace negotiations with the Government of Afghanistan.

In between my accepting the job in 2020 and heading out to Kabul in 2021, President Biden succeeded President Trump in the White House. After a short review, Biden confirmed Trump's decision that all US and allied military forces would leave Afghanistan over the summer of 2021.

Even though US, UK and allied military forces were to be withdrawn, the diplomats were to stay on. We would still have work to do. But it was not clear how long we would be able to stay, in a dangerous and rapidly worsening security environment. For the previous 20 years the diplomatic missions had been dependent on the military and their infrastructure. By the summer of 2021 these would be gone. There was not much time to put in place alternative arrangements. When I arrived in Kabul on 14 June 2021 there were still big uncertainties about what would happen when the US and NATO military forces completed their withdrawal during the weeks that followed.

Privately, I thought at the time that there was a high likelihood that the peace negotiations between the Government of Afghanistan and the Taliban would fail. If that happened, and if the Afghan Government lost the war with the Taliban, then the

Islamic Republic of Afghanistan in which we had invested so many lives, so much treasure and so much political capital would collapse on my watch. That would mean that it would fall to me to close the embassy, one of our biggest and most complex in the world. I did not believe that our diplomatic mission would be able to continue for any length of time as we had done for the previous 20 years, when the Islamic Republic of Afghanistan and our support for it had been underwritten by tens of thousands of NATO troops. But even the most pessimistic analysts did not predict that the whole thing would be overturned within weeks of the completion of the US and NATO military withdrawal.

Being an ambassador involves several different things. One is influencing the decision makers in the country you have been sent to. Another is advising and influencing the decision makers in your own government. A third is leading the people you are responsible for, setting direction and delivering results but also looking out for their welfare and safety. The last of these is particularly important when asking civilian staff to work in a war zone. You hold other people's lives in your hands.

In Kabul, as when I was in Moscow previously, a large part of the job was about asking the right questions and setting out the very difficult choices both we and our allies had to make, with clarity and realism about what those choices involved. It was about seeing decisions through, and leading people who were asked to do more difficult things than they ever thought possible. At times it involved putting aside illusions and self-deceptions, some of them deeply ingrained.

Someone had to do it. I do not regret that the task fell to me. I am indebted to all those who were there on the ground in Kabul in the summer of 2021, both soldiers and civilians. The friendships forged in such circumstances are like no others. We shared the highest of highs and the lowest of lows. We lived this story and will live with it for the rest of our lives. We lived with the fear and with the awful responsibility of deciding the fate of strangers. We discovered what we and the people alongside us were capable of in what were probably the most difficult circumstances we would ever face.

Above all, I am grateful to my family and friends, and the families and friends of my colleagues, who supported us selflessly while enduring the fear and anguish that service families go through when their loved ones are in harm's way. The spouses and partners carry the burden not only of their own fears but those of others – in particular, ageing parents, and children who are old enough to work out for themselves what is happening. Holding all that together is the toughest, loneliest job on offer.

I owe an unmeasurable debt to my wife Fiona for carrying that burden so that I could do what needed to be done. Her first question to me, when I asked her in late 2020 if I should take the job, was not 'Why do you have to go?' but 'Can I come?'

INTRODUCTION

NIGHT OF 16/17 AUGUST 2021

I awoke with a start as someone knocked sharply on the metal door, opened it without waiting for an answer, and flicked on the bright ceiling light. The room was small and cold from the aircon. A moment of disorientation, then I remembered: I was in Taipan, the British military base on the airfield at Kabul's Hamid Karzai International Airport. I felt dizzy and sick with lack of sleep. VHF radios beeped and crackled, crisp voices conveying urgent messages of information and instruction. I had slept through all that.

It was Jason, one of my armed close protection team and a former soldier. He was polite but very insistent. 'We need to move you to a safer location, sir. Immediately.' He stepped back outside the room. I pulled on clothes, shoes, body armour, helmet, grab bag. I had laid them out in a row across the floor of the room a couple of hours previously, in anticipation of a rapid move during the night. I pulled my phone and charger out of the wall socket and shoved them into the bag along with laptop and notebooks. Jason and Claire, another of my close protection team, were waiting outside the door, fully kitted up in body armour and helmets, carrying assault rifles. Claire double-checked the essentials: 'Have you got your passport, phone and charger, sir?'

We headed out into the night, moving quickly and deliberately across the blacked-out compound. Other members of the close protection team appeared out of the darkness, forming a box with me in the middle. We moved deeper into the base, picking our way carefully in the darkness across concrete kerbs and around deep potholes. I stubbed my toe on a random lump of concrete, unseen in the darkness. Through a gate in a chain link fence and towards some low buildings. Someone grabbed the handle on my backpack to steer me and to move things along. We broke into a brisk jog. I was glad of the time I had put in on the exercise bike since arriving in Kabul.

Around us, soldiers with weapons and night vision kit moved quickly, quietly and with purpose. They were heading out, beyond the high concrete walls and the relative safety of Taipan, onto the airfield. Later, as they came back in, it was all too clear that things were in a bad way. Out on the airfield was a vision of hell: hordes of desperate people who would do anything to get out of Afghanistan; gunfire and the beat of helicopter rotors as the military tried to move them off the runway and taxiways; smoke, flares and searchlights lighting up the sky. It could have been the opening scenes of a film – maybe *Apocalypse Now*. Except that this was for real.

From the darkness a short distance away, a soldier challenged us to identify ourselves. One of ours. A quick, tense exchange of words and we moved on, into one of the buildings and into the operations room. Everywhere a low, understated buzz of intense concentration and activity. We found seats and were offered coffee.

I checked the time. It was around 2 am. We watched the scene unfolding on banks of TV screens showing feeds from surveillance cameras and imagery from the huge blimp still keeping watch high in the sky over Kabul, from news media and social media. From time to time the military commanding officer updated me on developments. The airfield was overrun by thousands of desperate Afghans. There were people on the runway and the taxiways, in the airport terminal buildings. There were shooters among them. Who knew who or why.

Things were looking bad. Military flights could no longer land or take off. So there was no way out of Kabul, and no way in for the thousands of additional troops who would be needed to secure the airfield. The next few hours would be critical. Would we be able to run an evacuation? Would we get out alive?

I sent a message to the crisis leader working overnight in the Foreign Office back in London to let her know what was happening. Through the night the military kept their operational headquarters updated as they worked on plans to bring more soldiers in and to regain control of the situation.

I stayed put for several hours until the thing was sufficiently under control to allow me to return to my room and get a couple of hours of sleep. I used the time to catch up on a tsunami of emails and messages, many from people desperate to get out of Afghanistan. Every few seconds my phone pinged as a new message came in. People seeking updates. People seeking urgent evacuation. In the middle of a war zone, turning the phone off was not an option. If it rang you answered it, whatever the hour.

The pinging did not stop until 28 August, when, in the belly of a Royal Air Force C-17 transport plane, I switched the phone off.

Dubai airport, 14 June 2021

I was in transit to Kabul to take up my new position as Her Majesty's Ambassador to the Islamic Republic of Afghanistan. I travelled alone. This was an 'unaccompanied' posting. The exceptionally high security risks involved in working in Afghanistan meant that no spouses or partners, no family members, no visitors were allowed. Volunteers only: if any member of staff was no longer willing to accept the risks they could ask to leave. Very few did so.

Usually you feel a sense of excitement and nervous anticipation when travelling to a new job. This time it was a sense of foreboding. I had spent the previous three months in London leading a team putting in place the security arrangements the embassy would need to continue to operate after the US and NATO military forces had left Afghanistan during the summer. There were no good answers to the many questions this raised.

In Dubai airport, as we were called to board the flight to Kabul, I glanced up at the departures sign above the gate: 'Kabul: Final Call'. That seemed to sum things up.

I showed my boarding card and passport to the woman at the desk, and was on my way down the airbridge. The flight was full. Families, businesspeople, government officials, diplomats and others from the large international presence, and their even larger life support and security apparatus.

Twenty years earlier, people had been boarding airliners in Boston, Washington DC and Newark, NJ. Shortly afterwards, those planes would be hijacked and turned into weapons. Everyone who is old enough to remember 9/11 – 11 September 2001 – remembers where they were when they learnt about the attacks in New York and Washington DC. I was in the British Embassy in Turkey, as head of the Political Section dealing with our relations with this critically important country sitting between Europe, the Middle East and Central Asia. One of our Turkish staff called me from the media office: 'Something big's happening. You need to come and see this.' We watched the live TV pictures in shocked silence as smoke poured from one of the Twin Towers. The newscasters announced unconfirmed reports that a plane had crashed into it. As we watched, a plane banked across the screen and crashed into the other tower, removing any remaining doubt that this was a planned and deliberate attack. An hour or so later we saw the Twin Towers collapsing one after the other. A short while later we heard that a plane had been crashed into the side of the Pentagon. Another had crashed in a field as the passengers fought with the hijackers of the doomed aircraft, knowing that they had nothing left to lose.

The rest of my time in Ankara was dominated by the consequences of that day, as the USA and its allies – Turkey and the United Kingdom foremost among them – embarked on military operations to eliminate the threat from al-Qaeda in Afghanistan, to remove its Taliban hosts from power, and then to stabilise and rebuild Afghanistan. Our ways of thinking about foreign policy and national security had to be remade in a hurry, to address threats both from non-state actors and from failed or failing states that offered them safe havens from which to plan and conduct attacks against us and our allies.

In the second half of 2002 I spent six months at the NATO Defence College in Rome, working alongside American and European military officers and diplomats. Our understanding of the strategic threats we faced, and our instruments for addressing them, were changing almost by the day. Some of the military had already done tours in Afghanistan. By the end of our stay some knew they would soon be deployed to another conflict. Throughout that autumn, the Bush Administration and its allies were preparing for the invasion of Iraq.

Back in London I worked on the post-conflict planning for Iraq during and immediately after the invasion in March 2003. The decision to invade Iraq had been deeply entangled with the consequences of the attacks in New York and Washington for US and UK politics and the thinking about national security. And the invasion had a profound impact on the campaign in Afghanistan. The diversion of political attention and resources to the war in Iraq, which quickly went badly wrong, had a lasting effect on the ability of the USA and its allies to carry out the campaign in Afghanistan with the clarity of purpose needed, above all to put in place a stable political settlement and a viable military exit strategy. According to US Deputy Secretary of State Richard Armitage, 'The war in Iraq drained resources from Afghanistan before things were under control.'[1]

Much later, I worked on the metastasising threat from al-Qaeda, its affiliates and its murderous offshoots, including the rise of Islamic State (Da'esh) in Iraq and Syria, one of the calamitous consequences of the invasion of Iraq and what followed.

After 9/11 our armed forces, intelligence agencies, diplomatic service, homeland security and law enforcement agencies re-engineered themselves to address what was thought to be a near-existential threat to our country and our way of life. A generation of diplomats, soldiers, development workers and others learned the language of counterinsurgency, counterterrorism, stabilisation and state building. Many served multiple tours in Afghanistan and Iraq. In Afghanistan in August 2021 the fruits of their work and of their Afghan partners would disappear almost overnight.

The War on Terror had its dark side: Guantanamo Bay, networks of secret prisons, 'extraordinary rendition' (seizing terrorist suspects and moving them across borders), practices that amounted to torture. The USA built a covert drone strike programme to suppress the threat to itself and its allies from terrorists operating from safe havens in Pakistan, Yemen and elsewhere. These decisions had predictable consequences for the reputations of all concerned and for the motivations both of violent extremists and of others who were not terrorists but were caught up anyway.

The United Kingdom spent billions on the wars in Afghanistan and Iraq. The USA spent trillions. No further successful attacks were mounted on the United Kingdom from Afghanistan. But terrorist attacks against the United Kingdom and its citizens did not stop. Nor did the Afghan narcotics trade. The heroin kept flowing, in increasing quantities.

The USA and its allies expended vast amounts of political capital and goodwill, at home and abroad, as the conflicts dragged on. With no end in sight and as the costs mounted, the conflicts became electoral liabilities: no-win quagmires. Public support for the troops no longer translated reliably into public support for, or understanding of, what those soldiers were in harm's way to achieve.

For the United Kingdom, there was something else going on in parallel: our self-image as a global diplomatic and military power. And our vital national interest in being seen by the USA as America's foremost and indispensable ally, in which successive governments in London have invested so much since the 1940s.

Meanwhile, geopolitical rivalries between the world's Great Powers were coming back onto the international agenda. With attention and resources focused on the wars in Afghanistan and Iraq, and on countering terrorism, the threat from a resurgent and revanchist Russia under Vladimir Putin slipped down the agenda; now there were fewer senior diplomats, soldiers and intelligence officers with the depth of knowledge and experience needed to understand that country and the challenge it represented to the United Kingdom and its allies. As Ambassador to Russia in 2016 to 2020, I had worked at the coal face of the geopolitical rivalries that fed and were fed by the conflicts in Afghanistan and the Middle East, and the uneasy and shifting coalitions that sought to manage them.

Meanwhile China was on the rise, economically, politically and militarily. The People's Republic emerged as the major challenger to the USA and the West in the 21st century. And then there were big new challenges competing for attention, above all the onset of the Covid pandemic in early 2020, and the growing realisation that the world was running out of time to address the climate crisis.

By early 2021, the incoming Biden Presidency was clear that the US priorities had changed and that it was time to end America's longest war, in order to focus on those greater challenges. On this, at least, Joe Biden agreed with Donald Trump.

No less compelling than the fall of the Twin Towers were the images of the fall of Kabul 20 years later, in August 2021. Talibs driving pick-up trucks into Afghanistan's major cities, firing their guns triumphantly in the air. Talibs crowding around the desk in the Presidential Palace from which President Ghani had made a TV broadcast to the nation only hours before. An airport overrun with desperate civilians. People standing on planes and collapsing airbridges, walking aimlessly in droves across the runway and taxiways. People running alongside a US Air Force C-17 transport plane as it taxied, one of them laughing and waving his hands in the air as he looked straight into the camera, as if this was some sort of mad carnival. People falling to their deaths as the aeroplane took off, a terrible echo of people falling to their deaths from the Twin Towers nearly 20 years earlier.

And then the images of the evacuation. People handing small children to soldiers over razor wire and concrete blast walls. People being beaten with sticks and lengths of piping. Faces lined with tears of fear and despair. Soldiers and civilians offering small, and large, acts of kindness. A bottle of water. A helping hand. A huge British paratrooper carrying a tiny child on his shoulder, exhausted parents and grandparents shuffling along with whatever of their most precious possessions they could carry in a couple of bags. A puff of smoke as a suicide bomber detonated himself in a crowd of civilians and soldiers. The coffins of more dead soldiers being loaded onto a US C-17, just days before the final withdrawal of the US and allied forces.

In the United Kingdom, the violence and chaos in which the 20-year Afghanistan campaign ended provoked a bitter national reckoning. About what we had been trying to achieve. About why things had ended in the way they did. About the enormous human cost, and what was left to show for it. To the 457 British soldiers who lost their lives in Afghanistan, and the many more who were disabled or mentally broken. To our allies and partners. And above all to the Afghan people who themselves paid such a high price and who are now living with the consequences of the Taliban's return to power.

What happened is too important and too troubling for us to look away from its causes and consequences. The USA and its allies intervened in Afghanistan after 9/11 to prevent the country being used again to launch attacks against us. The public may no longer be much interested in Afghanistan, but – whether they know it or not – they certainly have an interest in the consequences of failure in Afghanistan.

We shall surely face again the dilemmas that a generation of policy makers and implementers faced in Afghanistan. Countering terrorism, insurgency, narcotics trafficking. Trying to build a state in a country where the state has not so much failed as never existed in a form recognisable to us. Addressing grinding poverty, illiteracy, misogyny. Dissuading people from migrating to the United Kingdom in large numbers to find better lives, many of them turning up in small boats across the English Channel.

We need to ask ourselves difficult questions, to recognise and account for avoidable errors and failures, self-deceptions and unwillingness to countenance what we could see was happening before our eyes.

It is also important to value the courage and resourcefulness of those who did the best they could with the hand they had been dealt – Afghans and their allies. This book is about the last few months of the republic and about the two extraordinary weeks in Kabul airport that brought the UK's Afghanistan campaign to a bitter end. It is about what the people who delivered Operation Pitting, the UK's evacuation from Kabul, achieved under the most difficult circumstances imaginable, and amidst all the anger and grief and recrimination that the end of the campaign brought forth.

It is also about why we had to carry out Operation Pitting. It is about the Afghan women and men and their children to whom we had an obligation to fulfil. Many of them were our staff and people we worked with. These people were not passive recipients of our generosity; they were people we had depended on to achieve what we had been in Afghanistan to do, and who depended on us in their time of need.

And it is about what was and is at stake in Afghanistan. It is about our moral and practical obligations as we exercise power and protect our national interests as we see them. It is about what we stand for and about our reputation as a nation, on which our influence and a large part of our military, diplomatic and economic power depend.

The people who delivered Operation Pitting were in most respects ordinary civil servants, diplomats and soldiers. Some were experienced non-commissioned officers, diplomats with multiple tours in conflict zones, experienced Border Force people who days before had been on passport control desks in Heathrow Airport. Many were not. The youngest British soldiers and civilians in Kabul were barely out of school or university.

Whatever their length of service, nothing in their lives could have prepared them for what they were asked to do. In 13 long, gruelling days they delivered the most difficult and dangerous evacuation in recent history, bringing over 15,000 people to safety and the chance of a new life.

Those diplomats and civil servants volunteered to go into the most dangerous city on the planet to bring to safety people they had never met and did not know. Many of the soldiers performed acts of extreme bravery, putting their own lives on the line to bring the most vulnerable people out of the crowds, and to keep some sort of order amidst the mayhem, violence and desperation. They did this only a few paces away from Taliban fighters who had killed and maimed British soldiers and would not have hesitated to do so again if the truce had broken down.

The aircrews kept the flights going, flying heavily overloaded aircraft day and night into and out of a war zone. There were some near misses. A British C-17 transport plane came within a few feet of hitting a minibus that crossed the runway as the plane took off. The skill of the pilots saved not only the hundreds of people on the plane and the bus; a plane crash taking out Kabul airport's sole runway would have put the entire evacuation at risk.

The medics patched up the injured; rehydrated old people and small children who had spent days in the blazing sun; delivered babies. And always in the knowledge that violent and extreme people were somewhere in the crowds. Maybe standing right there in front of you.

People paid a price. Everyone saw things you cannot unsee. A teenage boy in bright blue being physically carried out of the Baron Hotel compound, kicking and screaming, by a soldier whose face was set like stone in anger and frustration and disgust. A soldier hurrying to a medical point carrying a baby with bright red blood streaming from her mouth. The look in someone's eyes when you tell them that they, or one of their family group, do not qualify for evacuation. The look in your own eyes when you are told in return that you are condemning them to death.

Hardened soldiers coming off gate duty showed signs of shock: the thousand-yard stare. Living conditions were basic, especially for the soldiers. Stomach bugs were rife. Covid precautions were non-existent.

One of the Parachute Regiment officers in Kabul said to me: 'We train these young men and women for combat. This is much harder.' The same was true for the diplomats and civil servants, who are not trained for combat.

Inevitably, some have found it difficult to come to terms with what happened in those two weeks in Kabul airport.

Nine months after the end of Operation Pitting I gave a talk at an event in London about Russia's invasion of Ukraine. The first question was from an Afghan man evacuated from Kabul with his family in August 2021. He stood up and asked: 'How does it feel to save someone's life?'

There are British soldiers and others who in turn owe their lives to their Afghan colleagues. I pass the question on to the people who worked on Operation Pitting and to the Afghans to whom we owed that obligation. This is their story.

Part 1: From Doha to Kabul

This story begins in Doha, the capital city of the Gulf state of Qatar, 18 months before the fall of Kabul and the evacuation. On 29 February 2020 the US Government and the Taliban signed the Doha Agreement – the Agreement for Bringing Peace to Afghanistan. The agreement was negotiated bilaterally between the Trump Administration and the Taliban. The agreement was signed by Zalmay Khalilzad, the US Special Representative for Afghanistan Reconciliation, and Mullah Abdul Ghani Baradar, the political leader of the Taliban, at a ceremony attended by representatives of dozens of foreign states. It was published on the US State Department website at the time, and a copy of it is in the Appendix.

The Government of Afghanistan was not a party to the agreement, which was negotiated and agreed over its head. The Government of Afghanistan was nevertheless obliged under the terms of the agreement to make some major concessions to the Taliban, including the release of 5,000 Taliban fighters from government prisons. There was a parallel bilateral declaration between the US Government and the Government of Afghanistan.

At the heart of the Doha Agreement was an undertaking by the Taliban to enter into negotiations with the Government of the Islamic Republic of Afghanistan (GIROA) leading to a new power-sharing government, which would end the decades-long conflict. The USA undertook that its own and other NATO forces would withdraw from Afghanistan by 1 May 2021. The Taliban agreed not to attack US and NATO troops during the withdrawal period.

The Taliban were not required by the Doha Agreement to refrain from attacking the Government of Afghanistan or its forces, or the civilian population. Although a permanent and comprehensive ceasefire was on the agenda for discussion in the intra-Afghan dialogue and negotiations envisaged by the Doha Agreement, it was not a precondition for those negotiations or for the withdrawal of US-led NATO forces.

The Doha Agreement contained no requirement of the Taliban to negotiate in good faith or to reach a negotiated peace agreement before the US and NATO forces withdrew. Nor did it provide for the suspension or reversal of the military withdrawal if the Taliban did not do so.

The fundamental – and catastrophic – flaws in the Doha Agreement were obvious from the moment it was signed in February 2020. The US and NATO

1

military withdrawal was based on a timetable, not on conditions that the Taliban had to meet for the USA to implement its side of the agreement. By setting a timetable for withdrawal rather than conditions for withdrawal, and without a strong peace process, the Doha Agreement gave the initiative to the Taliban, putting the Government of Afghanistan and its allies under time pressure but with no corresponding leverage applied to the Taliban.

This fatally weakened the position of the Government of Afghanistan and of its international supporters. The Doha Agreement handed the Taliban a huge strategic advantage on a plate, and for no significant quid pro quo. It completely undermined the confidence and credibility of the internationally recognised Government of Afghanistan.

It was as if the Afghanistan that the USA and its allies had built and supported was an obstacle to peace rather than a partner in achieving a lasting peace. This was the country described by NATO in its Strategic Partnership Agreement with Afghanistan of May 2012 as a 'major non-NATO ally'.

Although the deal committed the Taliban to peace talks with the republic and to a temporary and undefined 'reduction in violence', the Taliban made no commitment not to attack Afghan Government forces. In reality, the beginning of the 2021 summer fighting season saw the Taliban mount a sustained and dramatic *increase* in violence: a nationwide, well-resourced and well-planned military operation to overthrow the republic. The Doha Agreement did, however, include private US undertakings not to help Afghan Government forces conduct offensive operations against the Taliban.

Nor did the Taliban refrain from assassinations of prominent civilian officials – judges, journalists, civil society activists – in a systematic campaign to gut the republic and its institutions. The United Nations counted over 700 such murders in 2020 *after* the signing of the Doha Agreement, with a sharp surge after political negotiations for a peace agreement began in September 2020. The methods used included drive-by shootings, bombings, and 'sticky bombs' – magnetic mines which could be quickly and simply attached to the target vehicle in Kabul's slow-moving traffic by killers who emerged from the crowds and melted back in again. I once asked my close protection team what the procedure was if we were targeted in this way in our armoured vehicles. The answer was not reassuring. 'Get out and run.'

Even if we were not directly targeted, there was always the substantial risk of what is euphemistically called 'collateral damage': being caught up in an attack on someone else. A consequence of this upsurge in violence for us was that by 2021 the embassies' security regimes in Kabul meant that Western diplomats were to all practical purposes locked down in the Green Zone, the heavily fortified city within a city in the centre of Kabul. That dramatically reduced our ability to read what was happening outside the bubble of diplomats and government officials in our relatively safe haven in the centre of Kabul. What we could see, however, was increasingly ugly and desperate.

The Doha Agreement also included commitments by the Taliban not to host al-Qaeda or other extremists, nor to allow them to threaten the security of the USA or its allies from Afghanistan. The worthlessness of this commitment was exposed graphically when the USA killed Ayman al-Zawahiri, the Emir (leader) of al-Qaeda and said to have been the mastermind behind the 9/11 attacks, in a drone strike in July 2022. Zawahiri was living in a swanky apartment in the very centre of Kabul, apparently with the full knowledge and consent of the leaders of the Haqqani Network, a group of extremely violent militants within the broader Taliban movement, who held top positions in the Taliban administration. Zawahiri's presence in the centre of Taliban-controlled Kabul was clearly contrary to the undertakings made by the Taliban in the Doha Agreement.

And what of the Government of the Islamic Republic of Afghanistan, with which the Taliban had undertaken to negotiate but refused to do so? Much has been written about the mercurial behaviour of that government's leaders, their corruption, factionalism and in some cases, predatory behaviour towards the population of Afghanistan. And about the international coalition's failures to address egregious behaviour in the allies it had helped install and keep in power. That factionalism and corruption fatally damaged the ability of the government to pursue an effective approach to the war with the Taliban or to build support and legitimacy in the eyes of the population, particularly once the USA had made it clear that it was withdrawing military support.

The September 2019 election in Afghanistan was particularly damaging to the ability of the republic to respond to the new situation created by the Doha Agreement between the USA and the Taliban. Ashraf Ghani, the incumbent president, was re-elected with just over 50 per cent of the votes cast. Like the previous election, in 2014, the result was marred by accusations of large-scale fraud; Ghani's opponent, Abdullah Abdullah, refused to accept the outcome. In 2014 the impasse had been resolved by Ghani and Abdullah agreeing to form a National Unity Government, with power shared equally between them.

In 2019, as in 2014, the standoff went on for months. Both leaders claimed victory and organised their own, rival, inauguration ceremonies in March 2020, after the signing of the Doha Agreement. It was only in May 2020 that the two agreed to work together, under heavy US pressure including a threat to withhold financial support. Ghani and Abdullah signed a power-sharing deal in which each would nominate an equal number of ministers. It would be Abdullah who would lead the peace talks with the Taliban that had been envisaged under the February 2020 Doha Agreement.

Throughout the summer of 2021, whenever Western politicians and diplomats like me urged Ghani, Abdullah and other members of the republic's leadership to act with greater unity of purpose, you could almost hear the grinding of teeth on the other side of the table.

For their part, the Taliban simply refused to recognise as legitimate the Government of the Islamic Republic of Afghanistan with which they had themselves undertaken to negotiate under the terms of the Doha Agreement. The Taliban did not consider their own ousting from power in 2001 to be legitimate, nor their replacement by leaders they saw as chosen by the West. Nor did they accept the legitimacy of the political structures from which they were excluded. When faced with an Afghan government whose leaders could not agree on who had won an election – an election, moreover, in whose legitimacy the Taliban themselves did not believe – why would they change that view?

The Doha Agreement's purpose in US domestic politics was to enable President Trump to be well on the way to extricating the USA from Afghanistan before the November 2020 presidential election took place. The internationally recognised Government of Afghanistan was not a party to the negotiations or to the deal, although it involved the USA agreeing with the Taliban that the Government of Afghanistan would take certain actions, including the release of up to 5,000 Taliban prisoners up front. Many of them were fighters who would return directly to the battlefield. Even more damaging to the Government of Afghanistan was the implication that it was the creation of the USA and had no say in the matter. Most damaging of all was the withdrawal of US and allied military support for a republic whose armed forces were by 2021 facing a full-on Taliban military onslaught.

The Taliban were careful to respect their undertakings not to attack US and NATO forces during the withdrawal. But the Taliban showed no such compunction regarding the Afghan Government or its armed forces, embarking on a ruthless, well-planned and executed military campaign to achieve military victory on the Taliban's terms. Taliban negotiators engaged in parallel in political talks with the government, which began in September 2020. But it was perfectly clear from early on that the Taliban had no intention of negotiating in good faith. Their strategy was very clearly to run the clock down in the intra-Afghan negotiations while pursuing military victory.

That would only change if the course of events on the battlefield changed to the Taliban's disadvantage, or if their supporters and sympathisers in Pakistan could persuade the Taliban leadership to seek a negotiated solution. For the United Kingdom, a central plank of our strategy involved working with the military and civilian leadership in Pakistan to use their leverage over the Taliban to create conditions for a stable political settlement.

That meant using the UK's long-standing relationships with the government and the military in Pakistan, and with the leadership in Afghanistan, to try to broker meaningful negotiations between Afghanistan, Pakistan and the Taliban. We were realistic about the prospects of success. Not least because this approach begged several questions.

First of all, which Taliban? The Afghan Taliban were, and are, not a single monolithic entity but a movement representing a spectrum of interests and views. Within that, the military campaign was run by a hard core of extremely violent militants including the Haqqani Network, designated as terrorists by the United Nations. They were winning. Why would they negotiate?

The second question was one that had bedevilled Afghanistan for years. The Taliban's ability to carry out military operations in Afghanistan depended on access to safe havens and facilitation networks in Pakistan. Pakistan had for many years permitted the presence of the Taliban leadership in Quetta, the capital of Pakistan's Balochistan province and close to the border with Afghanistan. The Afghan Taliban were furthermore supported by elements in the Pakistani military, particularly in the shadowy Inter-Services Intelligence (ISI), who were sympathetic to their aims and saw in the Taliban the best prospects of countering India in a proxy war in Afghanistan. The policy, called 'strategic depth', was driven by Pakistan's fear of facing India on two fronts. The logic went something like this: better to have a weak, Taliban-dominated Afghanistan on Pakistan's western border than a strong, Indian-backed Afghanistan.

The legacy of the British Empire was also in the mix. The Durand Line – the border between Afghanistan and British India – had been drawn by the British in 1893. After 1947 it became the border between Afghanistan and newly-independent Pakistan. As the Durand Line cut through the middle of Pashtun tribal areas many Afghan leaders, including Hamid Karzai, elected as President of Afghanistan in 2002, challenged this as the rightful border. Pakistan feared that Afghanistan, with India's support, would attempt to challenge Pakistan's sovereignty over the Pashtun areas on Pakistan's side of the border.

Successive governments in Pakistan had maintained an ambivalent attitude towards hosting Taliban militants who used Pakistan as a base from which to support their operations in Afghanistan against the government and against US and allied forces. This was a source of constant friction between Pakistan and the USA. Pakistan also had, and at the time of writing still has, a serious domestic terrorism problem, and was unwilling or unable to address the presence of violent extremists on its own territory. Under President Obama, the USA ramped up a covert drone strike programme against Afghan and Pakistani Taliban, and against al-Qaeda figures in Pakistan's tribal areas. The programme required the consent of the Government of Pakistan but was deeply unpopular in Pakistan and was regularly denounced by senior Pakistani politicians.

Even if Pakistan's military and the civilian government had wished to put real pressure on the Taliban to seek a negotiated agreement instead of a military victory, it was not clear that Pakistan had enough leverage with the Taliban to achieve this. Particularly not given the speed of the Taliban's military advances, and the US decision to pull its own and its allies' forces out of Afghanistan, in the process pulling the rug out from under the Government of Afghanistan.

It seemed to me that we were very unlikely to succeed in getting Pakistan to change the Taliban's behaviour. I could see no convincing reason to think that Pakistan could or would weigh in to change the Taliban's strategic aims so late in the day, any more than it had done so in the previous 20 years. Pakistan could see as well as we could that the Taliban had the upper hand on the battlefield. Some in Pakistan, particularly in ISI, Pakistan's military intelligence organisation, had gone to great lengths to make that happen. Even if the Pakistani Government or military had wanted to change that, there was formidable inertia in their own system to be overcome. There was just not enough leverage that we could bring to bear on Pakistan – and the leverage that anyone could bring to bear on the Taliban was visibly evaporating by the day as their military campaign gathered momentum.

But that was the policy we had adopted, and the risks and costs of not trying probably outweighed the risks and costs of trying – as long as we did not fool ourselves that this approach was likely to work. The Americans supported our activities, and they evidently had no serious plan of their own to change Pakistan's or the Taliban's calculations, having cast in their lot with the Doha Agreement. When I arrived in Kabul most of the senior people in the Afghan Government made a point of thanking us for our efforts and asked that those efforts should continue. I suspect they did this more in the hope than the expectation that something would come of it.

This work was led by General Nick Carter, the Chief of the Defence Staff, who was personally involved in trying to inch Afghanistan's and Pakistan's leaders forward. I had worked briefly alongside Nick in 2003 on the planning for the administration of Iraq after the invasion. He had served several tours in Afghanistan and knew many of the senior people. The plan for Afghanistan involved trying to get Pakistan's military leadership into the same room as senior Afghans – or in one case, the same British plane – to try to thrash out a realistic plan to shift the Taliban's approach in favour of a negotiated settlement. What that plan might look like was less well developed. These efforts would continue right up to the last day of the republic, by when the Taliban had won the war and there was no Government of Afghanistan with which to negotiate.

The Doha Agreement was President Trump's deal with the Taliban. But in January 2021 the White House had a new occupant. President Biden's presidency began with a national trauma, as Trump claimed, despite all the evidence to the contrary, that the election had been stolen. A mob stormed the Capitol building. America was bitterly divided. What to do about Afghanistan was one among many difficult and pressing questions facing the incoming president. Biden announced a review of Afghanistan policy and specifically the Trump Administration's agreement with the Taliban. The review was completed by mid-April.

The outcome was not a surprise, given President Biden's long-held views on the US military presence in Afghanistan. He wished to extricate the USA from what he saw as an expensive and unpopular legacy war with no prospect of an early resolution, in order to refocus resources and attention on the future challenges to US national security: the growing strategic competition with China; Russia's appetite to challenge the USA and the Western democracies; and global threats to US interests – in particular, climate change and the Covid pandemic.

Reversing Trump's decision to withdraw the military presence would mean being prepared for the likelihood that the Taliban would resume attacks on US and allied forces, with the near-certainty of renewed US casualties. This would have left the new Biden Administration open to political attack by Trump and his supporters on the basis that Trump's Doha Agreement had offered the USA a pathway out of America's longest war, which Biden was squandering at the cost of American lives. The new administration needed to demonstrate a big foreign policy win early on in Biden's first term, after the damage caused by the riots on Capitol Hill to the USA's international reputation and national unity.

On 14 April 2021 President Biden announced that the final withdrawal of US troops from Afghanistan would go ahead:

> I'm now the fourth United States President to preside over American troop presence in Afghanistan: two Republicans, two Democrats. I will not pass this responsibility on to a fifth … I have concluded that it's time to end America's longest war. It's time for American troops to come home.[2]

The final withdrawal would start, he stated, on 1 May and be completed before 11 September 2021, the 20th anniversary of 9/11. The Taliban were warned off any temptation to attack US-led forces during the withdrawal, which would inevitably run beyond the 1 May deadline agreed by the Trump Administration at Doha. Biden committed to supporting the republic, including through maintaining a diplomatic presence in Kabul, with the necessary security arrangements.

Although the nature of the new security arrangements was yet to be determined, it was clear that a substantial military presence would be needed to assure the security of the vast US Embassy and the Green Zone, in which it and most foreign embassies were located, as well as the Presidential Palace and many of the Afghan Government ministries. For the diplomats to stay after the completion of the military withdrawal, and for the government to which they were accredited to survive, the USA would have to act as the security provider of last resort, even after the modest remaining NATO presence, the Resolute Support Mission, had withdrawn.

As the planning progressed, it became clear that this meant a force of some 650 US Marines, with the attack helicopters and other capabilities needed to maintain a secure enough environment for the USA and its allies to keep a diplomatic presence.

It was hard to see how the Taliban would agree to such a military presence, which was clearly not permitted under the published terms of the Doha Agreement, despite the Taliban's protestations that they wanted foreign embassies to stay once they were in power. The Americans' plan did not involve asking the Taliban for their permission.

Biden showed no interest in renegotiating the terms of the deeply flawed Doha Agreement with the Taliban. He kept Zalmay Khalilzad, the architect of the agreement, in position as the US Special Representative for Afghan Reconciliation.

Biden's decision to stick with Trump's Doha Agreement presented a big dilemma to the US Administration, and to us in the United Kingdom. How were we to support the Government of Afghanistan once the military presence had withdrawn? The Taliban were not the government, and we did not view them, or wish to deal with them, as a government in waiting. The Taliban were an insurgency waging war on the internationally recognised government. They had killed and maimed large numbers of Afghan, US, UK and other allied soldiers, and murdered large numbers of Afghan non-combatants. Although they had committed to enter into peace negotiations with the Government of Afghanistan, there was no sign of them planning to do so in good faith.

Whatever its faults, the internationally recognised Government of Afghanistan had consented to the presence of foreign forces, and the purpose of foreign embassies being in Kabul was to work with the government in pursuit of our shared interests. These included security, stability, counterterrorism, counter-narcotics and development. The Taliban were on the other side of the argument on all the big issues that mattered most to us.

When it came to our ability to maintain a presence to achieve those goals after the NATO withdrawal, the picture was no clearer. Regardless of the undertakings in the Doha Agreement, would the Taliban meaningfully distinguish between their military opponents and the Western backers of those opponents? And if they fought their way into power, rather than reaching power through a political settlement, what then? There was no reason to take at face value the assurances that they would guarantee the safety of our staff given by representatives of a movement that had killed over 400 British soldiers over the last 20 years and had repeatedly attacked the diplomatic presence in Kabul. Would agreements made with the Taliban's Political Commission in luxurious hotels in Qatar be honoured by the violent extremists who would dominate the movement in Kabul and across

Afghanistan – the people who had fought their way into power? Would anyone have significant control over the fighters and hardened killers who had been released from prison, either through negotiations between the USA and the Taliban or as the prisons were overrun by Taliban forces? Would the Taliban be able to prevent Islamic State Khorasan Province (ISKP) – the offshoot in Afghanistan of the murderous death cult that had grown out of al-Qaeda in Iraq and Syria – from attacking us or the Taliban or both?

We all knew what failure could look like: the bombings of the US Embassies in Tanzania and Kenya in 1998; the bombing of the German Embassy in Kabul in 2017; the killing of US Ambassador Christopher Stevens in Libya in 2012; the Iran hostage crisis in 1979. Maybe none of this would ever happen in Afghanistan. Nonetheless, our job was to think through how to reduce the risk that it might happen, and what we would do if it did. Hope is not a plan.

And what of the supposed change in the Taliban's outlook since they had last been in power – the so-called Taliban 2.0? There was no reason, other than wishful thinking, to believe that their values had changed during their 20 years in the wilderness. It was not hard to predict what their approach would be to governing Afghanistan if and when they came to power.

The Taliban declared that they wanted international recognition and repeatedly claimed that once they took power they wanted foreign embassies to remain open. But they obviously had little understanding of or interest in what might cause foreign governments to grant or withhold that recognition, or what international donors would be seeking to achieve in continuing to work with Afghanistan under Taliban rule, or what it would take for foreign embassies to stay in the conditions that would likely follow a Taliban takeover. Before the fall of Kabul and since, it has always been abundantly clear that the Taliban want to deal with the outside world on their own terms. Their view of the outside world is through the prism of their long war against what they consider to be foreign usurpers and their Afghan puppets.

Two months into Biden's presidency and with his review of Afghanistan policy still under way, the USA set out a draft 'Afghanistan Peace Agreement', dated 28 February 2021. It was intended to kick-start the peace negotiations agreed in the US–Taliban Doha Agreement a year previously. The draft agreement proposed options for power sharing between the republic's leaders and the Taliban.

The draft Afghanistan Peace Agreement, and a letter from US Secretary of State Blinken to President Ghani and Abdullah Abdullah, were subsequently leaked to Tolo, Afghanistan's leading news agency. Blinken's letter was blunt, setting out in plain language the administration's intention to accelerate peace talks, and the administration's wish that that both sides should engage urgently. Blinken made clear to Ghani and Abdullah that the USA was 'considering the full withdrawal of our forces by May 1st, as we consider other options'.[3]

Blinken's letter ended with a stark warning:

> Even with the continuation of financial assistance from the United
> States to your forces after an American military withdrawal, I am
> concerned that the security situation will worsen and that the Taliban
> could make rapid territorial gains. I am making this clear to you so
> that you understand the urgency of my tone regarding the collective
> work outlined in this letter.

The USA proposed a senior-level meeting between the Government of
Afghanistan and the Taliban in the coming weeks, to finalise a peace agreement.
The meeting was to be hosted by Turkey, with Qatar and the United Nations as co-
convenors. The USA intended to enlist the cooperation of the major regional players
through the United Nations: Russia, China, Pakistan, Iran and India.

Ghani rejected a US proposal that a transitional government should be formed
with the Taliban, proposing instead the formation of an interim government that
he would lead until elections could be held. But the Taliban refused to accept any
government headed by Ghani, and refused to engage seriously with the Istanbul
peace talks while foreign forces remained in Afghanistan.

The Taliban then declined to attend a peace conference in Turkey in early April,
stating that the timing was not right. Undaunted, the United Nations, together with
Turkey and Qatar, announced that a conference would take place in Istanbul starting
on 24 April and running through to the first week of May, to accelerate the intra-
Afghan peace process.

The Taliban again pulled the plug. Taliban spokesman Mohammed Naeem stated
on Twitter that:

> Until all foreign forces completely withdraw from our homeland, the
> Islamic Emirate will not participate in any conference that shall make
> decisions about Afghanistan.[4]

In other words: the Taliban would only negotiate with the Government of
Afghanistan once the Taliban's position had been immeasurably strengthened, and
the government's position fatally undermined, by the completion of the withdrawal
of the US-led forces. In the meantime the Taliban would fight on.

The fighting season was getting under way, and the Taliban were the ones with
the momentum. Biden's 14 April announcement that US and allied military forces
would be withdrawn by 11 September could hardly have come at a worse time. As
the fighting intensified the republic and its army were subjected to a double blow:
the loss of vital military support, and the loss of confidence in the determination of

the USA and its allies to continue to support the republic in which we had invested so much over the previous two decades.

Even before the announcement, Afghanistan's armed forces had had little prospect of turning the tide of the war decisively in their own favour. The best realistic scenario was that Afghanistan's armed forces might somehow struggle through to winter and achieve what negotiators call a mutually hurting stalemate. This could have stood a chance of changing the Taliban's incentives in favour of negotiating a power-sharing agreement. But Biden's 14 April announcement and the rapid military withdrawal that followed demolished any realistic prospect of achieving even that low level of ambition.

Why did the Biden Administration do this? I think they had concluded that there could be no realistic conditions-based approach without an open-ended commitment to keep US forces in Afghanistan. US officials told the media that Biden had concluded that a conditions-based approach, which had been the approach for the previous two decades, was 'a recipe for staying in Afghanistan forever'.[5]

The US Administration judged that the terrorist threat to the USA emanating from Afghanistan had been reduced to a level where it could be addressed 'without a persistent military footprint in Afghanistan and without remaining at war with the Taliban'.[6]

The political priority for Biden was to get the US military out of Afghanistan. The strategic priority was to refocus US resources and energy on higher-profile challenges.

The missing elements in the equation were, unfortunately, the likely effect on Afghanistan, and the negative impact on the global reputation of the USA and its allies far beyond the immediate consequences for Afghanistan.

Dissenting voices within the US system and the wider alliance argued that a modest continued military presence would make all the difference, changing the balance of power between the government and the Taliban and giving the intra-Afghan negotiations a better chance of delivering a negotiated agreement. That would, however, involve going back on elements of the Doha Agreement, and would bring with it the risk that the Taliban would resume attacks on NATO forces. There was no cost-free or risk-free way out.

The Doha Agreement had committed the USA to reducing the number of US military forces in Afghanistan to 8,600 within 135 days of the agreement being signed (that is, by 13 July 2020), and to withdraw all remaining forces within 14 months (by the beginning of May 2021). But at the beginning of 2021, NATO's Resolute Support Mission still had 9,600 troops in Afghanistan. Of these, the US contingent comprised about 2,500 and the UK about 750.

This was a far smaller presence than at the height of the war. The Resolute Support Mission was not a combat mission fighting the Taliban. But it did provide vital underpinning to the Government of Afghanistan's forces through provision of training and equipment, support to key capabilities, in particular the air force, and through the political support that such a presence provided to the internationally recognised Islamic Republic of Afghanistan. Above all it provided a tangible commitment to the future of the republic that the USA and its allies had helped bring into being and had supported for 20 years.

Following President Biden's announcement, NATO Foreign and Defence Ministers formally agreed to begin the withdrawal of NATO's Resolute Support Mission, and to complete the task 'within a few months'.[7]

As mentioned earlier, the withdrawal was planned to take place starting 1 May 2021, and to be completed by 11 September – the 20th anniversary of the 9/11 attacks. The exact timetable was deliberately ambiguous, to give the military commanders flexibility to carry out the withdrawal safely, and to keep control over the political timetable and the public narrative. The military and political risks were substantial because of the scale and speed of the military withdrawal, the uncertainties about how the Taliban and others would behave as the withdrawal took place, and the perception that the USA and its allies were walking away from Afghanistan after a 20-year campaign.

The US military commanders moved quickly to implement the President's decision. With the political decision made to withdraw, it was clear that force protection – the safety and security of the troops – during the drawdown was paramount. The security risks were real. They would materialise in the most hideous way with the terrorist attack at the Abbey Gate on 26 August.

The political risks of the withdrawal were real as well, and were visible even as the military withdrawal was taking place. On 30 June, as the NATO withdrawal was nearing completion, General Miller, the US Commander of the NATO Resolute Support Mission in Afghanistan, briefed the media:

> The security situation is not good right now.... Civil war is certainly
> a path that can be visualised if this continues on the trajectory it's on
> right now. That should be a concern to the world.[8]

But the political decision to leave had been made, and the consequences of that were for those who had made the decision.

The 20-year Afghanistan campaign had cost the lives of thousands of NATO soldiers and many tens of thousands of Afghans. It had also brought the promise of a better, freer life to an entire generation of Afghan girls and boys. It had cost the USA over $2 trillion, most of that on the military campaign. It had also involved huge resources being put into building an army; health and education systems; a legal system; a state. What would become of that legacy?

Would the withdrawal of foreign military forces catalyse the warring parties to agree a path to a political settlement? Or would it bring about the opposite? Would government forces be able to contain an accelerating Taliban insurgency? Would the republic hold together? Would Afghanistan in effect disintegrate, with a return to the warlords and multi-sided civil war after the withdrawal of the Soviet Union in 1989?

It was clear that we were in for a difficult summer. The Afghan Government's best hope was to hold onto key cities, and to achieve a stalemate on the battlefield, with neither side able to advance and both sides feeling pain. And over time to change the Taliban's calculations to the point when they believed their interests would be better served by negotiating a power-sharing agreement than trying to take Kabul and other big cities by force.

Achieving this would be a tall order. It would require the Afghan National Defence and Security Forces to hold the Taliban's advance during the summer fighting season while being rapidly weaned off the practical and moral support of NATO's Resolute Support Mission. It would require effective leadership, strategy and logistics, and the ability to motivate Afghanistan's armed forces to fight a ruthless and determined opponent without the underpinning provided by NATO. With an army that had been designed and built to work with US-led international forces, not to fight alone.

It would also require much greater clarity and unity of purpose among the senior politicians in Kabul and across Afghanistan than had ever before been seen. The republic was less a coherent political entity, more an ever-shifting kaleidoscope of personal ambition and rivalry, ethnic and geographical allegiances, warlords and deal-making. Any Western politician, diplomat or soldier who thought they really understood how power and patronage worked in Afghanistan was probably missing something important.

Part 2: The Transition

Following Biden's April 2021 announcement that the USA would withdraw the US and NATO forces, the UK's Prime Minister and senior ministers decided that we should try to maintain an embassy in Kabul for as long as possible. The purpose of doing so was to provide support to the Afghan Government, in particular in its efforts to achieve a negotiated deal with the Taliban; to carry out our top priority counterterrorism, development and counter-narcotics work; and to support the Afghanistan Relocations and Assistance Policy (ARAP), the resettlement scheme for Afghans who had worked for us and whose lives were at risk as a consequence. Alongside these priorities, we needed to put in place contingency plans in case things deteriorated further or faster than expected.

There was a degree of conflict between these aims. Afghanistan had been for some years one of the UK's top foreign policy priorities. In 2010, Prime Minister David Cameron had identified Afghanistan as the UK's top foreign policy priority.[9] The UK Embassy in Kabul was one of our largest and most complex, reflecting both the importance of the mission and the difficulty of achieving it. We had major national security, stability and development interests in Afghanistan which would, if anything, become more important and much more difficult to sustain once NATO forces had withdrawn. And there was a clear political imperative: to stay the course, and to 'protect the gains' of the last 20 years – the improvements in governance, women's rights, education and health compared to the Taliban years and the civil war that had followed the Soviet withdrawal.

None of these things would be possible without a functioning Afghan state to work with. Nor would they be possible without a properly staffed and defended embassy capable of operating in a conflict zone without military support. If and when the situation became untenable and we had to leave, we would need to do so quickly, and as safely as possible. That meant reducing the number of embassy personnel to the bare minimum needed to function. It meant pressing ahead with relocating those Afghan staff who were most at risk, even though we still needed them to run the embassy. As time wore on, we were increasingly trying to keep the embassy working while taking steps that would make its closure all but inevitable.

There was also a wider picture. If we moved too early to close the embassy, reduce its size, or relocate from the Green Zone to the airport, we could be the trigger that set off a rush for the exit by the international community, in turn contributing to the collapse of the Afghan state. But we could not run the risk of moving too late, putting our people in unacceptable jeopardy. A big terrorist attack against the embassy, or losing people who had been caught up in fighting for control of Kabul, would have major political consequences for the UK Government, on top of the personal consequences for the people injured or killed.

And if we had to close the embassy, there would still be things we needed to do in Afghanistan – but working from outside the country, 'over the horizon'. In particular, we would need to put in place measures to protect the United Kingdom and its interests from terrorists operating out of Afghanistan, in a world where we would no longer have eyes or ears or hands or allies in Afghanistan. That too required advance planning, and any arrangements would take time to put in place.

The Joint Intelligence Committee (JIC) is the committee of senior officials, drawn from the relevant ministries and agencies, whose job is to look at all the available information and to advise the UK Government on major developments affecting defence, security and foreign policy interests. So it was the JIC who reviewed the outlook for Afghanistan following Biden's decision to complete the military withdrawal.

No one has a crystal ball, and the JIC is no exception. Usually, such assessments set out a range of possible scenarios. In the spring of 2021 the JIC's central scenario was that Kabul was unlikely to fall in 2021. But we all recognised that this was only one of many scenarios: the collapse could happen sooner than expected, or the Afghan Government might hold on until the end of the fighting season.

In the event, the rapid fall of the provincial capitals then of Kabul itself came as a shock to everyone, including the Americans, the European allies, and even the Taliban themselves.

But in the months before that, the high level of uncertainty about what would happen, and the scale of the risks involved, meant that we were trying to do three things at once. First, the military withdrawal: ending our 20-year military presence in Afghanistan, at speed and while trying to minimise the risk to our military personnel. Second, transitioning to new arrangements to support a very large embassy in a war zone, to meet ministers' decisions to stay and deliver top-priority work after completion of the military withdrawal. Third, contingency planning for how we would evacuate from Kabul if things fell apart. This would almost certainly depend on bringing back to Kabul the very military that we were withdrawing. For the United Kingdom, the timetable for the first and second of these was set by the US military withdrawal timetable. For the third, by events on the battlefield.

There was a personal dimension to all of this. My private view was that we might still be there in a year's time but that the odds were against it. I went to Kabul knowing that the embassy would probably have to close on my watch. If that happened, the responsibility to get our people out safely would fall in part to me. And I did not want to be the person explaining to the parents or partners or children of our staff why their family members had been killed, maimed or captured so that we could keep an embassy open for a few more days or weeks to achieve goals that were no longer clear or had become unachievable. A generation of military commanding officers had already been in that position. I did not envy them.

The political decision had been made to withdraw NATO forces, and the military withdrawal was under way to a tight timetable. The race was on to transition to new arrangements for our embassy without the support of a large military presence. In April 2021 I set up a Transition Task Force, based in the Foreign Office (FCDO) and drawing in a team across Whitehall, to take on the huge amount of work involved. As the incoming ambassador, I had a personal interest in getting this right; those of us based in Kabul were going to have to live with the results of the Task Force's work. We worked closely with the outgoing ambassador, Alison Blake, and her team in Kabul, with Nigel Casey, who as Afghanistan Director was the senior official responsible for day-to-day policy and operations, and with the FCDO's specialist security team in London.

There were no good options, in a poor, war-torn and landlocked country 3,500 miles away with a Taliban offensive that was gathering momentum with each passing day. All options involved substantial costs, for an embassy that had for many years been one of our largest and was still by far our most expensive anywhere in the world. And substantial risks, for the dozens of diplomats we needed to keep in place there; Kabul was already the most dangerous environment in the world, and about to get even worse.

We asked a lot of our staff, in Kabul and London. Everyone knew that mistakes could have serious consequences. More than once, individual members of staff confided to me their unease about the highly dangerous situation we would be putting our colleagues in if we kept them in Kabul after the military withdrawal. I listened carefully to their reasoning, and used it to test and improve our planning.

More than once, the options we put forward prompted sharp questions and barely concealed anguish from senior officials and ministers. On several occasions Nigel and I were told by a very senior official that we would have to find ways to offset the mounting costs of keeping the Kabul operation going. Easy to say, not possible to achieve. On another occasion we were accused by a senior minister of optimism bias.

Their comments completely missed the point. The bottom line was this: the government had taken the decision to keep an embassy in Kabul. That would inevitably involve increased costs and risks, which needed to be balanced against each other and against what ministers wanted us to achieve. I wondered more than once whether I should remind those people that it was not their lives that depended on the security arrangements in Kabul. I bit my tongue.

To keep the risks within manageable limits, we put tighter constraints on the number of staff allowed to work in the embassy at any one time. In April 2021 there were over 800 people working on the site – a mixture of British, Afghan and third-country staff, diplomats, security and support staff. In May 2021 we reduced the maximum number of British staff in Kabul at any one time from 115 to 75, and an overall cap of less than 500. Now, although Kabul was still one of our largest embassies in the world, it was a more manageable proposition if we had to evacuate in a hurry. In effect, we were reconfiguring the embassy so that it could stay open and deliver its core functions while getting it into a state where it could be closed quickly and with the lowest risk we could achieve to the lives of the people working there.

My rule of thumb was that the only people who should be in Kabul at all were those doing essential, top-priority work: work that had to be done, and had to be done in Kabul. But this put additional pressure on an already heavily loaded team. And the size of the security and logistical challenge in keeping an embassy open meant that it would be hard to reduce the guard force and logistics support regardless of how many, or few, 'front-line' diplomats we kept in Kabul. The vast majority of staff were life support and guards, and the nature of the environment meant that there was limited scope to reduce their numbers without fundamentally compromising the embassy's security or viability.

One of the hardest questions to resolve was whether we would be better off keeping the embassy on its current site or moving elsewhere. By April–May 2021 we had narrowed the options down to a short list of realistic options: one was to keep the embassy where it was, with necessary adjustments; a second was to move it onto the former NATO Resolute Support Mission compound, which the US Embassy planned to take over and make available to friendly embassies, with security and other services to be provided by the USA, at a substantial cost and an unknown timetable; another option was to move to the airport, where we already had a heavily fortified military base, Camp Taipan, next to the runway.

All had downsides. The current embassy was large and rambling, spread across three interconnected compounds on the edge of the Green Zone. An embassy – particularly this one – is a complex machine. Keeping it secure and capable of functioning was a major undertaking, particularly in a deteriorating security environment. But it was what we already had and it worked. The security and life support systems were well tried and tested.

Moving into the NATO Resolute Support Mission compound would involve major upheaval and we would have to make significant infrastructure improvements to create even a rough and ready functioning embassy. I was concerned that if we went down that route we would do little else beyond moving house during the decisive period following the end of the NATO military withdrawal, when events would be moving quickly and we should instead be delivering what we were there to do.

Taipan, our military base at the airport, was out of the city centre and much less difficult to defend. Located on the airfield just south of the runway, it had obvious advantages if we had to evacuate in a hurry. But if we were working from an improvised office at a military base out at the airport it would be much harder for us at the embassy to do what we were there to do. Every meeting with the Government of Afghanistan and international partners would involve a difficult, risky move across town. There would be frequent times when security lockdowns meant that moving off the base would be out of the question. And the political message given out by our camping at the airport would not be great, implying that we had set up shop in the departures lounge. We would rapidly lose relevance.

A longer-term option was to build a new embassy in the Green Zone. This had been under consideration for some years. A site had been identified. But this would take years to complete, and the cost would be huge. I knew from previous postings how much time and attention building a new embassy, or refurbishing an old one, would take. That would end up being our main task for years to come. At exactly the wrong time for it to be soaking up time and attention.

The least bad overall option was to keep the embassy where it was for the time being but to develop contingency plans to use Taipan as a fallback site. Even so, we had to fend off a steady stream of interjections from senior people around Whitehall, particularly in the Ministry of Defence, who wished to share their sometimes trenchant views but who had not actually looked at the details and did not bear any responsibility for making it work.

In Afghanistan, the fighting season was under way. Things were not going well for government forces. The Taliban were making progressive gains on the battlefield, gaining momentum in the north, seizing control of major supply routes and putting regional capitals under pressure.

On 21 April 2021 the UK's FCDO changed its travel advice for Afghanistan. The government had previously advised against all but essential travel to Afghanistan. The FCDO now advised against *all* travel to Afghanistan. The intention was to send a clear message: against a darkening sky, actively to discourage people from travelling to Afghanistan, and to encourage those already there to leave. One effect of the FCDO advising against all travel is that it makes it all but impossible to get travel insurance, and in most cases invalidates existing cover, incentivising people who do not have to be there to leave. As the crisis unfolded in July and August, the travel advice would harden further. In one or two cases, we contacted individual British citizens at particularly high risk to urge them to get on the next plane.

But you cannot make people leave. Nor is it possible to keep an accurate and up-to-date record of every British citizen's whereabouts in a country that is sliding into chaos. We did not have accurate numbers of British citizens in Afghanistan, or of British citizens of Afghan origin. The UK Government does not keep tabs on its citizens as they leave the United Kingdom and travel the world. In a crisis abroad, an inaccurate and out-of-date record is worse than useless; you waste time and scarce resources chasing people who are not even in the country or do not need your help – time which could be better spent helping people who are in trouble and do need help.

As the crisis unfolded, we were aware of Afghan-British dual nationals travelling to Afghanistan to try to get their Afghanistan-based families out. These arrivals were British nationals of Afghan origin living in the United Kingdom, and who had wives and children living in Afghanistan: families who had never lived in the United Kingdom and did not hold UK passports or, in some cases, had no documentation of any kind. During Operation Pitting in August 2021 this led to extremely complex cases presenting at our Evacuation Handling Centre, which we set up at the Baron Hotel next to Kabul airport. Changes to the UK's immigration rules made in 2012 meant that many of these dependents did not qualify for settlement in the United Kingdom, often because the spouse could not speak English to the required level or because the family could not demonstrate sufficient income to qualify for a visa. In mid-August, at the beginning of Operation Pitting, the Home Office temporarily waived these requirements, faced with the impossible task of applying them in the chaos and desperation of Kabul airport.

There was one young British man who travelled into Kabul as the republic fell, on a form of extreme tourism. He was found and put on an evacuation flight. I doubt that he considered for a moment the dangers faced by the soldiers, officials and Royal Air Force people running the evacuation flights, or by the Afghans being evacuated on those flights, for whom this was anything but a game.

Throughout April and May work continued to put in place the arrangements needed for allied embassies to stay after the completion of the NATO military withdrawal – above all, a secure Green Zone, a secure airport, and a major trauma hospital capable of keeping casualties alive after a terrorist attack. Without any one of these, our embassy, like others, would have to close.

This work was led by the Americans, who intended to keep their huge embassy open. In place of the security blanket provided by NATO's Resolute Support Mission, the USA created what was initially named the Diplomatic Assurance Platform, later renamed US Forces – Afghanistan, which replicated much of the security infrastructure for the Green Zone and the airport previously provided by Resolute Support Mission, with substantial contributions from the United Kingdom, Turkey and other allies. But it was going to take time to put the arrangements in place, and Afghanistan in 2021 was not a place where you wanted to keep people if you were not certain that the arrangements to keep them safe were adequate. The existing military arrangements were being rapidly dismantled.

Throughout April and May and into June there was a real possibility that we would be forced to suspend or close the embassy despite our best intentions, through our inability to meet our legal and moral duty of care to our staff.

Closing an embassy of this size and complexity, in this environment, would be a very big operation and would need to be done quickly if it was to happen. Doing so as part of Operation Cattalo, the UK military withdrawal, would be by far the safest and least costly option. The timetable for Operation Cattalo was in turn set by the US and NATO withdrawal timetable, since NATO and US forces needed to leave Afghanistan in a set order to minimise the risks to the military. Operation Cattalo allowed a short window – a few days in June – for the military to assist with evacuating the embassy. Once the embassy close-down was started, it would quickly become irreversible. But if we stayed on when Operation Cattalo was completed, the UK military would be gone and we would be on our own.

Until ministers took the decision to stay, we were doing an increasingly tricky juggling act, trying to keep our options open for as long as possible. In turn, the ministerial decision depended on whether we had sufficient assurance from the Americans about security arrangements to keep embassy staff in Kabul after NATO's departure.

In these circumstances, putting off a decision to leave with the military meant that in reality we were taking a decision to stay, and to risk a more dangerous, hurried and expensive departure later. Our UK military colleagues showed flexibility within their own withdrawal timetable, allowing us to defer decisions until the last possible moment to keep all options open while we worked on putting in place the necessary arrangements.

By early June, and with vital pieces of the jigsaw puzzle yet to fall into place, the timetable for taking a 'stay/go' decision for the embassy loomed large. Contacts intensified both with the US Administration, as we worked on the detail of the arrangements, and with the Turkish Government, who were in discussions with the Americans about taking over responsibility for the security of the airport.

Others were drawing their own conclusions. On 28 May the Australian Embassy suspended activities and withdrew its staff.

President Joe Biden and Prime Minister Boris Johnson met on 10 June, ahead of the G7 Summit in Cornwall. Our continued presence in Kabul was on the agenda. Biden gave Johnson an assurance that the key enablers would be in place before the final departure of NATO troops. The discussions gave us enough confidence in the arrangements being put in place to take the decision to stay. I handed over my work in London, packed my bags and travelled to Kabul a few days later.

When a newly appointed ambassador arrives in post, there is an important formality to be observed: handing over Letters of Credence to the Head of State. These are letters signed by the Queen (since September 2022 by the King) and addressed to the Head of State of the country to which you are being sent, naming you as the ambassador and 'recalling' your predecessor. Although written to a set formula, Letters of Credence are an important part of the theatre and the practicalities of diplomacy. They reflect the fact that you are the representative of the state that has appointed you, with full powers to speak and act on behalf of its government. Hence the rather grandiose title of 'Ambassador Extraordinary and Plenipotentiary'.

Meanwhile, though, there were more mundane matters to attend to. During the early summer, with the decision still to be taken in mid-June on whether the embassy could stay open, we had debated whether it made better sense for me to go to Kabul or for Alison, my predecessor, to stay on and close it down, if that was where things were headed. By early June there was enough confidence that the decision would be 'stay' to allow us to go ahead with the handover. But it did mean a very tight timetable for putting all the arrangements in place.

Farida, the FCDO's friendly and efficient protocol officer in London, worked with Buckingham Palace to get the Letters of Credence signed and delivered quickly to the Foreign Office. The Palace played their part, and I received scanned copies of my Letters of Credence by email at the beginning of June. But that left us with a tricky logistical question; although I would be leaving for Kabul in a few days the originals were still in transit to me, taking their time, and the Afghan Government would only accept the signed originals for presentation to President Ashraf Ghani. A printout of an email would not do.

I really needed to take the originals to Kabul in my backpack. It was not as if you could courier them to the Green Zone and expect them to arrive. Apparently it was not as if you could courier them across London and expect them to arrive, either.

I left for Kabul without them, wondering if I would be the person who had to ask the Queen to sign a spare set. Fortunately, the ever-resourceful Farida recovered them from the courier firm, and Simon, one of my senior staff, flew out to Kabul with them just in time for my meeting with President Ghani.

In the week before departure, a new ambassador would expect to be in regular contact with key staff about their arrival arrangements: who will meet you in the VIP room at the airport, will there be media, when you would like your first staff meeting, that kind of thing. My pre-departure exchanges included one with Leo, my chief of staff, about sizes for body armour and helmet, which the close protection team would need to bring to the airport for the journey into town. And with Matthew, the embassy's press officer, to agree media lines in case all the planning fell through at the last minute and I arrived just in time to announce that we were closing the embassy. If things fell apart I might be turning round and coming back within a few days or weeks of arriving in Kabul. If so, I would need to make carefully worded statements for Afghan, UK and international audiences. But not before telling senior members of the Government of Afghanistan. And especially our Afghan staff, so that none of them would find out from the media, and we would be able to explain what would happen to them next.

My most important exchanges were with Alison Blake, my predecessor. We had known each other for many years, and had worked closely together during the transition period, putting in place arrangements for the embassy and its staff to stay in Kabul beyond the departure of NATO, UK and US military forces. Alison had had an incredibly tough posting, leading the embassy through a year of Covid lockdowns, major security scares and the difficult decisions about whether the embassy could stay or would have to leave. Normally a departing ambassador would leave a few weeks before the arrival of the new ambassador. Alison stayed to the very end, only leaving the day before I set off from London.

Part 3: Her Britannic Majesty's Ambassador to Afghanistan

SUNDAY 13 JUNE – MONDAY 14 JUNE

I set off for Kabul on 13 June 2021. An overnight flight changing in Dubai, then a three-hour hop across the Gulf, Iran and Pakistan, before descending over majestic mountains and desert into Kabul. I travelled light: a couple of large bags and a backpack. The first rule of such postings is: do not take anything you are not prepared to leave behind. You might have to leave in a hurry.

I arrived early afternoon on 14 June at Hamid Karzai International Airport, Kabul's civilian airport, universally referred to as HKIA and named after the first president of the post-Taliban Islamic Republic of Afghanistan. I was met at the door of the aircraft by the armed close protection team and quietly hustled off down some side stairs to the VIP room. A quick 'getting to know you' chat with the close protection team while we waited for passport formalities. Then kit up in body armour for the drive into town in a three-car formation of armoured Land Cruisers – Civilian Armoured Vehicles, or CAVs. I was slightly surprised that the convoy set off not towards the main civilian terminal but along a dirt road parallel to the runway, bouncing across deep ruts and broken concrete service roads, stopping at a blank steel gate set into high concrete walls. The gates swung open and we entered Taipan, the UK military base on the airfield, before slipping out onto the highway into town with all the anonymity that a trio of armoured and armed Land Cruisers can muster.

This was my first sight of Taipan – our fallback location if it became necessary to close the embassy.

We headed into the centre of town, the drivers weaving deftly through Kabul's anarchic traffic, always keeping moving, eyes everywhere. Both the driver and the close protection officer had assault rifles tucked beside their seats. At the Wazir Akbar Khan roundabout we turned out of the traffic, passing quickly through concrete chicanes and security barriers to the relative safety of the heavily fortified Green Zone, behind high concrete blast walls and watchtowers. Through a series of security checkpoints and into the embassy. The lead and tail car blocked the approaches to the gate as my car turned into the Residence Compound: my new home.

The Kabul embassy was a sprawling network of fortified compounds, the size of a small town, improvised over 20 years. A spartan place of just-about-serviceable offices and utility buildings. Among the 130 or so buildings were garages and workshops, a canteen, a generator farm, a water purification plant and a sewage plant. Dotted along the streets were thick concrete shelters into which you would dive for protection from indirect fire (mortars, rockets, artillery, shrapnel and falling debris) if the need arose. Armoured vehicles were always on standby in case we needed to move quickly and unexpectedly, day or night. There were guns everywhere, carried by people who knew how to use them.

A modest brass plate by the residence door bore the royal crest, and announced: 'Residence of HBM Ambassador to Afghanistan'. (HBM stands for Her/His Britannic Majesty.) The same formula is used on the diplomatic bags.

My previous Ambassador's Residence, in Moscow, had been anything but modest: a grandiose 19th-century sugar baron's trophy mansion on the banks of the Moscow River, overlooking the Kremlin. It had hosted an incredible array of historical figures: Her Majesty the Queen, Princess Diana, H.G. Wells, Winston Churchill, Anthony Eden, a string of foreign secretaries, and some of the less savoury Bolsheviks, from Stalin on down through the Soviet pecking order. We did our best to use it to attract Russia's brightest and best as well as the people who actually held power in Putin's Russia.

The arrangements in Kabul were rather different, and the list of past visitors had a different profile. We had long since given up the magnificent old Legation Building at Karte Parwan, intended by Lord Curzon to be the grandest house in Asia but now fallen into disrepair and impossible for us to keep secure. In its place we had a heavily fortified suburban villa which I shared with the on-duty close protection team. Downstairs were some comfortable but not opulent reception rooms for official entertaining. An incongruously shiny baby grand piano stood under the stairs next to the operations room and armoury, where the duty team monitored the CCTV feeds and the VHF radio. Upstairs was a small private flat with sitting room, office and bedroom. My predecessor, Alison, had thoughtfully installed an exercise bike; although there was a gym and sports facilities on site it would be all too easy to get no exercise at all, particularly under Covid lockdown conditions. Outside was the haven of the garden, with a small lawn, trees and potted plants – a pleasant place to sit during the hot summer – and a drained and covered swimming pool.

The trees were populated with mynah birds. The UN compound went one better, with great strutting peacocks, who liked to sit on top of the outhouses. and kept us entertained with the occasional fan display.

I held many of my meetings in the garden, with tea and chocolate brownies for those who wanted them; the soldiers always welcomed the brownies. It was not the Moscow Residence. But I've lived in much worse places.

In the private flat was an armoured refuge into which the close protection team hustled me during security lockdowns. If the alert was particularly serious one of them would sit with me in case we needed to extract from the building. It is a bit like sitting in a wardrobe, with a heavily armed young man or woman, radios and adrenalin crackling, the occasional bead of sweat running down your neck. Under the benches were water, snacks, sanitiser, masks and a full first aid kit. A tip from a predecessor was to leave a book in there. You could be there for minutes, or hours. Nothing too cerebral. You are not likely to be in the mood for Tolstoy.

My close protection teams were the A-team. All ex-military. Professional, upbeat, ever polite and helpful, friendly while always maintaining a correct distance. And always alert. Reading my book one weekend afternoon, I became aware of strange clicking sounds outside. It was the sound of rifle bolts as Nick, the head of the team, put his people through weapons drills on the lawn. The very best. They needed to be. Later, in Kabul airport, I came to understand just how much we depended on these people to get through the day in one piece.

A few weeks earlier I had attended the obligatory week-long Hostile Environment training course in the countryside near London. The course included several days of training in first aid, and exercises on how to maximise your chances of a good outcome when caught up in tricky situations involving hostile people with guns. We practised getting into body armour at speed. It is harder than it sounds. Body armour is heavy, and it is difficult not to whack yourself in the face with it when swinging it over your head. It is especially hard to get into or out of when in the back of a car. It seems to get quite a lot harder when the President's protocol people are waiting for you to step out of the vehicle or to wave you off after a meeting. Occasionally the close protection team rescued me, with tact and good humour, when I trapped myself in it.

Even when at home or in the office, you need to be able to put your body armour on in seconds. That might be all the time you have before incoming rounds hit the building or the windows are blown in. You might, or might not, get a few seconds' notice from a loud siren linked to sensors warning of indirect fire or some other form of attack. I had a set of body armour in my apartment, another in my office in the embassy building, and a third in the car. There were spare sets for staff on racks at the bottom of the stairwell in the main office building, away from windows.

If you are under fire or a bomb has gone off, get low and get under cover if you can, and get your body armour on as soon as possible, while lying down if necessary. There may be casualties: your friends, your staff, your close protection team may be among them. Always position your body armour and helmet where you can find them quickly, in the dark. You don't have to wear them in bed (you can if you want, though it is not recommended except in the most extreme circumstances). But put suitable clothes and shoes nearby. You could be moving at speed, in the dark, across broken glass and rubble. Being hustled into a bunker by your close protection team, in your second-best underwear with one shoe missing and your body armour on back to front is not a look to aspire to. Especially if you are the ambassador. The close protection team's job is to keep you alive. Looking good is a secondary issue.

Like all embassies in Kabul, we observed strict Covid protocols. A Covid outbreak could quickly overwhelm the medical support system. And with people living and working in close proximity, a single case of Covid could quickly become a big outbreak. Everyone, ambassadors included, had to observe strict quarantine protocols including daily testing and working in isolation in the week after arrival. Our no-nonsense nurses administered the Covid tests, robustly if necessary. In the cars, the front and back seats were separated by thick plastic sheeting, adding to the surreality of the experience. If you were in quarantine but had to move around the compound, you wore a hi-vis vest so that others could keep their distance. If there was a significant outbreak the embassy quarantined itself. When I arrived in Kabul in June, both the Americans and the Russians were in Covid quarantine.

The 14 June NATO summit took place in Brussels. President Biden and President Erdoğan of Turkey met, with the intention on the USA side of securing Erdoğan's agreement that Turkey's capable military should take lead responsibility for securing Kabul airport. Erdoğan agreed in principle, but subject to further negotiations on the details, and a final political decision. Negotiations continued into late July.

The Taliban made it clear that they did not agree to Turkish forces being deployed to the airport.

Also on 14 June we passed our hard deadline for a decision on whether the embassy could stay open after the NATO withdrawal or would have to close, with all staff and sensitive materials withdrawn as part of Operation Cattalo. Even though the UK's decision had been taken in principle a few days before, following President Biden's assurances to Prime Minister Johnson, this deadline felt like a significant moment: a moment when you realise that you are crossing a threshold and there is no going back to how things were before.

Early on in the transition planning, it had become clear that once the military had gone we would need our own systems to track and try to predict a rapid deterioration in the security situation that would call into question our ability to stay in Kabul. We developed a matrix of 'indicators and warnings', borrowed from the military, to spot any significant changes in a range of military, political and logistical factors which could trigger a decision to leave. These included some unglamorous but essential services that were potential show-stoppers if they broke down. Such as: does the water purification unit work, and can we get the embassy sewage tanks emptied? If the answer to either of these was No, the embassy would become uninhabitable very quickly, making the decision for us. We knew how much water we consumed per day and how many days it took for the sewage tanks to fill up. Checking into a local hotel while we sorted things out was not going to be an option. The Taliban had a history of attacking the hotels.

The purpose of the indicators and warnings was to inform decision making: do we stay or do we go? If the signals are flashing red and it's time to go, the aim is to recognise that the situation is changing while you still have time to do something about it. If things deteriorate quickly you may be left with few options, none of them good. Nor do you want to be a boiled frog.

By any rational standards, unless we were confident that we would see a crisis coming and either keep people safe or get them out quickly, we should not be in the middle of a war zone without military back-up in the first place.

Each week, the indicators and warnings matrix, in whose design I had been involved in London, came to me for final sign-off before being sent back to London for the formal decision on whether to stay or close. Each week I asked my colleagues and myself the key questions: Is this an accurate reflection of the relevant facts and judgements? How confident are we that we know what is actually happening? Where do we expect things to be a few weeks from now? Should we still be here? Those were the questions and their answers that we needed to put each week to the foreign secretary, with our best advice on what to do on the basis of that information.

Each week the Red–Amber–Green ratings crept inexorably in the wrong direction, from Green to Amber to Red.

Pakistan's Foreign Minister Qureshi, speaking at a conference in Islamabad on 14 June, said that Pakistan's long-standing policy of 'strategic depth' was now obsolete. For many years Pakistan had seen its relationship with Afghanistan through the prism of its difficult relationship with India. Pakistan had pursued a policy of strategic depth, seeing Afghanistan as a means by which India could put Pakistan under pressure on two fronts, and therefore a country in which Pakistan had to maintain a strong position. What that meant in practice was hotly contested.

Pakistan's government was now trying to pivot away from a geopolitical approach towards relations with its giant neighbour India towards a geo-economic approach, which would enable Pakistan to benefit from India's economic dynamism. Foreign Minister Qureshi claimed that a 'paradigm shift' had taken place and that Pakistan was no longer seen by others as part of the problem but as part of the solution in Afghanistan.

But it was hard to read Pakistan's real intentions, or even to ascertain whether Pakistan's military and civilian leadership were pursuing the same strategy in Afghanistan. The Taliban were certainly pursuing a united and very effective strategy – to seize power by military means. Their strategy was working, and it depended on their continued access to their own version of 'strategic depth' in Pakistan: Taliban leaders and militants had for many years used Pakistan as a safe haven from which to pursue their aims in Afghanistan. But by many accounts there was more to it than that: how far did they receive active support from at least some elements of Pakistan's military, in particular from ISI, Pakistan's military intelligence organisation?

In this fast-moving and increasingly dangerous situation, who was setting the agenda? Who had leverage over whom?

TUESDAY 15 JUNE

For any ambassador a key part of the job is to keep in close touch with your political masters back home. You need to understand what London needs from the embassy and make sure London gets it. And also to make sure that London knows what is actually happening on the ground, what that means for the UK's interests and objectives, and that the objectives set by London are grounded in reality.

You are also the senior representative of the United Kingdom in the country to which you are sent. To do the job properly you have to get out and about. You have to get to know the people who take the big decisions and the people who influence them. You have to earn their trust, and you have to learn how far to trust what they tell you. Building that trust can take years. It was clear that I was not going to have years. More like weeks.

Being an ambassador is not all about high politics and grand strategy. You are also responsible for running a complex organisation. A big part of the job is about your responsibilities to the people working for you. Especially when working in a war zone, where the lives of your staff are at risk.

The day after my arrival Katrina Johnson, one of my senior staff, and that day's close protection team took me round the embassy site. It was a good opportunity to get to know Katrina. Dependable, practical, kind and down-to-earth: someone you would definitely want on the team in a place like Kabul.

Known to all as BEK, short for British Embassy Kabul, the embassy was the size of a compact small town built around two roads in the centre of Kabul. They had once been through roads – ordinary city streets. But for the last 20 years the Green Zone had been walled off from the world outside by high blast walls and heavily fortified check points. Then since 2017, when a huge truck bomb had exploded near the German Embassy, killing over 150 people and blowing out the windows in the British Embassy a short distance away, the approaches to the Green Zone had in turn been protected by an Enhanced Security Zone. Now, at the entrances to the Enhanced Security Zone stood truck-sized security screening equipment.

Like all the roads in the Green Zone, the streets running through the British Embassy were now a complex web of checkpoints, concrete chicanes, heavy steel barriers and guard houses with firing positions, under our control and not open to the public. On the edge of the heavily fortified Green Zone, the British Embassy was responsible both for its own security and for one of the main gates to the world outside the zone. A large contingent of contracted guards – former soldiers from the Indian subcontinent, and Afghan guards – provided security. Everyone would say a cheery hello and wave each time I passed. It was common to pass members of the guard force doing their fitness routines in the intense midday heat.

The Ambassador's Residence was located in the Archipelago, a row of villas with gardens along 15th Street, off the Wazir Akbar Khan roundabout. The Archipelago was uncomfortably close to the Green Zone perimeter wall. As security deteriorated and we looked to deepen our defences, the future of the Archipelago came increasingly into question. We started to move people deeper into the compound, further away from the Green Zone's external boundary and behind more layers of defence.

A short walk across 15th Street, and through two heavily fortified security checkpoints, lay the main embassy compound, known as the Bulgarian site after its original owners. At its heart was the main embassy building, a functional office block, heavily reinforced and with a large satellite antenna on the roof. The Bulgarian site included the canteen, a generator farm and numerous work buildings, centred around a small garden area and a war memorial. Two antique cannons from an earlier Afghan campaign served as a reminder of the long and difficult history of the UK's involvement in Afghanistan. And, as if we needed reminding, of how badly things could go wrong in Afghanistan.

Next door was the German Embassy and a large area of walled-off waste ground, abandoned after the huge truck bomb in 2017. On our site I was shown shrapnel damage to a steel shipping container building; the shrapnel had gone straight through the metal walls of the container, and the holes had been patched over. Later, visiting my German colleague, I saw the scale of the damage done to their embassy in 2017, still visible in shuttered and unusable buildings. Since the attack the Germans had maintained a minimal staff in Kabul.

Other near neighbours included the Canadians and the Japanese. The Japanese Embassy was protected against rocket attacks by high steel curtains. And, nestled between my residence and the Canadians, the home of Foreign Minister Hanif Atmar. Some months after the fall of Kabul, Hanif told me that our houses were now being lived in by senior Taliban.

Across the road, through more big steel gates with watchtowers, lay more of our embassy: the Egyptian site. The origin of the name is obscure, though I have heard that it comes from 'Egyptian PT', army slang for sleeping. Workshops; the medical centre; a gym, tennis court and swimming pool; and 'Pod Land', where most of the embassy staff lived. A pod is a tiny one-room flat based on a metal shipping container, unique to the more 'expeditionary' (meaning dangerous) environments in which the Foreign Office operates. Stacked two high, the pods in Kabul included steel shutters on the windows and sandbags on the roof to give a degree of protection against blast and shrapnel. A modest baggage allowance meant that people could personalise their pod to make it a bit less like living in a tin box.

31

Watching over the Green Zone was the Blimp, also known as the Aerostat – or, for the technically minded, the Persistent Threat Detection System. A huge tethered helium balloon hovering day and night high above Kabul, the Blimp was our eye in the sky, sending video and data feeds to operations rooms across the Green Zone. Later, after the Green Zone had ceased to exist, we watched from the airport as the Blimp, the target of countless small arms fire, slowly deflated, collapsed and then one day disappeared.

In the background beyond the Green Zone were the spectacular and austerely beautiful mountains that encircle Kabul. An instant way to get your bearings was to look for the antennae mountain – the forest of TV and radio masts on the top and upper slopes of Koh-e Asamai – due west of Kabul. It must offer quite a view of Kabul. The one time I asked the close protection team about the feasibility of taking a ride up there the hint was met with worried frowns, and I let it drop.

The perimeters of the Green Zone, and most roads inside it, were lined with high blast walls, known as T-walls because of their shape (an inverted T). Driving along a road lined with T-walls was like travelling along a concrete canyon, punctuated by fierce speed humps which the drivers of our heavy, armoured Land Cruisers negotiated with respect. Every few hundred metres there were security checkpoints with chicanes at intersections and entrances. The more sensitive the location the more alert the guards and the thicker the concrete. By late July the guards' nervous energy could be palpable, even in the heat of the afternoon, particularly on the approaches to the Arg (the Presidential Palace complex), the US Embassy and the NATO Resolute Support Mission headquarters. And at each checkpoint, a special bay for safely clearing weapon chambers, usually consisting of a steel barrel filled with sand with a pipe sticking out of the top. Even inside the Green Zone, we tended to travel in two- or three-car convoys, the close protection team ever alert. Each journey started with a security briefing. It was wise to listen carefully to it each time.

Travel by CAV is far removed from any caricature of ambassadors in feathered hats making stately progress in their Rolls Royce with the Union Flag flying. First, no Rolls Royce and no flag – and no other distinguishing marks on show. Not even diplomatic numberplates. These were on the sun visors, to be displayed only briefly on approaching checkpoints. The CAV of choice is a Toyota Land Cruiser. The vehicles are heavy, with uprated brakes and suspension. Survivability is a much higher priority than comfort or elegance. The outside world looks slightly odd when viewed through thick bullet-resistant glass. The onboard electronic countermeasures equipment (against remote-controlled bombs) puts out a lot of noise and heat, which the air conditioning barely keeps up with in a Kabul summer. The armour plating makes the door entrances smaller than expected. Body armour and helmets make you fatter, taller, heavier and less agile than you are used to; there is a knack to getting in or out with any decorum, and it is easy to get stuck. The close protection teams kept the vehicles supplied with hand sanitiser, face masks, a map.

British Embassy Kabul was a posting where you could walk to work. But with a difference. To set foot outside the residence, even to get to the office five minutes away, meant being accompanied by at least one close protection officer, armed. I preferred to walk to meetings where I could. For the exercise, but also to see and be seen around the embassy; you quickly become seriously detached from reality and from the people with whom you work if you see the world through an inch of armoured glass. Beyond the embassy, the options for walking to meetings were severely limited. Only the UN compound was sensibly possible, and even then with a close protection team and an armoured vehicle hovering in the background.

Meetings outside the walls of the Green Zone required advanced planning, and usually an advance recce team. More than once my team expressed serious unease with a venue. The first time they did this they were clearly worried that I would overrule them, putting all of us at serious risk. I made it clear that I would always respect and follow their expert advice. If their advice was that the risks were too high, we would make alternative arrangements. After that, they told me what I needed to know, not what they thought I wanted to hear.

I was glad to see that our drivers tried to be considerate towards other road users. It was hard to do this when navigating the teeming swirl of beaten-up goods vehicles, antiquated Ladas, heavily laden handcarts, pedestrians, bicycles, small children and animals while also keeping a beady eye out for suicide bombers, sticky bomb operatives and gunmen. It seemed as if the majority of men carried guns. Safety depended on being assertive and keeping moving where possible, despite often gridlocked traffic with no obvious rules of the road. We regularly encountered fast-moving cavalcades of black SUVs with blacked-out windows, which showed no consideration for anyone. It was hard not to see the looks of impotent hatred and contempt these vehicles aroused in the eyes of the ordinary people.

Kabul street life was insanely photogenic. But in the summer of 2021 it would have been insane to get out of the vehicle and start taking photos. I had to be content with watching through inch-thick glass, and remembering.

As with any newly arrived ambassador, my first month or so was taken up with rounds of meetings. The top priority was to get to know the people who ran the country and their closest advisers, starting with President Ghani, whom I met within days of arrival, to present my credentials.

A close second in Kabul were the key members of the international community – the USA and other NATO allies, the United Nations, the European Union delegation and the big humanitarian agencies. And also the ambassadors of the big regional powers, with whom we had more complex relations: Pakistan, India, Russia, China, Iran.

No less important than this is to lead and motivate your team. Diplomatic posts and development offices in conflict areas attract resilient, highly motivated people who relish making a difference and doing consequential work despite the hardships and the dangerous working environment. Morale is often higher than in the more comfortable first world posts.

But Kabul was a seriously difficult and stressful environment. Things were moving quickly, the stakes were high, and the worsening security situation meant that we needed to keep staff numbers in Kabul as low as possible, inevitably increasing the load on those who stayed on. But the highest priority work still had to be done, and workloads were very heavy, with most people working long days and seven-day weeks.

On top of the high and rising security risks, the Covid pandemic had made a difficult situation much worse. Covid protocols had severely constricted the lively social life that often goes with people making the best of adversity. The rotation pattern (six weeks in Kabul, two in the United Kingdom or elsewhere) was essential if staff were to work under these conditions for a year or more, but only barely feasible under global pandemic conditions. Particularly when airline routes closed down and quarantines became the norm.

You needed the team to be focused on what really mattered and to be at the top of their game. And to be working as a team: the diplomats, our military colleagues, and the large number of people who kept the show on the road providing life support and security services.

Covid made it much harder to do any of this. Yet despite the difficulties morale was high, and people were there because they believed in what they were doing. Many of the British staff had a deep personal attachment to Afghanistan and its people. Some had served multiple tours.

Nevertheless, uncertainty about the future hung heavily over everyone – particularly our Afghan staff, who did not have the option of two-week breather breaks every couple of months, and whose families were not safely in the United Kingdom. During the height of the global pandemic, most had been unable to work on site at the embassy. Those who did were often required to live on site to minimise the risk of bringing in Covid cases. This was on top of the mounting risks to them and their families from Taliban reprisals for working for the foreigners.

My first week, still in Covid quarantine, was dominated by briefing and planning meetings, usually in the residence garden to take advantage of the warm summer and to stay within Covid isolation protocols. One of my first meetings was with COMBRITFOR (Commander of British Forces), Brigadier Olly Brown. His arrival was preceded by the growling of Foxhounds, mine-resistant ambush-protected military vehicles (MRAPs), pulling up in 15th Street in front of the residence. Young soldiers with sunburn and nervous, watchful eyes took up defensive positions in the street. Many of them were about the same age as our sons. Olly was straightforward, brisk and to the point; like all the military I worked with in Kabul, the sort of person you would want to have alongside you in that environment.

I asked Olly if we were testing our judgements and analysis rigorously enough. Were we reading the situation accurately? Were others reading the situation differently? If so, why was that? We needed to make our own judgements but also to understand why others were reaching theirs – especially if these were different from ours or the Americans'. Above all, we needed to be vigilant against optimism bias and groupthink: seeing what we wanted to see rather than what was actually happening.

It crossed my mind to ask Olly if, when the military pulled out, he could leave a few Foxhounds behind. Maybe some helicopters too. Although rather more conspicuous than a Toyota Land Cruiser, a Foxhound is also considerably more heavily armoured. Just the thing if and when the time came to extract ourselves from Kabul. The Foreign Office does not have its own army. The diplomats rely on the real thing for that.

I had met most of the embassy leadership team before, in person or online. Everyone knew we were in for a busy and difficult summer. With my deputy, Alex Pinfield, and the heads of section I set out my priorities and how I wanted us to work together. A relentless focus on delivering top priority work and dropping lower priority work. But we would only succeed in this environment if we all worked together to build a mutually supportive working culture and looked after our people. In such a high-intensity, high-threat environment, with people working and living under pressure in close proximity, small problems can quickly become big problems. Conversely, teams thrive in a difficult environment where people actively look out for everyone else's welfare. In particular, we all needed to spot any signs that one of our colleagues was not coping. Such postings are volunteers only, and no one could or should be required to stay against their will.

When a new ambassador arrives there is a degree of curiosity and some nervousness among the staff. What is the new boss like to work with? Will they want to change everything? In Kabul in June 2021 this was compounded by the bigger uncertainties. I held an all-staff 'townhall' meeting online because of Covid restrictions. It was important that everyone saw my face and heard what was at the top of my priorities, on my first working day. Doing it online meant that it was far more difficult than usual to sense the mood in the 'room'. Many of our staff were Afghans, working remotely from their homes outside the Green Zone. All were desperately worried about their future, and considering whether they and their families would have to leave. Most were hoping they would be accepted onto ARAP, the British Government's Afghan Relocations and Assistance Policy resettlement scheme. Yet although they listened intently to what I had to say, there were few questions.

Just how do you lead a team through this?

Later, I went over to the office for a discussion with seniors in London on a secure video conferencing system, about our efforts to encourage the Pakistani military to push ahead a meaningful political negotiation between the Taliban and the Afghan Government.

We heard that gunmen had killed five polio workers in Jalalabad. The Taliban denied involvement. The murders were probably the work of Islamic State – ISKP. We put out a statement condemning the attack. While it was important to express sympathy and solidarity with the victims, we knew this had not the slightest prospect of changing the minds of the people who had carried out the attack. What kind of people kill health workers administering polio inoculations to children? Wrong question. IKSP see the media coverage and the revulsion that such attacks generate as the point of the exercise, not an unfortunate by-product of it. Their aim was and is to maximise the bloodshed and mayhem, and profit from it, with the ultimate aim of pushing the Taliban aside and emerging as the rulers of their own Caliphate.

WEDNESDAY 16 JUNE

My first meeting with a senior government official took place within two days of my arrival. Still in Covid quarantine, I dialled into a video conference between President Ghani's National Security Adviser Hamidullah Mohib, and a group of ambassadors from the major donor countries. The subject was Women, Peace and Security, a theme of UN-sponsored development work. During the 20 years of the republic gender equality had come a long way from the Taliban years. But there was still a lot to do. There had been reports of sexual abuse of women police officers in the Interior Ministry. We needed the government to understand that this kind of incident risked damaging the confidence of the major donors; in addition, the republic's treatment of women and girls was a fundamental and defining difference in values between the republic and the Taliban with whom it was at war.

I made a more general point, which became a central theme in my meetings with senior Afghan politicians over the weeks that followed. The republic's leaders needed to explain to ordinary Afghans in very clear and compelling terms what was at stake for them – why it mattered deeply to them that the Taliban should not fight their way back to power.

I asked: 'How can we help?'

Mohib replied: 'I like your style,' and asked for support from the international community to build a more effective strategic communications capability.

Later that day I joined an internal embassy meeting to discuss progress on the Afghanistan Relocations and Assistance Policy – ARAP. The question of what to do about Afghan military interpreters and civilian staff had been growing for years, reflecting the scale and duration of the UK's military, diplomatic and development programmes in Afghanistan going back to 2001. The Americans and other allies had the same question. The problem was now urgent.

ARAP had been announced by the home secretary and defence secretary in late December 2020. It was a development of earlier schemes aimed primarily at Afghans who were at risk from having worked with the UK military as interpreters and in other roles where their identities could become known to the Taliban. The scheme also covered staff who worked for the UK in civilian roles. The purpose of ARAP was and is to resettle Afghans and their immediate families who face a high and imminent threat to life because of their employment with the UK Government. ARAP was set up as a single cross-government scheme, with the Ministry of Defence and the Home Office jointly leading on its delivery.

ARAP had begun operating on 1 April 2021. The target was to relocate about 3,000 people by the end of August that year. A small team of Ministry of Defence staff were located at the British Embassy in Kabul to carry out those parts of the processing that had to be done in Afghanistan. This included receiving documents, taking biometric data, issuing visas. As I came and went from the residence, I would meet ARAP applicants including members of our embassy staff and their families coming and going from a nearby embassy villa where the ARAP team in Kabul were working. Some applicants smiled and waved. Others looked worried and preoccupied. Many had small children with them. We had brought nearly 2,000 people to the UK on charter flights during the early summer of 2021, before the start of the evacuation.

All parts of the embassy had Afghan staff, and looking after their interests was everyone's responsibility. We needed to ensure that the resettlement programme was implemented quickly and effectively, while keeping the embassy functioning as its Afghan staff were relocated to the UK. Several of my British diplomatic staff were switched from part of their official jobs to help process applicants and improve our support to them. But I did not think things were moving quickly enough in the Ministry of Defence or the Home Office in London. It was clear that we needed to force the pace. We established a system of weekly progress-chasing with London.

I dropped by at a staff farewell (and hello to me) in the villa next door to the residence. Drinks and a barbecue on the lawn. It was a pleasant warm evening and people were in good spirits. I wore a yellow hi-vis vest, in accordance with Covid protocols, to remind people to keep their distance while trying to put staff at ease with the new ambassador. The following morning I dropped by the pod of a staff member who had Covid. We sat outside in the sun for a while, chatting. He was upbeat and looking okay. Still, this was not a great place or time to be ill. Earlier Covid cases in the Green Zone had put serious pressure on very hard-pressed medical resources, which had been built for dealing with major trauma cases, not a pandemic.

THURSDAY 17 JUNE

Brigadier Tom came over for a meeting in the garden. Tom was the senior British military representative in Afghanistan and the Deputy to Admiral Vasely, the US commander of USFOR-A Fwd (US Forces Afghanistan – Forward). He was to become one of my most important colleagues in the weeks that followed, and a close friend. He brought with him a small team of high-quality analysts. They told things as they saw them, and they were invariably right. I quickly learned to trust Tom's judgement and wise advice. As the situation in Afghanistan deteriorated he called it right every time, to the evident irritation of some in London, who complained that we were 'catastrophising'. I ignored this. Tom and I met at least weekly, and stayed in touch throughout each day as events unfolded. I updated him on the political context, the mood in London and our planning, and in exchange Tom gave me vital insights into US military thinking and planning, as well as his own insights into developments on the battlefield and what was likely to happen next.

I joined the weekly coordination meeting of NATO ambassadors. Online. It is hard, on a Zoom call, to size up people you have never met before. The main item was a briefing by General Miller, the outgoing commander of the NATO Resolute Support Mission. With NATO military forces still in place but the drawdown well under way, the most important thing to do was to listen to General Miller's assessment of the security situation and the direction of travel, and to read between the lines of his carefully worded reports. And to ask ourselves: are we all seeing the same things, and drawing similar conclusions?

There had been discussion with London of whether I should join a call between General Nick Carter, Chief of the Defence Staff, and former President Karzai. Nick and I had first met when we both worked on Iraq in 2003. More recently, we were in regular contact when I was Ambassador to Russia and he became Chief of the Defence Staff, the UK's most senior military officer. Nick, who had served with UK and NATO forces in Afghanistan and knew many of the key players in Afghanistan, led on our efforts to broker contacts between the Government of Afghanistan, the government and military in Pakistan, and the Taliban, in pursuit of a negotiated political agreement. He was due to speak to Karzai ahead of a planned visit by senior republic politicians to Doha, to meet senior Taliban, and to test their (and Pakistan's) intentions.

I decided not to take part in the meeting with Karzai. I had not yet presented credentials to President Ghani, Karzai's successor and rival. It would make no sense to risk offending Ghani before I had even had my first meeting with him. Both Ghani and Karzai could be prickly characters, and the relationship between them was complex. My decision turned out to be the right call: Ghani and Karzai disagreed on the approach to be taken to the talks with the Taliban.

FRIDAY 18 JUNE

Friday was a non-working day in the Islamic Republic of Afghanistan, in principle. In reality, embassies in war zones do not work a five-day week; every day is a working day, just with a different rhythm depending on events and on the requirements from London. Also, Kabul is 3 hours and 30 minutes ahead of British Summer Time. Apart from the tricky mental arithmetic required, this meant that working late into the night was the norm. Crisis working happens when the crisis occurs. You don't get to pick the timing, and you don't get to say: 'I'll sit this one out.' I encouraged the team to take what down time they could.

I took the opportunity to go through the security operating procedures with Nick, the head of my close protection team. We walked through the layout of the house and the escape routes across the sprawling compound and we went through car drills; lockdown procedures; how the teams operated during daytime and silent hours; how the various communications and surveillance systems worked.

This procedure was the result of a tip given me on my Hostile Environment course in the UK. As well as familiarisation with the layout and procedures, it helps establish a good working relationship with the close protection team. I would be living with them, and relying on them, every day that I was in Kabul. We needed to trust each other so that each could do their job.

SATURDAY 19 JUNE

My end-of-quarantine Covid test came back negative. I could now get out and about and do the job properly, after a frustrating first week in Kabul.

Covid was on the rise again across the country, including among the international community. Several of my close protection team had tested positive, and the US Embassy was locked down, so I had to make do with a phone call to Ambassador Ross Wilson to introduce myself. I asked Alex, my deputy, to keep daily track of the numbers of cases in our embassy and to work up plans for more restricted working if that became necessary. It was hard to imagine how we could even continue to operate if there was a major outbreak. Meanwhile, we would have to ask all staff living on the embassy site to take daily Covid tests.

Mid-morning, Alex contacted me with an update about presenting credentials to President Ghani. There was a possibility it would happen tomorrow if the palace could squeeze in a time. As a newly arrived ambassador, you are only fully functional once this ceremony has taken place. Until then, depending on your host government's flexibility or lack of it, you are usually allowed only limited interactions with senior government office holders. With events moving quickly, and with Covid numbers rising, I was keen to get this done soon in case we or the government had to impose a lockdown.

SUNDAY 20 JUNE

Each Saturday morning an informal breakfast club of the major international donors met, chaired by Special Representative of the Secretary General Deborah Lyons, a senior Canadian diplomat in charge of UNAMA, the UN Assistance Mission for Afghanistan. Deborah was a class act, and had a good team.

The conversation was free-flowing, usually well informed, and focused on real world issues. As always in such conversations, ambassadors trade in snippets of information and analysis as each tries to form a coherent picture of what is going on, share views on what to do, and influence thinking – both back home and with allies and partners.

There was growing concern about Taliban military gains in the provinces. The Taliban were blocking Afghanistan's road network and progressively isolating regional capitals. The government's response was ineffective; its military were running short of serviceable helicopters and were putting too much of their effort into maintaining checkpoints and positions of questionable value, soaking up people and resources. There was an alarming lack of grip or cohesion within the republic.

The Taliban had told the United Nations that July would be a 'tense month', and requested that the United Nations 'let us know if your people are moving' – to reduce the risk that United Nations and other international staff would be mistakenly attacked in the course of Taliban military operations against government forces. We were particularly concerned about the risks to NGOs (non-governmental organisations) and aid workers. They needed to send people into local communities to help the ordinary people whom they exist to serve. This put their staff at significant risk of being caught up in fighting or deliberately targeted.

It was clear to me that the republic's unity and clarity of purpose needed to be greatly reinforced, now and in the coming weeks, if they were to turn the situation around. Afghanistan's allies needed a strategy to help the republic survive through the summer fighting season. We needed to look at what levers we had over both the Taliban and the republic to maximise the chances of a negotiated settlement. And we needed to impress on the big neighbouring countries that now was the time to prioritise achieving an acceptable negotiated outcome and that they should throw their weight behind that. A Taliban military victory would benefit no one.

A week since my arrival, and with the military withdrawal happening at full speed alarm bells were ringing about the security situation.

There were persistent rumours that a state of emergency was under consideration. President Ghani was reported to lack confidence in senior members of the security forces. I guessed that the feeling was probably mutual; Ghani was well known for having difficult relationships with some of his senior appointees, and it was clear that his closest security advisers had been appointed for their personal loyalty rather than their military expertise.

There were regular reports of soldiers and police going over to the Taliban, or just taking off their uniforms and going home. Villages and towns would often change hands not as a result of fighting but in accordance with deals negotiated between the Taliban and local commanders or elders. No surprise really, when so many of the soldiers lacked food, water, medical support, ammunition resupply or clear objectives. Men who had not been paid or resupplied, in many cases for months, saw no reason to fight and die for a republic whose leaders evidently had little regard for them and no strategy worth dying for, and whose foreign allies were making for the door.

Meanwhile Afghanistan's most capable forces were being severely stretched, often on tasks of little or no strategic significance. The losses among the Afghan National Army's élite Special Forces were particularly worrying.

President Ghani's appointment of two key new ministers was the week's big news. The new Defence Minister, Bismillah Khan Mohammadi (usually known as BK), was a political ally of Abdullah, Ghani's long-time rival and the second most senior politician in the government. BK was a Tajik with a long record of fighting the Taliban, going back to his time as a senior commander in the Northern Alliance under the legendary Ahmed Shah Massoud. The Northern Alliance had fought a war against Taliban rule from 1996 to 2001 and, backed by the Americans and others, had won it.

BK had been named Acting Interior Minister only a few days before his appointment as Defence Minister. General Abdul Satar Mirzakwal was appointed Minister of Interior, replacing Hayatullah Hayat, who had only been in the post for three months. These two appointments sought to address long-standing leadership problems in the Defence and Interior ministries, and a wider lack of coherent leadership across the security and defence forces. The appointments also needed to address questions of balance and patronage within the government, in particular between Ghani and Abdullah. Some saw Ghani's decision to appoint BK as a belated effort to reach out to former Northern Alliance leaders.

But it was hard to discern a concerted wider effort to rally round the survival of the republic. The merry-go-round of key appointments, which went on up to the very end of the republic, did not inspire confidence. Nor did the continual jockeying for position among senior politicians within the republic. Even if the individual appointments made sense, was this all too little, too late?

Ramiz Alakbarov, the Deputy UN Representative, talked us through his recent contacts with senior Taliban. Ramiz is an Azerbaijani with a well-developed sense of humour and an even sharper intelligence. Over coffee, he and I reminisced about Baku, his home town, where I had been sent as ambassador in 2004–2007.

Unlike most senior members of the international community, he had been managing to travel extensively around Afghanistan, despite the very serious and growing security risks, and to engage with a wide range of people. He generously shared the insights he picked up on his travels. The picture he painted was sobering, both on his encounters with the Taliban and on the disarray on the side of the republic out in the big provincial cities. It was clear that on the republic side greater cohesion and clarity of purpose was needed. Time was of the essence; the cohesion and clarity were needed now and in the coming weeks, not the other side of summer. I suggested that we should keep pressing all senior contacts on the seriousness of the situation and on the urgent need to rally together if the republic was to survive. What I did not say, but all understood, was that cohesion and clarity of purpose was also needed within the international community if Afghanistan was to avoid another catastrophe.

MONDAY 21 JUNE

I presented credentials to President Ghani, accompanied by Alex Pinfield, my deputy. Not many people have been to a presentation of credentials ceremony. It is an ancient ritual, but still central to what an ambassador is and does. The purpose of the meeting – handing over the personal letter from the ambassador's Head of State, appointing them to speak on behalf of their government and to act as a trusted conduit for the two countries to talk to each other – goes back to the days when an ambassador was a personal envoy from one Sovereign to another. In a sense, you still are, though these days you represent His Majesty's Government. The title makes it clear: His Majesty's Ambassador, usually shortened to HMA.

The letter of credence is handed over in person to the Head of State. Diplomacy depends on personal contact, as much personal trust as you can build with the people you are dealing with, and good judgement – both to read the intentions of your host government, and to get across those of your own government in the most convincing way. Having such a channel is no less necessary between governments that dislike and distrust each other than between allies and friends.

This occasion was rather different from when I had presented credentials to Russian President Vladimir Putin in 2016. That meeting took place in the great Alexander Hall of the Kremlin. A vast, gilded palace conveying imperial might, the staircase lined with soldiers in ceremonial uniforms whose eyes tracked you as you passed. You were not meant to feel at ease, and what followed was not a cosy fireside chat. Sixteen ambassadors lined up at one end of the hall, in protocol order (by date – and, if necessary, time – of first arrival in the country). When your name was called, you walked the length of the hall to hand over your credentials, past a phalanx of TV cameras. It was a long, somewhat lonely, walk. It was important to spot the trip hazard – a fold in the carpet, right in front of the cameras. And equally important to remember it on the long walk back. It was a kind of metaphor for the political environment that Western ambassadors inhabited in Moscow, liberally strewn with banana skins and worse.

On that occasion Putin gave a speech about Russia's foreign policy and her relations with the 16 countries whose ambassadors were presenting credentials. I still have a copy of Andrei Kolesnikov's sardonic word picture of the event in the newspaper *Kommersant*. Putin ran through how great Russia's relations were with Uruguay, Bolivia, India, Kyrgyzstan, Samoa etc. Then he got to the UK. Broadly summarised: 'Russia's relations with the UK really suck, and it's all your fault!' There was no right of reply. Welcome to Moscow. It crossed my mind that he might take the envelope containing my credentials, look at it quizzically, and hand it back. In fact, he just looked bored by the whole thing.

The meeting with President Ghani was very different. The military guard of honour at the Arg was maybe less immaculate than at the Kremlin, but impressive in its own way. Immediately before the credentials ceremony I met Foreign Minister Hanif Atmar for 30 minutes, quickly getting through the pleasantries and down to substance: the NATO withdrawal and its impact on the Taliban's calculations. Atmar was polite but frank: we had all wanted a conditions-based NATO withdrawal, but that had not happened; we had to press ahead with the peace process, and reverse the Taliban momentum on the battlefield; the Taliban had not met any of their commitments on cutting ties with extremists, reducing violence or engaging in meaningful talks. It was hard to disagree with Atmar's analysis.

The credentials formalities took place in a tasteful and modest room in the Presidential Palace, and were over in seconds. I handed my letters to President Ghani with a few words for the cameras about the strength of our relations and the uniquely pivotal moment. President Ghani took the envelopes, eyes smiling, and said some gracious words of welcome. Then we sat down for a friendly chat over tea. Ghani and Atmar were in white shalwar kameez and black jackets. Both are soft spoken (as am I), and we were all wearing masks, making the conversation harder than you would wish. Alex took careful notes, leaning forward to hear what was being said.

This was my first opportunity to meet President Ghani and his senior officials since my arrival and mandatory quarantine. Above all, I wanted to establish quickly the kind of open and frank relationship with Ghani and Atmar that would allow us to pick up the phone to each other when there were urgent and important matters to discuss. There was also an important demonstrative aspect to the event, with the UK showing its continued commitment to Afghanistan by sending a senior diplomat with a track record, even as the NATO withdrawal was gathering pace and our embassy reducing in size for security reasons. Both sides were keen to demonstrate to their publics that the UK was investing heavily in supporting the republic even as the NATO mission and its UK military component withdrew, changing the political and military dynamic in Afghanistan and the wider region.

Ghani thanked the UK for the sacrifices of its soldiers, for its continued support and for its efforts on the peace process. We talked about the prospects for the peace talks with the Taliban, and about Pakistan's role in bringing the Taliban to the negotiating table. And we discussed Ghani's forthcoming visit to Washington. Ghani knew that the US decision was not reversible. But the speed of the military withdrawal was putting Afghanistan's military forces under huge pressure; three years of transition were being compressed into three months. All of Afghanistan's neighbours needed to be clear about what sort of Afghanistan was in their interests.

I set out the UK Government's aims and priorities in an uncertain and rapidly developing situation. We were entering a new and critical phase in Afghanistan's relations with the UK and other close partners.

In my report to London, I commented: 'Time is of the essence. Events are running fast.'

The news and social media reports of my arrival prompted a large number of messages of support from friends and colleagues. One, from Konstantin von Eggert, a Russian journalist I have known for years, seemed to sum it up: 'I saw you handing in credentials, on Twitter. This IS QUITE A CHALLENGE.'

Later in the afternoon Sadat Naderi, the Minister of Peace, came to see me, for a rather more informal chat in the residence garden. Sadat is a youngish man, from a well-known family, educated in the UK, urbane and articulate. He was knowledgeable and realistic about the prospects for the peace negotiations with the Taliban. We got on well.

That same day the Taliban Supreme Leader Haibatullah issued a decree saying that Afghan soldiers who surrendered to the Taliban would be treated well. The Taliban released a series of videos purporting to show this: surrendering soldiers being given some food and money and sent home. The Taliban also released a stream of videos showing in graphic and gory detail what would happen to those who did not surrender. Over the coming weeks we would see ample evidence of a concerted, sophisticated and effective Taliban propaganda campaign to break the Afghan army's will to fight. From the government, nothing.

To add to the humanitarian burden, the country was in the grip of a measles outbreak. On top of conflict, Covid, drought and hunger. It was as if the apocalypse was descending on Afghanistan.

Andy McCoubrey, the UK's Development Director in Afghanistan and one of my senior leadership team, talked me through the complex humanitarian crisis unfolding before our eyes, and what we and the international community could do about it. Andy ran our big aid and development programme in Afghanistan, covering some of the most politically sensitive and high-profile areas including education and opportunities for girls and women. Andy's background was in the Department for International Development, before it was merged with the Foreign Office in 2020. He was smart, politically astute, compassionate. And also – as it turned out in the August evacuation – incredibly brave.

Tuesday 22 June

The first ARAP charter flight took off from Kabul, taking Afghan former interpreters, embassy staff and their families to new lives in the UK. It felt like we were making progress, though still with a mountain to climb in that we were planning to relocate several thousand people by the end of August. Nearly 2,000 people were in fact relocated under ARAP before Operation Pitting, and some 4,500 during the operation. The work goes on to this day.

The first ARAP flight featured in the UK media, despite a previous agreement in Whitehall to keep things low-key, to protect the security and privacy of the people being relocated. The briefing had clearly come from the UK Ministry of Defence. I puzzled for a while about why they had done this, and concluded that it was about deflecting long-running criticism in the UK press that the Ministry of Defence had not moved quickly enough to resettle Afghans who had worked with the British army over the previous 20 years. There was a large caseload of former military interpreters and others still to be worked through. Some had previously been denied resettlement because of minor offences that had led to their summary dismissal.

The scheme had its limitations. The capacity of the UK Government and local authorities to resettle large numbers of people at short notice was limited. The Ministry of Defence and the Home Office, as the lead departments for implementing ARAP on behalf of the whole government, had to work with the domestic departments and local authorities who would need to find significant numbers of people housing, education and health care, and help them with finding jobs and settling into a new way of life.

There were questions about which embassy and other UK Government staff qualified for resettlement. ARAP required decisions based on whether the applicant had made a material difference to the UK's mission in Afghanistan and on the degree of exposure to personal risk this brought. The scheme needed to be applied consistently and fairly to the different cohorts of staff who had worked for the UK in very different capacities and circumstances over the previous 20 years. Very large numbers of people had worked for the military and civilian agencies during that time, in very different roles. Military interpreters and embassy staff, people in public-facing roles and support roles, contractors and direct employees. One group among many included people who had worked for the British Council. They had not served on the front line, as the military interpreters had done. But their jobs had involved public-facing roles, promoting education and opportunities for women and girls – anathema to the Taliban. Should they qualify for resettlement?

There was potentially a very large and ill-defined category of people who had worked *with* us but not *for* us. This included people who had worked for the Afghan military and security forces alongside UK personnel on joint military and national security objectives. It also included civilians who had worked on UK-funded programmes to improve governance or to strengthen the rule of law or to build the accountancy profession, or any number of other areas essential to a modern society. The lists of people who had worked with us and who could therefore be at risk from the Taliban widened and lengthened. Distinguishing consistently between those who were eligible and those who were not became ever more complex. There was usually lobbying by senior and influential people in favour of 'their' groups.

Candidates for ARAP were and are assessed under four categories, reflecting the nature of the applicant's role and the risk of threat to life. Category 4 allowed for case-by-case assessment for those who were at risk because they had 'worked … alongside, in partnership with or closely supporting' the UK's military and national security objectives in Afghanistan. Some of these people were in very high-profile and high-risk areas of work: soldiers and officials who had worked with us on counterterrorism. Politicians, human rights activists, journalists. Lawyers and judges who had sent Taliban fighters and others to prison for terrorism offences, or worked on narcotics and corruption cases. If the people they had put away were let out of prison, inevitably some would come looking for vengeance in the form of a bullet or a sticky bomb. Women judges were at particularly high risk; the Taliban did not take kindly to a 'mere woman' exercising power over them.

Some ARAP cases were straightforward, with staff whose lives were at risk being eligible for resettlement by default. But many cases were not straightforward. Some were complex due to Afghanistan's extended family structures. There were particularly difficult issues around unmarried daughters and other single women over the age of 18. In the UK, they are considered independent adults. In Afghanistan, they may be dependents until they marry and leave home. Their fate, if the Taliban came to power, would be something you would not wish on anyone: loss of any personal freedoms, inability to work or even to leave the home without a male chaperone, forced 'marriage' to a Talib. For many families, leaving them behind was not an option.

In all of this, the policy needed to be applied as fairly and consistently as possible. And the numbers needed to be manageable for the domestic government departments and local authorities in the UK who would need to provide housing, schooling and other support for Afghans building new lives there.

Increasingly, the decisions had to be made under time pressure. People accepted for relocation had to assemble their documentation, and uproot their and their families' lives, in a matter of weeks. Among the embassy's Afghan staff, almost all who qualified to leave asked to do so. As they left their jobs, we had to decide what to do about replacing them. Without them, the embassy would quickly stop working.

I looked in on an FCDO worldwide all-staff meeting chaired by senior officials in London, focusing on the FCDO's Country Based Staff. These are the staff that embassies employ locally – typically but not always nationals of the country in which the embassy is located. In our case, Afghan nationals: the people being considered for resettlement under ARAP. No embassy can work effectively without the local knowledge and continuity brought by the Country Based Staff. But they do not have diplomatic status, and can be caught in the mangle when things go wrong between their employer and their country's government. This was a particular problem in Russia, where the government had no scruples about attacking our Russian staff as a way of attacking the UK Government.

In Afghanistan the problem we faced was different but very acute: what is the extent of our responsibility to the Country Based Staff when their country collapses into civil war or is taken over by violent and vindictive men who see them as collaborators with a hostile foreign power? In both cases, our reputation as a nation and as a diplomatic service depends on us repaying their loyalty and service to us in extreme circumstances. That was and is what the ARAP resettlement scheme was about.

The humanitarian situation was bad and getting worse. Afghanistan was in the grip of a third wave of Covid, on top of the conflict, the consequent displacement of people, and successive droughts leading to failed harvests. President Ghani formally declared the drought that had already been gripping the country for many months. This was the second major drought in three years, compounding a humanitarian crisis that was already one of the world's worst. Even before the drought started to bite, the United Nations had assessed that a third of the country was in crisis or emergency food insecurity, and half of children under five were acutely malnourished.

As always, the burden was and is borne primarily by women and children. There were persistent reports of families selling their land and animals, or selling their daughters into early marriage – storing up more poverty and more lost opportunities for future years.

The failures of governance that led to this situation were compounded by the war the Taliban had waged on the republic whose responsibility it was to build a better life for Afghanistan's citizens. But it is too easy to blame everything on the Taliban or on the many weaknesses of the republic's political leaders. We too played a role in this. How had billions of dollars of foreign aid, trillions in military expenditure, and countless hours spent designing and implementing reconstruction, aid and development programmes led to a situation where half of all children under five were still malnourished? In such circumstances, for ordinary people looking at a republic that had so abjectly failed to deliver the basic necessities of life, and at their international backers, how many would conclude that the right answer was 'more of the same'? The Taliban capitalised ruthlessly on these failures.

WEDNESDAY 23 JUNE

Mid-afternoon, I called on Second Vice President Muhammad Sarwar Danesh, with Esther, my senior political officer. Fifteen years previously I had worked with her father in Azerbaijan, where I had been the UK Ambassador and he the European Union's Head of Delegation. The setting was relatively formal, with interpretation. Danesh was a senior member of the Hazara community, a Shia minority who were regular targets of oppression and violence by the Taliban.

It was a sombre meeting. On 8 May the Taliban had bombed a Hazara girls' school in western Kabul, killing dozens of civilians, most of them schoolgirls. I offered my condolences and said that the attack should provoke a debate within Afghanistan about what sort of country Afghans wanted – one where girls went to school or one where schoolgirls were murdered? Danesh replied that there was no ethnic or cultural cohesion in Afghanistan. The only way for Afghanistan to find peace was to put ethnicity aside.

We turned the discussion towards the peace negotiations. I said that there needed to be clarity and unity of purpose among Afghanistan's leadership. The overriding common interest within the republic was to reach a negotiated settlement with the Taliban. I did not need to say that the alternative was not military victory over the Taliban but the prospect of defeat. Danesh was sceptical that the Taliban would negotiate. The political process had not been well handled. The Taliban had been handed legitimacy and leverage. He had no ideas to offer for how to take the initiative back from the Taliban.

A year later, in April 2022, a further series of bombs would explode outside schools in Kabul's Hazara district, killing and injuring yet more schoolchildren.

After my meeting with Danesh I spoke by secure video conference with Rob Macaire, our ambassador in Tehran, to compare notes about Iran's interests in Afghanistan and our readings of the situation. For the Iranians, the large US military presences to their east and west, in Afghanistan and Iraq, had long been seen as a strategic threat. Where would the balance of threat and opportunity lie for Iran in the cauldron of sectarian violence and warlordism descending on Afghanistan as the US military and its allies left? Rob and I go back over 30 years, to our very first postings in Bucharest in the early 1990s. He is cool, collected, with a dry sense of humour. He needed all of that in a tough posting in Iran.

Next, Stephen, the FCDO's London-based security adviser, and a visiting team of security experts called by to talk through their findings. They had been in Kabul to look in more detail at what we could do to improve security at our current site after the military withdrew, and to compare alternative options, such as they were, for the embassy. My view was that there was no obviously better option – i.e. more secure, lower cost, with enough functionality, and available now or in the near future – than the existing arrangements.

Someone at the top of the Ministry of Defence shared their view that we should downsize further, faster – without, needless to say, offering coherent proposals for how to do so. That was a fine idea in principle, but not achievable with the options we had in the time available. Nor was it compatible with ministers' instruction to stay and deliver our top-priority work for as long as possible, including pressing on with the much-delayed relocation of military interpreters and others under the ARAP scheme. The view clearly had more to do with not wanting to take responsibility for the consequences of the decision that ministers had taken. The real choice amounted to stay on after the military withdrawal or leave. I did not need reminding that either option carried heavy risks.

The contingency planning for an evacuation gathered pace; it had come a long way since my first run-through with Ministry of Defence and embassy teams back in May. The plan for a full-blown evacuation was centred on the Baron Hotel, a large and heavily fortified hotel and resort complex just outside the airport perimeter. The embassy had begun scoping possible locations for an Evacuation Handling Centre in January 2021. In April we had signed a contract with the Baron Hotel and paid a substantial deposit, giving us first refusal should we need to take up this option. This would give us a large, self- contained and defensible facility close to the airport. No other embassy in Kabul had such a facility.

An Evacuation Handling Centre is the best option for managing a large evacuation of civilians. It allows you to set up and run the evacuation in a relatively secure location, rather than improvising in the open air or in tents. We had judged – correctly, as it turned out – that the airport's civilian terminal would be out of action, or too dangerous, from day one.

Once on flights, people would first be flown out of immediate danger on military transport aircraft to a Temporary Safe Location in Dubai, from where they could be moved to the UK or elsewhere on wide-bodied airliners. This would allow us to concentrate scarce military assets at the sharp end of the operation – the difficult and dangerous flight out of Kabul. The combination of the Evacuation Handling Centre in Kabul and the Temporary Safe Location in Dubai meant that we had a comparatively short end-to-end evacuation pathway, allowing us to make best use of very scarce capacity in Kabul and on RAF flights.

We were the only country to plan and implement this system. The difference showed. Throughout the two weeks of the evacuation we received constant requests from governments and others to put their evacuees through our system. One message, which accompanied a plea for help from a civil society group, is typical of many similar requests I received: 'You are the only ones with a system that works.' During August we helped around 30 allied nations, including the Americans and the French, to get their people out.

As our planning progressed, we heard increasingly large figures being thrown around about the scale of the possible US evacuation if Kabul fell to the Taliban. One figure I saw put the number of people to be evacuated as high as 175,000. That would put the airport under enormous pressure, making our own evacuation much harder. The airport and every road leading to it would be gridlocked. What the American plan involved, we could not say. It was hard not to draw the comparison with the chaotic withdrawal from Saigon in 1975. That was something we wanted to avoid getting drawn into.

Apart from the colossal size of an evacuation from Kabul, its complexities grew with each iteration of the planning. Afghanistan is a landlocked country, so evacuation by ship was out of the question. So too was evacuation overland: there were no safe routes to the border, and no neighbouring countries where a large-scale overland evacuation would be possible. That left air.

Kabul airport – Hamid Karzai International Airport – is a single-runway airport with limited facilities. It is a difficult operating environment for aircrews. An accident or mishap can bring the whole thing to a halt. For us, the nearest back-up airport was Bagram, 50 km north of Kabul, and due to be handed over to the Afghan armed forces in early July. By mid-August it was in the hands of the Taliban.

Once civilian airlines had stopped operating into Kabul, military transport planes were the only realistic way in and out. That required agreements with host countries on basing and overflight agreements, and onward transit arrangements for those being evacuated. Aircraft and people would need to be moved into the region. The nearest basing options were in the Gulf, where the UK and others had existing defence relationships, but which would need scaling up. Overflight options meant Pakistan. It was not going to be possible to mount an air evacuation of this size and nature across Iran or the post-Soviet Central Asian countries.

Any evacuation would be taking place under conditions of war or its immediate aftermath. No roads in or around Kabul would be safe, nor would we have sufficient armoured vehicles to move large numbers of people from the centre of Kabul to the airport. We would not be able to rely on basic infrastructure working – telephones, electricity, water. The military presence in Kabul after the completion of the US and NATO withdrawal, due to be completed by 11 September 2021 (later brought forward to the end of August), would be very modest and focused on the defence of the Green Zone and its embassies. If we needed more soldiers or equipment to support an evacuation, they would have to be flown back in. Most likely, in a hurry. Quite possibly under fire. If embassy staff were trapped or captured and it came to mounting a rescue, assembling the right military forces would take time that we might not have. I had talked this through with the military planners in May and June during earlier stages of planning for Operation Pitting. The discussions were sobering ones.

Thursday 24 June

I called on Hamid Karzai, Afghanistan's first president after the overthrow of the Taliban in 2001; when his second term ended in 2014 he stepped down and was succeeded by Ashraf Ghani. Karzai, wearing traditional Afghan clothes, received me in a modest, comfortable sitting room in his residence. He was accompanied by a few advisers and note takers; I was accompanied by Alex Pinfield.

Hamid Karzai is a charismatic personality. A Pashtun from the southern city of Kandahar, he had for many years played a central role in Afghanistan's politics. After 2001 he became instantly recognisable on the world stage, wearing a distinctive green robe and Karakul hat which increased his gravitas. He also has a reputation for being mercurial, and as president his relations with the Americans were sometimes difficult.

On this occasion, he was welcoming and bantering, the conversation going from light to dark and back in an instant. But it was hard to pin him down to anything concrete. I guessed that he had seen many dozens of Western diplomats, politicians and generals come and go in his time. It was hard to know what to make of his joking references to the desirability of 'bringing back the Raj' (the British rule over the India), or his description of Afghanistan as 'an old, crumpled Lord in the midst of a tournament of shadows'. He was probably seeing how I would react.

Now serious, Karzai spoke of Afghanistan being at the fulcrum of the Great Game between the UK and Russia in the 19th century, and now, in the modern world, centred between China, Russia and the USA. India was an old friend and a huge power; Russia a massive reality; China a new player who wanted to help Afghanistan.

Karzai's key message for the UK was to keep trying to get Pakistan to help with shifting the Taliban's calculus away from fighting and towards negotiating. But he offered few ideas on how to strengthen the unity and effectiveness of the republic and its armed forces in holding back the rising threat of a Taliban takeover. My overriding sense was of a wily fox hedging his bets. I wondered whether he had already concluded that Ghani would fail, and was keeping his own options open for what would happen after that. Nothing that happened in the following months significantly changed that impression.

I travelled out to Hamid Karzai International Airport for a low-key but important flag-lowering ceremony with the final contingent of British troops deployed to

Afghanistan under Operation Toral, the UK contribution to the NATO Resolute Support Mission. The last rotation under Operation Toral was the Black Watch, the Third Battalion of the Royal Regiment of Scotland.

There was no appetite in the Ministry of Defence for a media event to mark the end of our 20-year military campaign in Afghanistan, out of concern not to fuel the growing narrative that the USA and its allies were abandoning Afghanistan. I was clear in my own mind, though, that these young people serving the UK should hear the words 'Thank you' in person from the UK's most senior representative in Afghanistan, for their service, and for that of a generation of other young people who had served and fought in Afghanistan. And in particular, for those who had lost their lives, their limbs or their mental health. During the Afghan campaign 457 British soldiers had died. Many more had suffered life-changing injuries.

It was a short, dignified ceremony, in blazing sunshine and intense afternoon heat. A crescent of flagpoles stood around a car park outside a new red brick building in the military terminal on the north side of the runway. The UK flag was lowered and carefully folded. One of my staff took charge of it. After the lowering of the flag, the troops gathered in a tight semi-circle. Brigadier Olly Brown, General Scott Miller (the US general in overall command of the Resolute Support Mission) and I each gave a short speech to thank the troops for their service and, through them, their predecessors.

Afterwards I spent some time chatting with the soldiers. Several said they wished they were staying. It was not just bravado or putting on a good showing for a senior officer; there was a strong sense of unfinished business – a sense that we were leaving without having completed the job.

Before leaving to return to the Green Zone in central Kabul, I took the opportunity for a quick tour, with General Miller and his entourage, round the Norwegian-run medical facility in the building next door. This was a critical part of the infrastructure, without which we would not be able to stay in Kabul. I needed to be able to tell London that I had personally seen it and spoken to the people running it. It was impressive: four fully equipped operating theatres, with a casualty reception exercise going on as we arrived. A group of medics crowded round an operating table working on a lifelike dummy patient. The exercise did not look as if it had been laid on for our benefit. They'd had no notice of us coming, and looked up quizzically as we arrived. Then they quickly got back to work on their patient. I hoped I would never see them doing that for real.

We had driven out to the airport in the usual three-car convoy, weaving through the Kabul traffic. General Miller asked with a grin if I would like a ride back into town. We walked out to his flight of UH-60 Black Hawk helicopters waiting on the ramp, rotors turning. You saw a lot of these criss-crossing backwards and forwards above Kabul, usually in pairs; they have a distinctive, slightly humped silhouette.

General Miller's security detail sat up front, guns trained outwards. The rest of us crammed into the rear cabin. As we buzzed over the streets of Kabul, it was hard to get the Ride of the Valkyries out of my head – the *Apocalypse Now* version, not the Royal Opera House one. Helicopters are noisy places and General Miller kept his counsel. I imagine he was wondering what the diplomats thought they were doing, staying here after the military had left.

Later I asked Nigel Casey, the Director for Afghanistan back in London, if the Foreign Office budget would stretch to a UH-60; more convenient, though maybe less picturesque, than road moves in a trio of armoured Land Cruisers. I gather a UH-60 starts at around $20 million. Nigel and I share a similar sense of humour. But there was a serious point too: were we trying to achieve something that was not actually possible?

That evening, the Norwegian Ambassador hosted a dinner with Yunus Qanooni, a senior Afghan politician and former vice president. An ethnic Tajik from the Panjshir Valley, Qanooni had been a powerful figure in the Northern Alliance and in the early years of the republic but was sidelined by Karzai following the 2004 election, in which Qanooni came second. He was pessimistic about the outlook. For their part, the Norwegians are big players in the world of peace negotiations and reconciliation, and it was a good opportunity to hear their take on the prospects for some sort of political deal. Their residence was outside the Green Zone, in a small and heavily fortified compound; my move outside the Zone, returning after dark, had involved a significant amount of pre-planning.

Friday 25 June

The night was broken by an earthquake in the small hours, enough to shake the building but not enough to need further action. I spent a few minutes sitting in a doorway in case the ceiling fell in, then went back to bed. Almost exactly a year later, a bigger earthquake killed large numbers of people.

The following morning I spoke with Paul Wojciechowski, the Australian Ambassador. Working from a borrowed desk in a European capital, he clearly wished he was still in Kabul. I talked him through the political and security developments and, in less detail, our contingency planning. In late August, after the fall of Kabul and at the height of the evacuation, the Australians sent a highly capable military team in to help. They made a very substantial contribution.

General Miller put in what was billed as his last appearance at the weekly NATO ambassadors' meeting. He updated us on the security arrangements that would be in place after the termination of Resolute Support Mission, which would be completed by 11 September 2021. These included a contingent of 650 US military personnel to guard the US Embassy and secure the Green Zone. Less encouraging was his professional assessment of the state of the conflict: the Taliban were intent on a military takeover, not a negotiated outcome, and were making much faster progress than expected. The government had plans to stand up people's militias – organised and armed citizens – to bolster the regular armed forces and defend their towns and villages. Good, if they were well disciplined, working to a single plan, and fought back against the Taliban. Not so good if this plan led to further fragmentation on the republic side and ultimately to back to the warlordism that had plagued Afghanistan in the past. Miller warned that we should be prepared for things to move quickly.

Others spoke of several northern regional capitals now at risk of falling to the Taliban. Mazar-e Sharif, Afghanistan's fourth largest city, was close to being cut off and isolated. Loss of Mazar would be a strategic blow to the republic. The Taliban's campaign in the north seemed to be centred on suppressing the re-emergence of the Northern Alliance, which had played a decisive role in overthrowing the Taliban in 2001. The consensus view was that the Taliban had every intention of taking over Afghanistan by military force, even if they were not – yet – poised to make an end run on Kabul.

Later on I joined a video conference with colleagues in London to discuss options for setting up a British Embassy in exile somewhere in the region. An obvious candidate was Doha, where the Taliban Political Commission was based; In a note to London I commented: 'I think there is a substantial possibility that we'll be doing this over the summer/early autumn.' And that was indeed where a small team would set up shop after the fall of Kabul and the evacuation.

President Ghani and Dr Abdullah visited Washington for crucial meetings with the Biden Administration and with their supporters in Congress. In their meeting with President Biden in the White House, the Afghan side put a brave face on it – but there was no getting away from the fact that the US and international military withdrawal was going ahead at full steam and would be completed within a few weeks. From the Oval Office, Biden spoke of the USA's 'enduring partnership' with Afghanistan: 'Our troops may be leaving, but support for Afghanistan is not ending.' But it was for the Afghans to decide 'what they want ... The senseless violence, it has to stop. It's going to be very difficult.' [10]

For the cameras, Ghani spoke of Biden's 'historic' decision, which he respected and supported. In private, he asked for military assistance: air cover, helicopters, and continued logistical and maintenance support from US military contractors to keep Afghanistan's air force flying. Without this support, the Afghan air force's advanced Western aircraft would quickly become unserviceable, as the contractors were unwilling to stay in Afghanistan beyond the US military withdrawal. But instead, the USA planned to organise long-distance support for Afghan maintenance crews, with contractors providing advice by video conference. It was not hard to foresee problems arising with such arrangements.

Ghani also asked Biden to hold off evacuating Afghans at risk, to avoid creating a sense of panic and a loss of confidence in the government. Ghani and his officials later made similar requests to us.

A few days before Ghani's visit to Washington, the US media had reported a new US intelligence assessment that the government could fall to the Taliban within six months of the completion of the military withdrawal.

SATURDAY 26 JUNE

Relocating our Afghan staff at greatest risk was a moral imperative and a political necessity, and we needed to accelerate the programme because of the worsening situation. But we also needed to keep the embassy open and operating, and we needed to find answers as to how we would do this as we progressively stripped out the people we depended on. I made clear my view that we could not and should not try to compel anyone who qualified for resettlement to stay in Kabul against their will.

I wrote to two of the most senior officials in the Foreign Office, setting out the practical implications of the ARAP relocation scheme for the embassy. We needed to find ways to keep the embassy functioning: to keep the infrastructure working; to deliver political analysis and reporting; to support the Afghan Government's education, development, justice and security programmes; to support the peace negotiations.

Keeping the show on the road in Kabul would depend both on finding creative ways to employ the staff we were evacuating so that they could continue to do their jobs in the UK, and on putting in place different ways of working in Kabul. We needed the Foreign Office to show creativity and flexibility in coming up with solutions quickly. There were puzzled frowns in London, but no real answers. Six weeks later the question would be overtaken by events, with the fall of the republic and the closure of the embassy.

At least once a week all NATO ambassadors met in person for a coordination meeting. The NATO Resolute Support Mission HQ was a huge, sprawling site next to the US Embassy in the Green Zone, which had grown into its current form over many years. It still had a curiously improvised feel amid its high blast walls and security checkpoints. In the summer heat, and with Covid precautions in force, NATO ambassadors' meetings took place outside in a small garden, under a tent awning. The flies buzzed and hovered over the refreshments. Occasionally the conversation was drowned out by the much louder buzzing of a helicopter landing or taking off from the next-door helipad.

On each ambassador's arrival, their close protection team was required to hand over charge of their ambassador to Resolute Support Mission HQ security and then hover in a nearby holding area under the shade of a high blast wall. I am short-sighted, and on the way out I sometimes failed to spot my close protection team immediately. Working out which close protection team to go home with each time made me giggle irrationally. It was like some sort of deranged speed dating arrangement with unusually heavily armed participants.

Driving out of the Resolute Support Mission compound, we passed the C-RAM installation. C-RAM stands for Counter-Rocket, Artillery, Mortar. It is a high-speed, high-precision automatic gun whose purpose is to detect and shoot down incoming ordnance threatening the Green Zone. We slept safer and better for having it. But it does look disconcertingly like a very angry R2-D2, the dustbin-shaped robot from the Star Wars films.

This week, the discussion in the NATO meeting focused on the Taliban's capture a few days previously of the Sher Khan Bandar border crossing point, the main route to and from Tajikistan, and fierce fighting over Hairatan, on the border with Uzbekistan. This was a big blow to the government and a major coup for the Taliban, increasing their grip on Afghanistan's supply arteries and communications with the outside world.

The outline of the Taliban's war strategy was becoming clear. At its heart was a military campaign to exhaust the Afghan National Defence and Security Forces, and to wear down the wider population's willingness to resist. On the battlefield the Taliban were pursuing several linked goals: to isolate the south of Afghanistan from the north, neutralising the government's ability to draw on the non-Pashtun north's resources; to take control of highways and border crossings, starving the government of resources and making resupply of government forces harder; and to encircle – but not yet attempt to take – the major cities.

The Taliban's strategy was putting huge pressure on the Afghan Government's most capable but scarcest resources: air transport, close air support, and well-trained, highly motivated special forces. In response, the government was implementing a 'national mobilisation', raising local militias, known as Popular Uprising Forces, in the hope that these formations might be motivated to defend their home towns and cities against the Taliban. But this would not address the Taliban's systematic filleting of the country, and could not substitute for the shortfall in the government's most capable forces.

In support of their military operations, the Taliban ran a powerful propaganda campaign, making adroit use of social media. The messages were simple and devastatingly effective. *Why fight for a government that does not care about you? Surrender to us and we will give you food and some money and send you home. Fight us and you will meet a grisly end.* The Taliban were too often winning the war inside people's minds as much as on the battlefield. Afghan National Defence and Security Forces units, demoralised, isolated and cut off from resupply, surrendered when they ran out of ammunition, food and water. They had nothing to fight with and nothing convincing to fight for.

There were now Taliban-dominated districts within 25–50 km of Kabul, and a substantial Taliban presence in areas as close as 10 km from Kabul. Yet still there was little sense in Kabul of impending catastrophe. A few days later Eid, the Muslim Feast of the Sacrifice, would bring a rude awakening.

I heard on the grapevine that BK thought Kabul might fall to the Taliban by August.

Sunday 27 June

I went to see the Canadians. Although the Canadian Embassy was only a few blocks down the road, past Foreign Minister Atmar's house and in a part of the Green Zone secured by the UK, the move still required the close protection team to plan, to move cars, to hand off to Canadian security, and to pass through a heavily fortified checkpoint with a steel door the width of the road that could be used to close it.

The Canadians were very focused on our plans for staying or leaving. The same was true for many other Western embassies. The British Embassy was seen by many as the canary in the coal mine; if we left, or even significantly changed our defensive profile, that would change their risk assessment. Our intentions were scrutinised closely by our Western colleagues; at every meeting, I was asked for our latest assessment of the security situation and whether the British Embassy would be staying or leaving.

Early evening, I went to see Fazel Fazly, Director General of President Ghani's Administrative Office. A doctor by profession, Fazly was one of Ghani's top officials, one of those closest to the president and trusted by him: in effect, his right-hand man.

Fazly claimed to be relaxed about the state of the war. The latest military setbacks were a 'nosebleed' – nothing more than an interim period of instability until the end of the fighting season as winter closed in. He was unconcerned that the government might not last that long. He argued that the government had popular support. That the Taliban had not changed since the 1990s, but the population of Afghanistan had. He rather undermined his own argument, however, stating that with two thirds of population under 35, few had any recollection of how the Taliban had behaved when in power, or of the anarchy that had followed the Soviet departure.

I replied that the government should in that case raise its game, leaving the population in no doubt about what was at stake in the war with the Taliban. We agreed that I would swiftly work up with London a plan to support the government's strategic communications – its efforts to win hearts and minds in a fight to the finish with the Taliban.

I left the discussion seriously worried by the complacency and happy talk of President Ghani's key advisers. Did this reflect the quality and realism of the advice Ghani was receiving?

I asked my staff to set up a series of introductory calls on the ambassadors of a number of regional powers. Russia, China and Iran are some of our most difficult international partners. But they have important interests, and play significant roles, in the region. As NATO's forces withdrew, the leadership of each of these countries was having to reassess and recalibrate their approach. I wanted to get under the skin of how their thinking was developing, and to explore whether there was any scope for at least a partial alignment of interests, in particular over countering extremism, drugs and the growing humanitarian crisis.

We also needed to watch for any sign that these countries might take actions that damaged our interests. Diplomacy is not only about talking with people who like you or agree with you. More often it is either about finding ways forward with people who neither like you nor agree with you – or about finding ways to block them from causing you harm.

Monday 28 June

Alex, my deputy, messaged me first thing. Back in the UK, some Ministry of Defence documents had been lost and had found their way to the UK media. The story had broken over the weekend. According to first reports, some of the documents related to the security situation in Afghanistan. A damage assessment was under way. The immediate question was whether the papers contained any information that would compromise the security of our staff.

With the security situation in Afghanistan deteriorating rapidly and seriously, this was a problem we could do without.

I received a request from a well-known British journalist for an on-the-record interview on the unfolding situation in Afghanistan, or a background briefing – a convention whereby the journalist cannot quote you by name but uses what you say to inform their story. I passed the request back to the Foreign Office's media office in London for a decision. They in turn referred it to Foreign Secretary Raab's Special Advisers (SpAds) – the political advisers to senior ministers.

The reply came back quickly. A flat No from the SpAds. No reason given, and no discernible logic. Part of a pattern of micromanagement and controlling behaviour. This was self-defeating. The Afghanistan story was big, and growing quickly. It was going to get told in the media with or without our contribution. In my experience it is almost always better to try to work with the media on an important story than to hold them at arm's length. If you do not, and the story is factually wrong or unbalanced, you have only yourself to blame. And besides, some journalists are extremely well informed. You might even learn something.

A few days later the story of a 'secret' flag-lowering ceremony for the departing British troops appeared in the UK media, together with speculation about a continued UK military and Special Forces presence after the withdrawal of Resolute Support Mission. Given the Taliban's sensitivity to any foreign military presence after the completion of the NATO withdrawal, this story was not helpful.

The stories had obviously been briefed to the press by someone in the UK Ministry of Defence, despite earlier protestations that they wished to keep the event low-key to avoid feeding a narrative of abandonment. We should have done proper background briefings to explain the government's position including why and how we planned to stay after the NATO withdrawal.

The Afghan Parliament debated the escalating violence. There were divided views on the formation of the independent militias – the People's Uprising Forces. There were growing fears that the country could be sliding towards civil war. General Scott Miller, the Commander of Resolute Support Mission, had warned of this possibility in media interviews.

Towards the end of the day we sent our own, frank, assessment in a diplomatic cable. A diplomatic cable (called a 'diptel' in the FCDO – short for diplomatic telegram) is a concise piece of reporting, analysis and recommendations for action on key developments in an embassy's host country. It is aimed at a wide and senior audience, in London and in our worldwide network of embassies. By convention it is signed by the ambassador and addressed to the foreign secretary, and as such is to be read as the considered advice of the ambassador:

Afghanistan: Under pressure

Summary

Taliban make territorial gains across Afghanistan. Not yet a tipping point. But the psychological impact on Afghan security forces and population is significant. Taliban seem to be positioning to attempt to take major population centres when its strategic calculus allows.

More than 50 districts are reported to have fallen since the withdrawal of international troops began. Afghan security forces have retaken a number of the lost districts, but open source analysis indicates that of Afghanistan's 421 districts the Taliban now controls 156 to the Government's 82, with the remainder contested. In the last week fighting has threatened the outskirts of two provincial capitals for the first time this year. The Taliban has seized control of – and closed – Afghanistan's principal commercial border crossing point with Tajikistan.

From Pashtun heartlands to Northern Alliance strongholds, the Taliban has momentum. But so far gains have been largely in rural areas where the Taliban presence is long established and there is usually minimal security footprint. The strategic value to the Taliban has primarily been in the information space, with images of surrendering government forces and seized equipment spreading a growing sense of unease through Afghans and international partners alike.

The Government continues to hold all the major cities and provincial centres, and Kabul remains secure despite clashes in recent weeks in neighbouring Maidan Wardak and Laghman provinces. However, fighting in the north threatens to weaken the former Northern Alliance as an opponent to the Taliban.

To achieve its political aims in Afghanistan, the Taliban will need to take control of major population centres. It is unlikely to do so while it perceives an ongoing threat from US air power. From a Taliban perspective, doing so would risk provoking a slowing or a reversal of the US withdrawal, as well as taking significant casualties for little gain. It is more likely that the Taliban will wait until it believes international military withdrawal is irreversible before escalating its campaign. In the meantime, it will continue to encircle provincial centres and target key logistical and resupply routes around the country in preparation for future offensives.

The Afghan response

The Government of Afghanistan faces a number of challenges. Both Ghani and his newly appointed Defence Minister have called for a national mobilisation of local militia to support the Afghan security forces in their fight against the Taliban.

BRISTOW [11]

A delegation from the Halo Trust called by at the residence. The trust is a leading NGO which specialises in clearing the mines and unexploded ordnance which would otherwise kill and maim civilians trying to farm their fields and go about their lives. Those who work for Halo Trust and other similar organisations are brave, practical and down-to-earth people making a big difference to ordinary people's lives.

Two seniors from London and Dr Farid Homayoun, Halo Trust's immensely impressive, unshowy Afghanistan programme manager, briefed Andy McCoubrey and me about a serious attack on one of their demining operations in Baghlan Province on 8 June. The compound had come under attack, and in the subsequent massacre of Halo staff 11 people were murdered. The staff members, even when threatened by the gunmen, had refused to identify their team leaders or Hazara minority colleagues to the attackers.

This was the worst attack on Halo in its 30 years of working in Afghanistan. The Taliban had disowned the attack. It appeared to be the work of ISKP. As with the murder of the polio inoculators, the aim seemed to be to sow murder and mayhem, and to profit from it.

I made my introductory call on Dr Abdullah, at the Sapedar Palace, a concrete building in the Green Zone that served as his headquarters. Since the disputed 2019 election he had been the head of the High Council for National Reconciliation, a senior role in charge of the peace negotiations with the Taliban. He had previously been Chief Executive Officer of Afghanistan, an uneasy power-sharing arrangement with President Ghani created after the 2014 election which both Abdullah and Ghani claimed to have won. Like all Afghan elections since the overthrow of the Taliban, the outcomes in 2014 and 2019 were tainted by suspicions of massive fraud.

Abdullah had just returned from an official visit to Washington with President Ghani. Abdullah and I sat in large upright armchairs, with long sofas for his officials and mine, in front of an ornate bookcase. Unlike most other Afghan top officials, Abdullah generally wore a Western suit and tie when meeting foreigners. His style was different in other ways from the other top officials I had met so far; he was more realistic about the prospects for some sort of settlement with the Taliban, and about the chances of achieving greater unity within the government and between the power brokers of the republic. Clearly, relations between Abdullah and Ghani were as complex as ever.

We talked about whether it would be possible to get across to the Taliban that if they entered power the attitude of the international community towards them would depend heavily both on how they got there and what they did with power once they had it. Abdullah spoke slowly, choosing his words carefully, his eyes sad. He observed ruefully that the Doha Agreement had not in any way addressed this question and that the insurgency was the result.

After the fall of the republic to the Taliban in August, both Abdullah and Hamid Karzai would choose to stay in Kabul to try to influence the future of Afghanistan from within. Very brave men.

I joined a sequence of calls with London. The most urgent was about the media story concerning the bag of Ministry of Defence papers. The bag had been left at a bus stop in the UK, and the person who had found them handed them to the media instead of the police. As the papers included documents relating to the security arrangements for the Embassy in Kabul, it was quite hard to imagine why anyone would think giving such documents to the newspapers was the right thing to do with them. But that was not a question for us. Our job was to consider what changes needed to be made to our security arrangements.

After that, a call to check in with Lord Tariq Ahmad, the Minister of State responsible for Afghanistan and Pakistan. A thoughtful and knowledgeable man, with good contacts across the region and a good understanding of the issues. I always enjoyed meetings with him.

Lowest down my to-do list was for me to drop in on a few online sessions of the Foreign Office Leadership Conference – the annual meeting of ambassadors and senior officials in London, to catch up on developments and to get our bearings for the year to come. This year the conference was all online; in the middle of a pandemic it was not possible to bring to London and into the same room 200 or so ambassadors and senior officials from all over the world. That sharply reduced its already limited appeal. After years of corporate homilies I could do without another dose of them. The value of the conference lay more in tuning into the political mood in London – doubly so, given the UK's post-Brexit politics and the Covid-enforced isolation in which we were all working. The most useful part was invariably the coffee breaks, catching up with friends and colleagues and finding out what was really going on. But it is hard to do either of those by video conference from a conflict zone.

This time, we were a year into the merger between the Foreign Office and the Department for International Development to form the Foreign, Commonwealth and Development Office. It was more than usually important to listen carefully to the messaging about the new Foreign Office itself, and to what was said or not said between the lines. Kabul was not only one of our highest profile diplomatic posts but also it delivered our biggest bilateral aid and development programme, in support of a government and a population under attack from a nationwide insurgency. It was essential that our work on development, aid, and the political and security priorities was coherent and effective.

The merger between the Foreign Office and DFID seemed to be going rather better on the front line in Kabul than back in the UK.

TUESDAY 29 JUNE

Paul Wojciechowski, the Australian Ambassador working from exile in a European capital, chaired an online meeting of the Friends of Afghan Women, an ad hoc group of embassies with a strong commitment to women's rights and, in many cases, programmes to deliver practical support. Everyone on the call understood very well what a Taliban return to power would mean for Afghanistan's women and girls, and no one had a clearer understanding than the Afghan women activists on the call. The demonstration of solidarity for their work by foreign ambassadors was needed, but to me it felt totally inadequate in the face of the calamity that was sure to come for those women, and for all Afghan women and girls, if – or, much more likely, when – the Taliban took power.

In the course of 2021 and beyond, after they had overthrown the republic and were back in control of Afghanistan, the Taliban rolled back the rights of women and girls inexorably. They pushed women out of the workplace and girls out of school. In late 2022 they announced that women students would no longer be able to attend university, and at the same time required national and international humanitarian organisations to stop employing women. These were the Taliban about whom there had in many people's minds been wishful thinking before August 2021 that they had somehow reformed during their 20 years out of power: that they had somehow become the Taliban 2.0. There had never been a shred of evidence for that belief.

Wednesday 30 June

Brigadier Nick Pond dropped by for coffee. Nick was the UNAMA Senior Military Adviser, and another of my weekly regulars. A level-headed, well-informed British military officer who knew his way round the politics, people and organisations in Afghanistan and beyond. I came to value highly his insights and advice, carefully balanced and modestly offered, and in particular his realistic military assessment of what was happening across the country.

I went to see Vice President Amrullah Saleh. Saleh was a big player in his own right, with an uncomfortable relationship with some other senior government figures. He was a fighter: during the Soviet invasion he had been a member of the mujahideen, and had later joined the legendary anti-communist and anti-Taliban leader Ahmed Shah Massoud's Northern Alliance. Highly intelligent and driven, bursting with nervous energy, and a feisty and articulate speaker, Saleh was not a man to hold back. He gave me an uncompromising view of the situation and the outlook, and of Pakistan's culpability for the Taliban's resurgence. After the fall of the republic he would regroup his fighters in the Panjshir Valley, a short distance north of Kabul, declaring himself the interim President of Afghanistan. His National Resistance Front conducted an insurgency against the Taliban until he was reportedly forced to flee to Tajikistan.

My next meeting was with Hamidullah Mohib, Ghani's National Security Adviser. Mohib could hardly be more different from Saleh in demeanour or background. He had studied at university in the UK, earning a doctorate in computing. In 2014, following Ghani's election as president, he had joined Ghani's staff and was later appointed Ghani's ambassador to the USA. Urbane and articulate but with no background in national security, Mohib, who owed his position entirely to Ghani, was something of a courtier as well as a close adviser. We had already met online, with a group of Western ambassadors.

The purpose of this meeting was to establish the kind of personal trust where we could speak frankly and if necessary urgently, knowing that we were speaking for and to our political masters in a situation where the future existence of the Afghan State was on the line.

In the evening I recorded a radio interview for the BBC Dari/Pashto service. The messaging was carefully calibrated, both for listeners who supported the republic and feared what could happen after the NATO military withdrawal, and also for any Taliban who might be listening. Some weeks later, after the fall of Kabul, the young journalist who had conducted the interview would be evacuated from Kabul airport.

Thursday 1 July

We received reports that the militias were being raised in 20 or so northern provinces. The underlying logic was that locally raised militias might be more motivated to defend their homes than the Afghan National Defence and Security Forces – the regular army and the police. The regular forces were, on paper, numerous and well equipped. But the reality was proving to be very different. They were losing the psychological war with the Taliban. The risk of reliance on these disparate militias was that this fragmentation would further damage the republic's cohesion, heightening long-standing tensions between local power brokers and the central government in Kabul, and raising the risk of a return to warlordism.

It was clear that for Ghani a concern was that reliance on the militias could also undermine his own authority and primacy as the President of the Republic. What personal authority he had was leaking away as the government over which he presided staggered from one disaster to the next, senior republican politicians manoeuvred blatantly for personal position, and Afghanistan's international allies continued to pull the rug out from under it all.

In London, a debate was still fitfully rumbling on about whether we would be better off moving to the former Resolute Support Mission HQ, now taken over by the US Embassy and rebadged as US Embassy Kabul South Compound. Some in the Ministry of Defence still seemed to think that South Compound offered quick and easy answers to the growing problem of how to keep a secure and functioning embassy in Kabul. As we had explained many times, however, there was nothing remotely suitable there to move into: just rudimentary buildings, most of which did not meet our security or technical requirements and would need significant work, time and expense before they could even come close to what we already had. And we would also need a lot more clarity on what security and other arrangements the Americans intended to provide for the foreign embassies who moved there. I had, though, received some useful intelligence from our military on the ground in the South Compound: 'the food is improving'.

FRIDAY 2 JULY

Overnight on 1–2 July US forces pulled out from Bagram airbase. Bagram, a Soviet-era airbase about 50 km north of Kabul, had been the linchpin of US and NATO operations throughout the 20-year campaign. As well as being the major operational and logistics hub, it was the site of a large detention centre where al-Qaeda suspects, Taliban and other fighters had been held and interrogated. The body of Osama bin Laden had been brought there following the Abbottabad raid in Pakistan in 2011. The Parwan Detention Facility next to the airbase, now controlled by the Government of Afghanistan, still held thousands of prisoners, many of them Taliban.

The news broke as the USA was going into the 4 July Independence Day holiday weekend. In Washington, President Biden made an upbeat speech, talking up the fastest US economic growth for 40 years, rising employment and a 90 per cent reduction in Covid deaths. He was pressed by journalists about the situation in Afghanistan. One asked him direct: 'Are you worried that the Afghan Government might fall?' Biden was clearly irritated by the questions, replying: 'I want to talk about happy things, man.' [12]

Both the French and Russian languages speak of leaving a place 'English-style' – that is, without observing the usual courtesies. It is not a compliment. According to the new Afghan base commander at Bagram, General Asadullah Kohistani, the Americans had upped and left in the night without telling their Afghan partners. Shortly afterwards the electricity went off and the base went dark. The last American soldiers to leave abandoned their vehicles on the runway, lights on and engines running. The Americans were reported to have left behind 3.5 million items including car parks full of vehicles, many without their keys. Looting began even before Afghan forces had taken control.

Everyone had known that the US presence at Bagram would close down. But it was a heavy blow when it came. Like many others, I was taken aback by the way it was done. Everyone understood immediately the significance of the moment. This was the definitive end of the US-led military intervention in Afghanistan. The fact and the manner of the Americans' departure from the most important gateway to Afghanistan of the 20-year campaign was taken by Afghans as a symbol of abandonment and betrayal. And it was presented in that light by the Taliban, whose message to the Afghan public and armed forces amounted to: 'Look – your so-called allies have left and are not coming back. We won.' So much for 20 years of partnership.

For many months afterwards an argument would rage in the international media about whether US forces should have kept control of Bagram, either as a better alternative to Kabul airport for running an evacuation or as a fallback option if Kabul airport was no longer available. The question would become acute during the evacuation in August, when the limitations of Kabul's civil airport became apparent.

The decision to leave Bagram had been based on clear if unwelcome choices. First, the Doha Agreement had committed the USA to withdrawing all forces from Afghanistan. It did not include a provision to keep forces in Bagram, Kabul or anywhere else. When President Biden confirmed that the decision to leave had been made and was not up for further discussion in Washington, the US military wished to prioritise force protection, minimising the risk of further casualties during the military withdrawal. Second, the number and disposition of forces staying behind to protect the US Embassy and the Green Zone were not large enough to carry out that task while also holding a facility as vast as Bagram. The US military were clear that it could be one or the other – but not both.

The bigger question was whether the inexorable collapse of the republic could have been halted by a different approach to the withdrawal of US-led military forces. It was clear by this time that the republic was failing badly and rapidly under the Taliban military onslaught. At the time and since, the weekend of 4 July felt like the last chance to rethink the military withdrawal. That chance was not taken; the republic and its international allies crossed the Rubicon.

The Taliban took control of Bagram airbase on 15 August 2021. The day the republic fell.

SATURDAY 3 JULY

Bagram changed the mood in our embassy. At the morning meeting of the senior embassy staff I asked the team to test the closure plan. Testing a contingency plan of this sort means going through it meticulously, working out what you would do in a range of scenarios, and trying out your responses for real, where you can do so. You need to get into the right mindset, where you have crossed over from thinking about it as something you hope you will not have to do, to something you know you probably will have to do.

The aim is also to identify the plan's weaknesses. If you do not find any, it almost certainly means you have not tested it hard enough. Every plan has weaknesses and points of failure. It can be something as simple as a key member of staff being away at the critical moment. Or an out-of-date phone number in a contacts list. As the boxer Mike Tyson said: 'Everyone has a plan until they get punched in the mouth.'

Each day at the embassy morning meeting, I nagged the team to press ahead with 'aggressive housekeeping' – making sure unnecessary files were shredded, and that nothing sensitive was kept in Kabul unless it was critical to the operation of the embassy, that we were ready to leave at short notice if we had to. We might soon have to do so.

Sunday 4 July

At the weekly breakfast club of ambassadors over at the UN offices, we discussed Qatar's efforts to act as a mediator between the Government of Afghanistan and the Taliban. The Government of Afghanistan agreed in principle with Qatar's doing so. But the Taliban's strategy was to fight and talk. On the battlefield the Taliban fighters strengthened their position with each passing day; in the Doha talks the Taliban's Political Commission were dragging their feet, seeking to build their political standing and sense of legitimacy through talks. They claimed not to trust the United Nations as an honest broker. This said a lot about the Taliban's attitude towards the international community, and towards how they planned to rule Afghanistan once they seized control.

In the political negotiations with the republic and international mediators, the Taliban insisted on the need for a new Islamic Afghan constitution. But they refused to engage on the details of what they wanted. Ghani meanwhile insisted on the fact that Article 149 of the existing constitution said that the only permissible changes were ones which strengthened its human rights provisions. That was a laudable position. But it no longer reflected how power was ebbing away from the republic that Ghani represented and flowing towards the Taliban. The Taliban had no interest in either the existing constitution or the human rights provisions it enshrined.

Ramiz Alakbarov, the enterprising and very courageous deputy head of the United Nations in Kabul, reported on his programme of visits to regional capitals. He described a mood of panic in Mazar-e Sharif, the capital of the northern province of Balkh. In neighbouring Kunduz, the government was in control of only the centre of the city. The Taliban were telephoning public servants to encourage them to walk away from their jobs, with the promise of a bonus and of returning to their jobs under a Taliban administration. The government had no effective answer to this increasingly effective psychological warfare.

I noted that former president Hamid Karzai seemed to be manoeuvring in some mysterious and unfathomable way. He seemed to blow hot and cold on the talks with the Taliban, supporting these discussions in principle but neither committing to attend them himself nor lending his personal authority and experience to achieving an agreement. I privately wondered whether he was more interested in letting others try and fail, then turning the situation to advantage.

I travelled across the Green Zone to the Ministry of Defence for an important meeting with BK, the recently appointed Defence Minister. Colonel Max, my defence attaché, accompanied me. After the fall of Kabul, Max was one of the team who stayed on in Kabul airport, working round the clock as my liaison and fixer with the UK, US and other allied military contingents.

BK came with a high reputation. He was a straight talker: he told things as they were about the prospects for the war. He stated frankly that Afghan's military strategy was unsustainable without coalition support. In particular, Afghanistan's armed forces needed urgent air support to move forces quickly to where they were most needed. The Afghan Air Force was down to a couple of serviceable C-130 Hercules transport planes – not enough to even touch the surface of what was needed. Military casualty levels were high, and new recruitment was not keeping pace. Morale in much of the regular army was low, giving way to panic as districts fell to the Taliban. The locally raised militias kept changing sides to the Taliban. BK was frank about the uneven and sometimes poor leadership within the Afghan National Army.

And, BK confirmed, the Taliban were winning the propaganda war. They often treated captured soldiers well, which undermined the army's will to fight. Why risk dying for a distant and dysfunctional government when the alternative is some food, some money and being sent home?

BK painstakingly outlined his strategy to turn the tide. The Taliban now controlled 80 per cent of territory in the north of Afghanistan, with government forces remaining in control of the provincial capitals alone. The government needed to consolidate its forces and reinforce key regional centres vital to the survival of the republic. And it needed to regain control of the border crossing points and highways.

I pressed BK on the lack of political unity among the republic's leaders. He chose his words carefully, but it was clear that this was a major problem for the conduct of the military campaign. In turn, BK asked me outright if I thought Pakistan wanted a Taliban military victory. It was a hard question to answer. If Pakistan did not, would they – could they – do enough to prevent the Taliban believing that a military victory was within their grasp?

It was Independence Day in the USA. In Afghanistan NATO's Resolute Support Mission was drawing to a close. That same day the *Wall Street Journal* published a story speculating that the US Embassy was gearing up to close down as well.[13]

This was news to me. Clearly, if there was even a grain of truth in the story this would be a game changer for us, and still more so for Afghanistan. It was hard to believe that closure of the US Embassy was in prospect without us knowing about it. I called the US Deputy Chief of Mission Ian McCary and asked him straight out. We also cross-checked with the Americans in Washington. McCary confirmed that the story was not true.

We were all going to need to be very clear in our communication in the coming weeks. Everything we were trying to achieve depended on others believing that we meant what we said about our continued commitment to Afghanistan after the military withdrawal.

MONDAY 5 JULY

One of my ambassador colleagues expressed the view that the Taliban wanted to 'normalise' the situation in areas they controlled so that they could 'feed on' the population: that is, rely on the local economy to provision themselves. That the Taliban seemed to be settling in for a war of attrition against government forces, blockading cities rather than trying to seize them, and waiting for the republic to collapse.

Mohammad Daudzai called by at the residence. Daudzai, a veteran envoy to Afghanistan's neighbours under the Karzai and Ghani administrations, was a key channel for contacts between Afghanistan and Pakistan. We discussed the glacially slow progress on two key bilateral agreements under discussion between Afghanistan and Pakistan: a Strategic Partnership Agreement and a Bilateral Security Agreement. Between them, these two agreements were intended to form the basis for a more substantial and stable relationship including managing the border and refugees, and economic cooperation. I updated Daudzai on our work with Pakistan to encourage the Taliban to make progress in the intra-Afghan negotiations.

Daudzai urged the UK to continue its efforts with Pakistan, as did most other senior Afghan officials who knew of them. But until the very end, personal animosities and poor judgement would continue to get in the way of Pakistan and Afghanistan working effectively towards a workable peace settlement. There had been a spectacular bust-up two months previously. On 10 May, the UK had brokered a meeting in Kabul between President Ghani and Pakistan's most senior military officer, General Qamar Javed Bajwa. Chief of the Defence Staff General Nick Carter was present in the meeting. Only a few days later, President Ghani's national security adviser, Hamidullah Mohib, one of Ghani's closest confidants, made a speech in which he compared Pakistan to a brothel. Not surprisingly, the Government of Pakistan refused to have anything more to do with Mohib.[14]

There was a growing sense that time was running out for the Ghani Administration. The Supreme State Council, a senior executive body formed only a few weeks previously to bind Afghanistan's fractious political leaders into a unified approach towards matters of war and peace, was already collapsing; the power brokers, sensing the end of the Ghani Government, were distancing themselves from it and positioning themselves as contenders for a future government.

David Martinon, the French Ambassador, invited me to his embassy for lunch. A table was set in the middle of a large lawn under the trees, with a gusty wind blowing. The embassy looked deserted apart from David and his close protection team. Dressed all in black with dark sunglasses, they looked the business.

David had worked closely in the past with President Sarkozy. Still only about 50, he was a canny and well-informed operator with a dry sense of humour. He told things as he saw them. In my experience the best French diplomats are highly effective, and he was one of those. We got on well. We shared a similarly gloomy perspective on the likely course of events. In mid-August David and his small team would be extracted from the French Embassy to the relative safety of the airport. He would stay there to the end, personally overseeing France's evacuation.

In Doha, the head of the Taliban Political Commission, Suhail Shaheen, told the BBC that any foreign forces or military contractors still in Afghanistan after the completion of the military withdrawal would be viewed as occupying forces. The demand that all foreign forces should leave was consistent with the Taliban's position going back to the Doha Agreement, and was not a surprise to anyone.

Even so, the Taliban at Doha said that they wanted foreign diplomats and aid organisations to stay. They claimed that since they were not targeting diplomats and NGOs, no foreign protection force would be needed.[15]

It was not wholly reassuring to be told that diplomatic missions and foreign NGOs would not be targeted by the Taliban. I doubted that hardline Taliban fighters would even be aware of, still less feel bound by, assurances given by political figures in Doha, or that such assurances would mean anything in the heat of battle. Particularly since a large part of the purpose of the diplomatic missions and their staff was to support the government that the Taliban were seeking to destroy. The security of the diplomatic missions and their staff was inseparable from the security of the government and other inhabitants of the Green Zone. There was obviously a very high risk of collateral damage if the Taliban tried to take Kabul.

And the Taliban were not the only game in town. There was also the threat from al-Qaeda, despite the Taliban's undertakings in the Doha Agreement not to allow al-Qaeda or other extremists to use Afghanistan to threaten the security of the USA or its allies. And above all from ISKP, those extremely violent militants implacably hostile towards the West, who considered the Taliban little better than apostates and who wanted control of Afghanistan for themselves.

The Taliban were using statements of that sort to build a sense of inevitability, that they were the government in waiting, and that the world would soon have to deal with the reality of a restored Taliban government. They intended to run Afghanistan on their terms, not ours, when they were in control of the country. When they said that they would be responsible for the security of foreign embassies in Afghanistan they were perfectly serious.

The problem was that I knew no one among the international community in Kabul who had the slightest confidence in the Taliban's assurances or in their good faith. In the same interview, Shaheen denied that the Taliban were behind the recent increase in violence and stated that seizing Kabul was 'not Taliban policy'.

TUESDAY 6 JULY

At short notice, Foreign Minister Hanif Atmar called Western ambassadors to the Storai Palace for a set-piece briefing over lunch. Earlier in the day he had hosted a similar, separate event for non-Western embassies. He described the level of Taliban violence as 'unprecedented'. He stated that although no provincial capital had fallen yet, Kunduz, Kandahar and Herat (in the west) were under severe pressure. Afghanistan's armed forces were facing their highest ever attrition rate, with 3,500 soldiers killed since April. There had been extensive destruction of infrastructure. Atmar said that while the Taliban had never been committed to the Doha Agreement and had fulfilled none of their obligations, the Government of Afghanistan had fulfilled its side of the bargain even though it was not a party to the agreement.

Atmar did not seek a reversal of the decision to withdraw NATO forces. He claimed instead that the departure of foreign military forces disproved the jihadists' narrative that Afghanistan was under foreign occupation. But he requested that Afghanistan's allies should provide urgent support to keep Afghanistan's air force flying. He acknowledged that for its part the Government of Afghanistan needed to strengthen national unity. The international community should tie its assistance to greater Afghan Government unity and effectiveness.

It was naïve, Atmar continued, to believe that the Taliban would cut their ties with al-Qaeda, whatever the Doha Agreement said. On the contrary, he said, the terrorist threat was rising.

I needed Atmar to spell a few more things out, both for my own report back to London, and knowing that others around the table would also be reporting back to their capitals. I asked him two questions. First, if there was scope to bring more pragmatic Taliban elements to the fore, increasing the chances of a negotiated outcome. And second, what we should learn from history.

Atmar understood the purpose of the questions. To the first, he replied Yes; we should press ahead with efforts to get the Taliban – and, by implication, the Afghan Government – to hammer out some sort of political deal to avoid catastrophe.

His response to the second question ought to be carved into the desk of anyone dealing with Afghanistan: 'You won't solve the problem by disengaging from it. Repeating past mistakes will simply lead to the same results.'

WEDNESDAY 7 JULY

A short drive over to the German Embassy to meet Axel Zeidler, the departing German Ambassador. Axel's embassy had been reduced to a minimal presence since the 2017 truck bomb, which had killed over 150 people. The Government of Afghanistan had blamed the Haqqani Network, an affiliate of the Taliban. The

Taliban had denied involvement. The German Embassy still felt like a ghost town, with abandoned buildings and shuttered windows. Axel's assessment of the situation was sober and downbeat.

THURSDAY 8 JULY

A few days after the 4 July Independence Day national holiday, and a few weeks after President Ghani's visit to Washington, President Biden spoke again about the progress of the withdrawal. The military drawdown was nearing completion. The situation on the battlefield was worsening by the day. There was growing disquiet in the US defence and foreign policy world about where things were headed. Some had recommended keeping a force of 2,500 soldiers in Afghanistan. General Miller, the US military commander in Afghanistan, had said on ABC a few days earlier that 'we should be concerned'.[16]

Speaking from the White House, President Biden sought to regain control of the public narrative. He confirmed that the US military mission in Afghanistan would end by 31 August – sooner than the previous target date of the 20th anniversary of 9/11. Biden quoted the advice of his military commanders that 'speed is safety'. The US mission in Afghanistan – to bring Osama bin Laden to 'the gates of hell' – had been completed, and the terrorist threat to the USA had been degraded. It was not in the US national interest to stay in Afghanistan.

> We did not go into Afghanistan to nation-build. And it's the right and responsibility of the Afghan people alone to decide their future and how they want to run their country.[17]

It was clearly the Afghan leaders, then, who were responsible for the country's future.

Biden asserted that the nearly 300,000 serving members of the Afghan military had been provided with all the training and equipment necessary to defend their country. The USA would maintain its embassy in Kabul and its commitment and funding to Afghanistan.

For those Afghans who had worked alongside US forces and who wished to leave Afghanistan, the USA had accelerated the Special Immigrant Visa programme, the US equivalent of the UK's ARAP scheme; 2,500 such visas had been approved since Biden's inauguration, with special flights and holding arrangements in third countries being stood up.

Returning to the reasons behind the decision to end the military presence, Biden was unwavering. The USA should not fight the wars of the past but focus on challenges such as China, emerging technology, Covid and climate change. Those who argued that 'one more year' was needed to create the conditions for withdrawal were misguided. History showed that 'one more year' was not a solution but 'a recipe for being there indefinitely'. Nor was staying indefinitely an option. It meant putting

> American men and women back in the middle of a civil war … How many more – how many thousands more of America's daughters and sons are you willing to risk? How long would you have them stay? … I will not send another generation of Americans to war in Afghanistan with no reasonable expectation of achieving a different outcome.

I was struck by the awful similarity between Biden's words and Hanif Atmar's response to my question the previous day: don't keep doing the same things expecting different results.

In the questions that followed, a journalist drew comparisons with the fall of Saigon at the end of the Vietnam War. Biden responded with words that would come back to haunt all of us, but especially the Americans. 'There's going to be no circumstance where you see people being lifted off the roof. It is not at all comparable.'

The reference was to one of the defining images of the fall of Saigon in 1975: the photograph of people climbing up a ladder onto the roof of the US Embassy in Saigon and into a helicopter. In mid-August, as Kabul fell to the Taliban, an enterprising press photographer would capture a picture of a CH-47 Chinook helicopter seeming to rise from the US Embassy compound. It was all in the camera angle. But the effect was the same.

In Kabul's weekly NATO meeting the military briefers raised concerns over the Taliban's ever-tightening squeeze on the national road network. This was critical to the government's ability to support and resupply its troops; to feed the population; and to maintain any degree of national cohesion and common purpose against the Taliban. It was also critical to our own planning, should Kabul be cut off from the rest of the country and from the border crossings into neighbouring countries. One scenario was that the republic could be reduced to a rump state based on Kabul. How would a besieged city-state of maybe 5 million people, swollen by refugee inflows, survive? How would we even be able to maintain a presence?

Only one highway in and out of Kabul was still 'green', meaning safe to use. In this context 'safe' had a somewhat different meaning from the normal usage of the word.

I spoke with Russian Ambassador Dmitry Zhirnov by phone, as he and his embassy were locked down by Covid. A courtesy call – and, I hoped, an introduction to a more developed discussion later. The Russians have a lot of history in Afghanistan, most recently from the USSR's disastrous intervention in 1979. Moscow's failures in Afghanistan had been a drain on the resources and prestige of the USSR. The Red

Army's necessary but humiliating withdrawal, completed in early 1989, had set the stage for the violence, chaos and eventual victory of the Taliban that followed.

Over the years I had found some senior Russians unexpectedly thoughtful and reflective on their, and our, experience. One of them was General Boris Gromov, the commander of the Soviet 40th Army and the last Soviet soldier to leave Afghanistan. In around 2009 I had taken a British parliamentary delegation to meet him in Moscow. Gromov, by then a member of the State Duma, the lower house of Russia's parliament, had growled his way through a list of the strategic errors made by the Soviet Union in Afghanistan. He had then growled through another, no less impressive, list of the mistakes the USA and its allies were still making.

Less valuable was Zamir Kabulov, the Russian diplomat and Special Representative for Afghanistan, who I had met from time to time when I was the UK's Deputy Ambassador in Moscow and later as Ambassador. He had previously been Russia's Ambassador to Afghanistan, and liked to joke that Kabul was named after him. He delighted in telling me that MI6 and the CIA were ferrying ISKP fighters around the country in unmarked helicopters. I asked him where he had heard this manifestly absurd conspiracy theory, knowing perfectly well that the source of it was Kabulov himself.

Despite Kabulov and his conspiracy theories, it made no sense to think about Afghanistan in isolation from its geography and its neighbours. This had been brought home to me some years previously. In 2012, as Regional Director at the Foreign Office for Russia, Eastern Europe and Central Asia, I had accompanied Defence Secretary Philip Hammond and Armed Forces Minister Nicholas Harvey on a tour of the five Central Asian countries, to negotiate greater access to the ground transport routes that would provide an alternative to the GLOC – Ground Lines of Communication – through Pakistan to Afghanistan.

NATO's involvement in combat operations was to end in December 2014 and the International Security Assistance Force (ISAF) was to be replaced by a much lighter 'train and equip' mission named Resolute Support. At its height in 2010–2012, ISAF had about 130,000 troops in Afghanistan. The UK's contribution, Operation Herrick, involved thousands of soldiers and their equipment. The exam question was: how were we going to withdraw vast amounts of UK and NATO military kit by the end of 2014?

Pakistan had temporarily closed the GLOC following clashes between NATO and Pakistani forces on the Afghanistan–Pakistan border in 2010 and 2011. Then in May 2011 the USA had located and killed Osama bin Laden at a compound in Abbottabad close to Islamabad. The compound where Osama bin Laden lived for five years was just a short distance from the Pakistan Military Academy, Pakistan's equivalent of Sandhurst. It was hard to believe that he had been there for five years without the knowledge and support of Pakistan's Inter-Services Intelligence. The

American raid caused outrage across swathes of Pakistani society.

We badly needed alternatives to the Pakistan GLOC, both for capacity reasons and to reduce Pakistan's leverage over our operations in Afghanistan.

The problem was that there were only two viable land routes in and out of Afghanistan. One was through Pakistan. Iran was out of the question: our relations with Tehran, tricky at the best of times, had gone over a cliff in November 2011, when diplomatic relations with Iran had been broken off following an attack on the British Embassy in Tehran.

That left the northern route: the rail and road network of Central Asia. Some of this had been built to service the USSR's catastrophic entanglement in Afghanistan. By far the most important railways and roads ran through Uzbekistan and Kazakhstan. So in February 2012 off I went with the senior UK military officer in charge of planning the logistics, first to Kazakhstan and Uzbekistan with Philip, then on to Kyrgyzstan, Tajikistan and Turkmenistan with Nick.

The British relationship with Uzbekistan was complicated by that country's impressively bad record on human rights and in particular by the 2005 massacre in the city of Andijan, when President Karimov's security forces had fired on demonstrators, causing mass casualties and prompting European Union sanctions. The meeting with Karimov was never going to be a meeting of minds. It was a haggle in the best traditions of carpet trading.

Our last meeting of the tour was in Ashgabat, the capital of Turkmenistan, at the end of a long week. I had been to Turkmenistan several times before and had a sense of how the place worked. Shortly before our visit, President Berdimuhammedov had been re-elected in the kind of election where all the candidates were from the governing party and most had publicly announced that they would be voting for Berdimuhammedov.

Berdimuhammedov duly won 97 per cent of the votes. Before the meeting I carefully coached Nick on the exact form of words to use to congratulate him. Nick delivered his lines word-perfect. Berdimuhammedov's interpreter was also a true professional, delivering in Russian exactly what Berdimuhammedov needed to hear. It bore only a passing relationship to what Nick had actually said. The interpreter knew perfectly well that I understood exactly what he had just said to Berdimuhammedov, and fixed me with a stare. I fixed him back. No words passed nor were any needed. We had said what we wanted to say. Berdimuhammedov had heard what he wanted to hear. Honour was satisfied on both sides.

The absent participant in these meetings was Russia. All concerned knew perfectly well that without Russia's consent the Central Asian routes would not be viable. Russia had agreed in 2009 to the establishment of the Northern Distribution Network – a network of overland, air and sea supply routes through Russia and Central Asia to support NATO operations in Afghanistan. Russia did this because

Moscow did not want a failed state in Afghanistan – a haven for terrorists and narco-barons – any more than we did. But it was an uneasy cooperation, which could be blown off course by Russia's increasingly difficult and ultimately confrontational relationship with the USA and its allies. And Russia was never going to be happy with a large, permanent US or NATO military presence in a region that had until recently been part of Russia's empire. I once asked a senior Russian official in Moscow to summarise Russia's views of the NATO presence in Afghanistan. The response was laconic: 'Don't fail, and don't stay.' I could not have put it better myself.

We did fail. We didn't stay.

Throughout 2013 and 2014, Operation Herrick drew to a close as NATO combat operations ended and ISAF was wound up. In a huge and complex logistical operation, large amounts of military equipment were brought back to the UK overland via both the northern routes and Pakistan. Equipment that was no longer needed was gifted to the Afghan National Army, to neighbouring countries, or destroyed.

Back to the present: our Afghan staff working in the embassy were getting increasingly concerned at the pace of resettlement under the ARAP. The scheme was run by the Ministry of Defence working to a policy owned by itself and the Home Office. The problem went wider than the speed of implementation. There were also unresolved questions about its scope: which staff were eligible for resettlement, and which were not. Not all embassy staff were eligible, with the decision turning on whether the individual concerned worked for or with the UK Government in exposed or meaningful roles. But bureaucratic distinctions based on whether roles were public facing, and on whether an individual was employed direct by the embassy or via a contractor, were looking increasingly detached from the reality on the ground.

I put a hold on two dozen ARAP rejection letters to a group of embassy staff before they could be issued; I did not consider that in refusing those members of staff we were in a defensible position. I asked the team to look at the applications again and take up with the Ministry of Defence and the Home Office a number of issues that the cases raised. We needed to look again at the purpose and spirit of the policy, which was about fulfilling our obligation to look after our staff, without whom we could not function in Afghanistan. As the situation in Afghanistan worsened we would be certain to come under increasing pressure to expand the scope of the policy. Better to think that through now. The scheme also needed a proper appeals process.

As well as our own staff, we started to receive appeals to evacuate UN staff and people who had worked with the UN system. The United Nations, which worked on behalf of the entire international community, had no country to which to evacuate its country-based staff. I was asked repeatedly by colleagues in the United Nations if we could include their staff in our resettlement programme. But our resettlement programme included no provision to do this, and we were not able to offer resettlement to UN staff.

I was invited to dinner with Fazel Fazly, who I'd met with on 27 June. Simon, the embassy political officer, and I drove out to a guest house compound on Wazir Akbar Khan Street, a short distance outside the Green Zone. We were joined by one of Fazly's staff, a tall young man who spoke good English. We talked late into the evening. I wanted in particular to get Fazly to focus on how to turn around the propaganda war in Afghanistan, as the Afghan Government was losing it, and had been for a long time. I offered to source some specialist help. Fazly agreed that we should swiftly work up a proposal for some rapid consultancy support.

On the drive back to the embassy late that evening, I saw two small boys standing at the edge of the road on the Wazir Akbar Khan roundabout, the entrance to the Green Zone closest to our embassy. Maybe eight years old, wearing traditional Afghan clothes. Solemn and dignified, children, yet older than their years, they were counting out each boy's share of the day's takings from whatever commercial enterprise they were engaged in.

Three thousand five hundred miles away, in the Palace of Westminster, Prime Minister Boris Johnson was making a statement to the House of Commons, marking the departure of the last British service personnel from Afghanistan at the close of Operation Toral, the UK's contribution to NATO's Resolute Support Mission. He spoke of the achievements of the 20-year campaign: the progress made in suppressing terrorism, and the gains made in health and education, particularly for women and girls. He pledged the UK's continued support for Afghanistan and for a peaceful settlement.

FRIDAY 9 JULY

General Nick Carter, Chief of the Defence Staff, gave a media interview in which he described the situation in Afghanistan as 'pretty grim'. There were reports that China was evacuating its nationals.

We were receiving a steady stream of letters from people in the UK asking for ARAP to be widened in scope, to include specific groups of people who had worked with us or on UK-funded initiatives. Today's appeal was from a group of British accountants on behalf of members of Afghanistan's Independent Joint Anti-corruption Monitoring and Evaluation Committee, who the accountants had worked with. This initiative had been funded by the UK's Department for International Development and launched at the 2010 London Conference on Afghanistan. The purpose of the 2010 London Conference had been to bolster Afghanistan's security, development and transition to democracy following the flawed 2009 election. On the agenda was planning for the eventual handover of responsibility for Afghanistan's security to Afghanistan's defence and security forces. So too were plans to draw the Taliban into peace negotiations – this, a decade before the Doha Agreement.

Taliban leaders attending a meeting in Moscow announced a temporary moratorium on attacking cities on the grounds that they needed to have a plan in place to prevent the looting of shops and banks. That same day, Taliban forces attacked Kandahar city.[18]

The international media drew attention to a spate of assassinations of Afghan Air Force pilots. This was a highly effective tactic by the Taliban, which lacked both an air force of its own and modern anti-aircraft weapons. As well as killing very scarce and highly skilled members of the military, this encouraged others to desert. Much simpler than shooting planes or helicopters down, much cheaper, and much harder to counter.

SATURDAY 10 JULY

I spent the evening at the residence of Deborah Lyons, the UN Head of Mission, a senior Canadian diplomat. The guest of honour was Ronald Neumann who, now in his late 70s, had been the US Ambassador to Afghanistan 15 years previously. His father Robert had held the job in the 1960s. The purpose of his visit was unclear, to me at least. But he asked good questions and was clearly getting very good access to senior people while in Afghanistan. I chalked it up as one of those events where you do plenty of listening, thinking and testing out ideas.

SUNDAY 11 JULY

I travelled out of the Green Zone and across town in the direction of the airport for my first meeting with the new Minister of Interior, General Abdul Sattar Mirzakwal. Like me, Mirzakwal was less than a month into the job. Like Bismillah Khan (BK), the newly appointed Defence Minister, he had been appointed to try to turn around the disastrous performance of the Afghan National Defence and Security Forces against the Taliban onslaught.

The ministry was a large military compound behind high concrete blast walls. Between the approach road and the wall ran an open sewer: a concrete channel filled with black, stinking liquid. There was heavy security, both on getting into the compound and inside the building that housed the Minister's office. I wondered how serious the insider threat to him was from infiltrators or disaffected staff. Not a question you want to dwell on when you are sitting in his office.

Mirzakwal had in front of him a voluminous briefing pack detailing the extent of the UK's substantial support to the Ministry of Interior. Although speaking through an interpreter, he was friendly and welcoming. A bear of a man with a bushy moustache and heavy beard stubble.

The Taliban's war on the Republic of Afghanistan and its security services meant that the Interior Ministry was in effect a branch of the military rather than a police force. Mirzakwal was heavily focused on defending cities and supply routes against Taliban military attacks. As with the military, this was, without reliable air transport and with the Taliban controlling most of the main roads, an increasingly tall order. Mirzakwal acknowledged that morale was poor and that the government was losing the propaganda war. He claimed, though, that the people under his command would 'fight with their bare hands to the very end'.

At the weekly breakfast club at the UN offices, we compared notes on the Taliban's approach to the peace negotiations in Doha.

The arrogance of the Taliban Political Commission and their disdain for the international community was palpable. When challenged by the United Nations on the very high levels of violence, which were contrary to the Taliban's commitments under the Doha Agreement, the Taliban replied: 'You call it violence; we call it victory!' They dismissed the social, economic and political progress of the last 20 years in health, education and human development, in which the international donors and development agencies had invested so heavily, as nothing but corruption and a drugs economy. The Taliban rejected UN mediation in the peace talks. They retorted that Afghans could talk directly with other Afghans, without the involvement of foreigners.

The Taliban did not seem to be in the least serious about agreeing a negotiated settlement. They were obviously using the negotiations to buy time for their military campaign and to bolster their legitimacy in the eyes of Afghans and – to the limited extent that the Taliban cared about this – the international community.

At the breakfast club we compared notes also on the republic's leadership. On the basis of my meetings with them so far, I reported that I thought Abdullah understood the trouble the republic was in, Ghani less so. No one could work out Karzai's game plan, if he had one, other than to keep his options open. I commented that it was probably too late to turn around the republic's lamentable strategic communications and to build strong public support for the war against the Taliban.

We knew, too, that senior members of the government, including Amrullah Saleh and Fazel Fazly, were becoming increasingly critical of the international community for failing to put real pressure on the Taliban. There was a lot of bitterness among senior government figures about the way in which the Americans had left Bagram airbase.

Brigadier Dan Blanchford and his team were in Kabul to work on the detailed planning for an evacuation – Operation Pitting. He and Brigadier Tom came to the Ambassador's Residence to talk through where things stood. Dan and his team, and the embassy, had done a lot of groundwork and the planning was in good shape. But Dan was concerned at the speed at which the situation was deteriorating. He was right to be concerned. I talked him through London's direction to maintain the embassy and its core functions for as long as possible. Operation Pitting was our back-up plan. Our role in Kabul was to tell things as we saw them, and to ensure that we were in lockstep on our contingency planning.

Later that afternoon, Alex Pinfield said that the time had come to consider moving the embassy onto a 'crisis watch' footing. This is one step short of moving into full scale crisis management mode. It would help focus minds and efforts on the very top priority business, including preparations for an evacuation if that was where we ended up. I agreed.

MONDAY 12 JULY

I went to see Foreign Minister Hanif Atmar, to get an authoritative update on recent peace talks between the republic and the Taliban. As always, although Atmar's demeanour was polite and courtly his analysis and prescriptions were laser-sharp. He got quickly to the point. He was deeply concerned. The Taliban had not changed. Their abuses of human rights continued unabated, as did their relationship with al-Qaeda. They would only engage seriously in peace talks if their progress on the battlefield was halted. Unless this happened, they had no reason to negotiate.

To halt the Taliban's military advances the USA and its allies needed to supply government forces with close air support, to help them get through the summer fighting season and allow the Afghan Air Force time to build up its own capacity.

Despite Atmar's unflappable demeanour I detected a hint of desperation. He was openly critical of Ghani's leadership and of the effectiveness of the government as a whole. He repeatedly urged me to press the Afghan Government and the wider political élite to agree and implement a single, coherent strategy. He agreed that the republic's ineffective strategic communications were undermining the Afghan National Defence and Security Forces' morale, at the same time leaving the field open for the Taliban to set out their own narrative.

We talked about the government's peace negotiations with the Taliban in Doha, and the diplomacy supporting them. The Taliban had demanded control of the Presidency and the security ministries, and proposed an interim constitution based on the 1964 version. But it was clear that they viewed the negotiations as little more than a veneer, a diversion, while they continued to fight. Their rejection of the United Nations' offer to mediate meant that they were rejecting the United Nations' capacity to offer workable and impartial advice on how to bridge the gap between maximalist demands and negotiable outcomes. The Taliban were also rejecting the route to international legitimacy offered by UN-sponsored negotiations.

A further round of senior-level talks was scheduled for the middle of July in Doha.

General Miller handed overall command of US forces in Afghanistan to General McKenzie, the commander of US CENTCOM in Tampa, Florida, with a forward base in Qatar. Admiral Peter Vasely assumed command of US forces on the ground. This marked not only the transition of command but also the transition of the mission, as NATO's Resolute Support Mission wound down and was replaced by USFOR-A – United States Forces Afghanistan.

TUESDAY 13 JULY

We were well aware that if we were to achieve a negotiated peace, Afghanistan's international supporters would need to create real leverage over the Taliban, soon, to incentivise them to seek a peace deal rather than pursuing outright military victory.

I sat in countless discussions in which we told ourselves that the Taliban wanted legitimacy and that this gave the international community leverage. But I no longer believed that to be the case, and I am not sure it ever was true.

In reality, in Taliban eyes legitimacy was not ours to confer. It came from their religious authority, and from military conquest if that was the Will of God. Some of them, at least, did apparently want international recognition. But those who did believed this was theirs as of right, and had been unjustly taken away from them in 2001. They planned to take it back from a government they had always considered illegitimate and imposed by foreign occupiers. I no longer believed that they were prepared to compromise in exchange for international recognition, in the form of better behaviour either on the path to achieving power or once they had done so. They had lived for many years untroubled by the fact that the international community did not recognise them as a legitimate government, and they had conducted a campaign of relentless violence to expel us from Afghanistan and take back what they considered to be theirs. The Doha Agreement deal had in any case, some Taliban argued, already given them a measure of recognition and legitimacy at no cost to themselves.

What the Taliban did want was a range of practical concessions: lifting of sanctions; release of prisoners (who would of course, as we all knew, promptly turn up on the battlefield); the lifting of sanctions on their leadership; access to resources to consolidate their grip on the population and on administrative functions. They wanted access to cross-border supply routes and customs revenues, and free movement for the Taliban seniors who lived in Pakistan. They wanted all this on their own terms, not ours. And they wanted to create a sense of inevitability that the Taliban would win.

As the Doha Agreement had given the Taliban many of these things on a plate, then if we, the international community, wanted to support a peaceful settlement in preference to a Taliban military victory, we would need to apply more coercive measures, and quickly.

But what measures could we apply, if we were not prepared to reverse the military withdrawal?

Overnight, the Taliban captured Spin Boldak, a major border crossing between Afghanistan and Pakistan, following heavy fighting in Kandahar province. Spin Boldak, on the road between Kandahar and the southern Pakistani city of Quetta, the home of the exiled Taliban leadership, was of great strategic value to the Taliban, and its loss was a major political and economic blow to the government. The ever greater Taliban control of the major border crossings and customs posts meant that the Taliban were ever more visibly exercising the functions of the state, as well as raising ever more revenue for their war and starving the republic of resources.

The embassy's economic and political teams summarised the situation in a diplomatic cable:

Afghanistan: Taliban Puts an Economic Noose on the Republic

Summary

Taliban capture key economic nodes such as trade ports and arterial roads. Loss of revenue, and an ambitious budget, may lead to a fiscal crisis in the coming months, requiring additional funds from donors to meet basic needs such as security and health. Control of trade routes is a strategic win for the Taliban. Taliban filling their war chest, putting a financial stranglehold on the government, and could, in time, blockade cities including Kabul. Fuel and food prices are rising.

The capture of the Shir Khan Bandar border crossing with Tajikistan has been followed quickly by the fall of Islam Qala on the Iranian border, with intense fighting at Spin Boldak on the Pakistan border. These are important border and dry ports in the North, West and South of Afghanistan. A host of smaller crossings and dry ports have also fallen.

On average 84% of Afghanistan's import are from its regional neighbours. Fuel and food are critical imports. As long as the crossings and key arterial roads remain open to trade comment and the Taliban continue to hold them, their ability to exert control over the economy increases, and their revenue base expands. At the same time it reduces Kabul's revenues and increases economic pressure on the government.

Comment

The fall of Spin Boldak and other border posts with Pakistan would signal not only a consolidation of the Taliban strategy [redacted].

So far, the Pakistan border crossings continue to be held by the government, along with the important border crossing with Iran at Zaranj.

BRISTOW [19]

After the fall of Kabul, I learned that around this time staff at the US Embassy in Kabul had sent a 'dissent cable' – a formal channel on which US officials could register in writing their disagreement with the direction of government policy. According to a Senate Committee on Foreign Relations minority report published in February 2022, the cable was highly critical of the US Administration's approach, warned that the Taliban were making rapid advances, and recommended that the Biden Administration should speed up evacuation planning. [20]

Wednesday 14 July

Lots of our indicators and warnings would be turning amber in this week's security report to London. This would inevitably cause a flutter back in Whitehall. One of my team in Kabul checked with me if this was the message we should be sending. I instructed that we should send the report: the purpose of the indicators and warnings was to give our honest and informed assessment of the reality on the ground. It did not necessarily mean that the embassy would have to close soon. But the picture was worrying enough to need drawing to London's attention.

France announced that it would be running commercial charters for any of its citizens wishing to leave Kabul. A flight left a few days later. In the aftermath of the fall of Kabul, a great deal was made in the UK press and parliament of France getting its people out in good time while we failed to do so. That is inaccurate, on several counts.

First, we did not offer charters to British nationals because there was no clear need to do so. The UK Government's approach was to encourage people to leave while the commercial airlines were still running, and commercial flights were still operating up to 15 August, with availability: we checked this every day. We were, however, running charters for Afghans being resettled under the ARAP scheme, where we needed the additional control and privacy for people at risk; 2,000 ARAP evacuees left between May and early August on these flights. France's profile in Afghanistan had been much lower than the UK's since at least 2014, and France had fewer people with a claim for evacuation or resettlement.

Second, no government succeeded in evacuating all the people it wanted to get out, either before or during the August 2021 evacuation. The French Government was itself criticised heavily for not doing more, sooner. As were the USA and

European governments. NATO and the United Nations had no plans for evacuating their Afghan staff before the republic fell.

This is in no way a criticism of my French colleagues in Kabul. Ambassador David Martinon and his team did their duty, acting with great courage, integrity and tenacity before and during the fall of Kabul.

It was clear at the time, though, that in many allied embassies the contingency plans were not as well developed as they needed to be. Few seemed to have concrete plans of their own, and most were over-reliant on the Americans. None had an equivalent of Operation Pitting in preparation. One senior European diplomat told us at the time: 'We are not prepared. Our head is in the sand. We are at physical risk, and our ministers are at political risk.'

Cihad Erginay, the Turkish Ambassador, came over for dinner. Cihad was one of the best ambassadors in Kabul: incredibly well informed, astute and witty.

I needed to hear from Cihad where things stood with Turkey taking on responsibility for the security of the airport. The Americans had been asking the Turks to do so for some months, and there were still unresolved questions about what Turkey was and was not prepared to agree to do. The Turkish military were very capable, and Turkey had a long-standing and serious commitment to Afghanistan. But the Turks were concerned about the scale and riskiness of what the Americans were asking them to take on.

The Taliban had made clear their opposition to Turkish forces staying on at the airport after the NATO withdrawal: 'The extension of occupation will arouse emotions of resentment and hostility inside our country towards Turkish officials and will damage bilateral ties.' They warned that any foreign forces staying in Afghanistan for any reason would be subject to the fatwa of 1,500 distinguished scholars in 2001 – the fatwa under which the Taliban's 20-year jihad against the republic and its international backers was being waged.[21]

The US Government announced Operation Allies Refuge, a programme which would speed up the evacuation of Afghans who had helped the USA under the Special Immigration Visa (SIV) programme. A week later, Congress approved an increase in the number of visas available. The first group of evacuees under Operation Allies Refuge would arrive in the USA on 30 July 2021.

There had been bipartisan criticism of the US Administration for not doing enough to protect Afghans who had worked in support of the US mission in Afghanistan. The question became pressing because of the decision to withdraw the military, and to press ahead with this even when it became clear that the Afghan defence and security forces were losing the fight with the Taliban.

But the question did not hit like lightning from a clear blue sky in mid-2021. Biden was the fourth US President since the 2001 attacks and the start of the US military mission in Afghanistan. Boris Johnson was the fifth UK Prime Minister since the UK's decision to send military forces to Afghanistan alongside the USA. The USA, the UK and other allies had had 20 years to come up with adequate plans to fulfil their obligations to their Afghan staff and partners if things went badly in Afghanistan. The problem was well known and long standing. The US SIV programme had been running since 2009. The UK introduced limited schemes for Afghans in 2010. And Trump's Doha Agreement with the Taliban in February 2020 had put everyone on notice that time was running out.

THURSDAY 15 JULY

Lunch was with the Japanese Ambassador, Takashi Okada, at his residence, a short distance from mine. Okada had previously been Japan's Ambassador to the UK. Japan was a major development assistance donor to Afghanistan and had hosted the Tokyo Conference on Afghanistan in 2012. At the Tokyo Conference the international donor community had set out its ambition to support Afghanistan's 'Transformation Decade' following the end of the International Security Assistance Force (ISAF), the NATO combat mission, in December 2014. The Transformation Decade was to be an Afghan-led process of building political institutions, the economy and lasting security, following a long decade of UN-led 'transition' from the legacy of the previous Taliban rule.

Our discussion ranged widely over the sushi and rice wine, only mildly inhibited by the substantial Perspex screen standing between us across the middle of the dining table. Diplomacy in a pandemic. Takashi probed on our intentions for our embassy; the Japanese, like the Canadians, were our close neighbours in Kabul, and depended on our security provision in the Green Zone. If we decided to leave, that would all but make their decision for them.

The Japanese Ambassador's Residence was an oasis of serenity. As is customary at Japanese embassies, at the end of the lunch the sushi chef emerged from the kitchen, bowing low as we thanked him.

A crucial round of talks was to take place in Doha on 16–18 July. But in the run-up the Republic of Afghanistan's leaders had gone out of their way to demonstrate disunity. Games were being played over who would and would not attend as individuals jockeyed to maximise their own positions and to ensure that their rivals took any blame for failure or for unpalatable concessions to the Taliban.

I put in an early evening call with Mohammed Masoom Stanekzai, the Afghan Government's chief negotiator. It took numerous attempts to get through, eventually successful from a garden table outside the embassy cafeteria. We talked through the outlook for the negotiations and what might follow. Stanekzai confirmed the list of participants on the republic's side (to the extent that anything is ever confirmed in Afghanistan until it actually happens). He joked that the list was not as big as yesterday's, when the whole of Kabul had been invited. In theory, the republic's delegation would include both Abdullah and Karzai. In the event, Karzai backed out at the last minute but was at least persuaded to go to the airport and make a supportive statement to the media.

I asked Kevin (the embassy press officer, now doubling up as my acting chief of staff) to schedule a video conference with senior colleagues in London in the next few days. We needed to force the pace on the implementation of ARAP, the contingency planning, and the preparations for crisis working over August.

Saad Mohseni, a prominent Afghan businessman and founder of the Tolo news and media group, contacted me to ask for help with protecting Afghanistan's cultural heritage as the threat of a Taliban victory loomed. This was the first of several such requests. The immediate question concerned the private collection of an individual in Kabul, who was terrified for his own safety and for the fate of his collection of Afghan cultural treasures. Apart from this person's individual plight, the wider risks from a Taliban takeover were hard to miss. The Taliban's fondness for cultural vandalism had been vividly displayed in early 2001 with their destruction of the Bamyan Buddhas. The Taliban had used artillery, anti-aircraft guns and dynamite to destroy these globally important statues, which dated from the 6th century. The Taliban considered them idolatrous.

Saad's question was simple: could the embassy take possession of the collection for safe keeping? I desperately wanted to say Yes on the spot and work out the details later. But in reality, the answer was nowhere near that simple. This was a minefield of legal and reputational problems. How would we know who in fact owned the collection or how it had been acquired? Who would take responsibility for packing and moving it? What would happen to it if we had to evacuate the embassy? How would we deal with similar requests from other individuals or state museums? What would we have to stop doing in order to turn our attention to this matter?

The hard fact was that we did not have enough staff or time to take on rescue missions for cultural objects, no matter how important they were. I asked colleagues in London to look into it quickly in case there were ways we could help. I wrote to the British Museum. I asked the United Nations – maybe UNESCO could do something? And I raised the matter with several top Afghan politicians over the course of the week.

A UN report to the Security Council assessed that al-Qaeda was present in at least 15 of Afghanistan's provinces. The report stated that al-Qaeda was operating under Taliban protection from the southern provinces of Kandahar, Helmand and Nimruz. The report also detailed the strengthening position of ISKP across the country, including in and around Kabul, and its efforts to recruit disaffected members of the Taliban who were opposed to the Doha Agreement. "

FRIDAY 16 JULY

News came through of the death of Danish Siddiqui, a Reuters photojournalist and a Pulitzer prizewinner. He had been killed while reporting on the fighting in Kandahar, where he had been embedded with Afghan forces. One of a very courageous group of war correspondents who put themselves in dangerous situations to inform the public of the facts.

Every day we received messages from current and former UK government and military colleagues about past and present members of staff, and about Afghans they had worked with, pressing for them to be offered evacuation. Afghan judges, and particularly female judges, were one such group. There were many others. When you work for a long time in difficult circumstances with courageous and principled people, it is natural and right to want to support them when their lives are in danger. With each new case it became clearer that we were going to need answers soon for the multitude of special cases who were not covered by the ARAP scheme.

SATURDAY 17 JULY

The USA began to speed up its SIV process. American colleagues told me that President Biden had directed that all SIV cases who had been processed and were cleared to travel should leave Afghanistan by the end of July. Another 600 cases whose applications were in progress would also leave with their families for the USA, for completion of the processing there. By early August applicants would be processed in a third country, yet to be determined.

In reporting this to London, I underlined the need to step up the pace further on ARAP: 'Our current timelines do not reflect the urgency of the situation or the likelihood that our capacity to do this work in country will reduce or disappear before the work is completed.'

Brigadier Tom passed on the advice being given to NATO embassies by Admiral Vasely, the senior US military commander in Afghanistan. It was short and to the point: 'Get small.' That is, reduce the size of your establishment to the bare minimum. And get on with relocating eligible Afghans out of the country. That was clearly the advice he was giving his own people. The US Embassy remained stubbornly large. I did not find this reassuring. It felt too much like disconnectedness within the US system, and a wish to believe that things were in better shape than they really were.

SUNDAY 18 JULY

The weekly breakfast club meeting at the UN compound took stock of the intra-Afghan negotiations taking place in Doha.

I came away with the sense that the Doha meeting was the last chance for any sort of negotiated deal rather than a hostile takeover by the Taliban. Afghanistan's political leaders seemed not to understand that their negotiating position was weakening with every passing week, and that as events on the battlefield took their course what might have been achievable a couple of months previously was no longer on offer. There was growing evidence of local-level deal making with the Taliban. I wondered if we might now be approaching a point where the most optimistic outlook was that the republic would be able to hold Kabul and maybe a few key regional capitals but would lose control of most of the country.

For some time I had been convinced that the only way we would change the Taliban's approach would be to dramatically sharpen the incentives on the Taliban to do a deal with the Afghan Government. Virtually the entire international community was – in public, at least – telling the Taliban not to seek a military victory. But this was clearly having no effect on their strategy. We needed to look yet again at what hard leverage we could apply, before and after they entered power, that would stand a chance of moderating their behaviour.

I commented to colleagues in Kabul and London that we should not kid ourselves that the threat to withhold international legitimacy was a strong lever. I said that there was no reason to think that the Taliban believed that legitimacy was ours to confer. In their view, this would come from their religious and political authority and from the facts on the ground. The Taliban seemed perfectly happy to create those facts through military conquest.

I had a visitor from London: Glen (not his real name), a senior military officer sent by the chief of the defence staff, Nick Carter, to assess the situation. Glen and I called on President Ghani. It was a hot afternoon. The peace and calm inside the palace were totally at odds with what was going on beyond the blast walls that protected the Green Zone.

Ghani was accompanied by Hamidullah Mohib and Matin Bek, his chief of staff. The meeting was polite in a courtly, otherworldly way. But our message was as clear as we could make it, within the boundaries of diplomatic courtesy. Time was running out for the republic. The Taliban was gaining momentum on the battlefield. Tough choices needed to be made. The republic needed to hold onto provincial capitals, sustain the army as a fighting force, and get through to winter and the end of the fighting season. The Taliban were also gaining momentum in the propaganda war, which was successfully projecting their gains and the strength of their fighting forces, demoralising the republic's armed forces and creating in the wider population a sense of the inevitability of a Taliban victory. We added that the republic needed to address urgently the reasons why the Taliban's propaganda narratives were working and the republic's were not. President Ghani and his colleagues needed to broadcast a compelling story of what Afghans would lose if the republic lost the war.

Ghani agreed with much of this, but without conveying to us much sense that he would or could act on what we were saying. He produced a one-page slide on how Afghanistan would be governed after the US and NATO withdrawal. A few days later I found another copy in the papers left for me by my predecessor in the office at the embassy. It looked like something intended for publication in an academic treatise. But it was of limited practical use in addressing the immediate challenges the republic faced on the battlefield.

Ghani gave us a quick summary of the latest talks with the Taliban in Doha, all of which I already knew from other contacts. The Taliban had as usual made no concessions of substance, and were not even willing to engage in serious negotiations. They had demanded a return to the 1964 Constitution. In reality, this meant installing an emir as Afghanistan's monarch. And the removal of any references to women's rights. The republic and the Taliban had at least agreed to a date for their next meeting. It seemed that was all they had agreed.

What was missing from Ghani's analysis was any sense that he had a plan or a counter-offer that would turn the situation around. Or the political weight, or even the low cunning, to assemble a coalition of people who might between them be able to do so. It was like talking to a university professor – which is what Ghani had been before entering political life.

Before the meeting with Ghani we had covered similar ground with Fazel Fazly, the Director of the Administrative Office of the President. The meeting took place in the spectacular Emir's Pavilion – Kuti-e Baghtscha – in a roasting hot room with poor acoustics. It was hard not to nod off in the stultifying afternoon heat. On the way out I grabbed some photos of the pavilion on my camera phone, suspecting that I might not be coming back there again. This earned me a stern talking-to from the palace's security men, which I ignored.

From our meeting with President Ghani, we went on to meet the former president, Karzai. The meeting was outwardly friendly and cordial; Glen handed Karzai a book of poetry. Karzai is a politician to his fingertips. But it was even harder than usual to tell what he was really thinking, or doing behind the scenes. To me, it felt increasingly as if he was hedging against the failure of Ghani's presidency and the peace talks with the Taliban, keeping his options open for the looming crisis and for whatever happened beyond that. I wondered whether he wanted Ghani's presidency to fail.

We finished the working day at the Turkish Embassy, to compare notes with Ambassador Cihad Erginay and his team. We sat on an outside terrace being served tea and Turkish cakes. Cihad, dapper and quietly spoken, once again demonstrated that he was one of the most astute diplomats in Kabul, deftly dissecting the situation and its likely consequences. We all agreed that the outlook was not good.

MONDAY 19 JULY

With Glen, we continued to work our way around the senior members of the Afghan Government, meeting with Foreign Minister Hanif Atmar at his residence, a few steps from mine. Atmar's residence was similar in many respects to mine: a villa in a compound off 15th Street, with high walls and unobtrusive but robust security. Atmar was as urbane and quietly articulate as ever. The pastries and tea were outstanding, discreetly served by his well-practised staff. But there was a note of despair in his voice about whether the leadership of the republic would get its act together. He once again urged me to use my position to make the gravity of the situation crystal clear to the republic's leadership, and to spell out the risk that unless they worked together all would be lost.

On the way to the meeting with Atmar, I dropped by the Canadian Embassy, a city block away from the UK Embassy and Residence. The small team of Canadian diplomats, who had been bolstered for the summer, were clearly concerned to get as much advance notice as possible if we decided to pull our embassy out of the Green Zone. I gave them what information and assurance I could. It was not much.

Back in the UK Embassy, I discussed again with senior colleagues what we could do to force the pace of the ARAP scheme. We identified a significant bottleneck in the system: the time taken for applicants to assemble the documents they needed to lodge an application, on the basis of which the Ministry of Defence in London considered whether they qualified. Passports, marriage certificates, birth certificates for children ... Afghans often lacked such documents, which people in the West have as a matter of course. The Afghan bureaucracy was slow, cumbersome and corrupt, and sometimes barely functional even in Kabul, still less out in the provinces. There was no prospect of that situation improving. If we needed to speed the process up, it could only be achieved by our taking a more flexible approach to the documents we required to support the applications.

Meanwhile the system continued to struggle to arrive at a clear sense of how narrow, or broad, the scope of ARAP was meant to be. Everyone understood what the problem was: to work out who was in scope, among the many Afghans who had worked with us over the previous two decades and who would be at risk from the Taliban. But it was proving much harder to get agreement on what the answers to it would look like, particularly under increasing pressure to do more, for more people, more quickly.

The ARAP documentation as it stood identified four categories of applicant. Category 4 was potentially open ended. This was the 'special cases' cohort: people who did not automatically qualify for resettlement but whose work for us or with us meant that their life was judged to be at risk from the Taliban. To complicate matters, individual UK government departments and the military had worked with very large numbers of people, over many years, in widely different circumstances. In London there was a great deal of discussion between government departments and agencies to ensure a broadly consistent approach across such a broad swathe of people. This was a question of fairness and meeting our moral obligations, but there was also a requirement to take into account our ability to resettle large numbers of people in the UK in a short time scale. We would need to advise ministers on the growing size and urgency of the problem and ask them for decisions, quickly, on how narrow or broad to set the criteria for evacuating people in a crisis.

To force the pace I called an online meeting with senior colleagues in the Ministry of Defence, Home Office and FCDO. I said that our current target of completing the existing programme for embassy staff and military interpreters by the end of August felt very risky, even if there was no slippage (there is *always* slippage). We needed to move faster. If our processing did not keep pace with events on the ground and we had to evacuate, we would time-out. If that happened, we would be leaving people behind who qualified for resettlement.

So we needed a clearer sense of what we were trying to achieve beyond embassy staff and military interpreters – in Category 4 in particular, where there was discretion to widen the scope of ARAP. And we needed clear decisions on what we intended to do for people at risk who were not our direct employees but were contracted via private companies. The Taliban were not likely to distinguish between people who worked *with* us and those who worked *for* us. They would kill the people they wanted to kill, regardless of the details of their employment contract.

TUESDAY 20 JULY

The Green Zone was under attack. Around breakfast time the centre of Kabul was rocked by a series of explosions. I heard rockets go overhead followed by loud explosions. They felt uncomfortably close. The close protection team quickly hustled me into lockdown in the fortified safe room in my apartment. One of them sat with me, fully kitted up and carrying an assault rifle. I quickly pulled on body armour and running shoes in case we needed to make a rapid move. We sat there in a space the size of a walk-in wardrobe, fizzing with adrenalin and making awkward small talk, the occasional trickle of sweat running down our backs. In the Operations Room, the close protection team worked quickly to get a fix on what was happening and what to do.

The Taliban had fired a salvo of rockets into the centre of the Green Zone, targeting the Eid celebrations attended by President Ghani and all the senior republic politicians and officials. The television crews covering the Eid celebration captured the moment in all its horror. Long lines of top public figures were kneeling at prayer. Explosions shook the cameras on their mountings. There was a moment of shock and confusion. Most participants maintained their composure but one or two people jumped up in panic, running in circles before looking round and rejoining the prayers.

Miraculously, no one was killed or injured. But the propaganda value to the Taliban was huge, demonstrating their ability and intention to attack Afghanistan's political leaders, in the very heart of Kabul, at will. They had come very close to killing a large number of leading government figures in a single spectacular blow. If the rockets had fallen slightly differently the consequences could have been grave. That fact was lost on no one.

And it was a sobering moment for us, too. The rockets had been launched from the back of a pick-up truck within the city, outside the Green Zone, and had passed overhead close to the embassy. Although we were not the target, there had been an obvious risk of collateral damage if the rockets had fallen short of it.

The Taliban had chosen one of the holiest events in the Muslim calendar to attempt an act of mass murder against fellow Muslims and Afghans, with whom they were supposedly conducting peace negotiations. That fact should have received more attention than it did from those claiming that the Taliban 2.0 were reformed characters.

Later that day Sadat Naderi, the State Minister for Peace, called by at the residence. A young man in his early 40s with a ready smile, Naderi was from a well-connected Ismaili family. In his youth he had attended Harrow, one of the UK's top schools, and now he had extensive business interests in Afghanistan, including in fuel distribution and insurance. He was just back from the talks with the Taliban in Doha, a couple of days before the rocket attack. His summary of the meeting was brisk: two steps backwards. It had been wholly unproductive. This was not because the negotiators could not find a way forward; it was because the Taliban did not want to find a way forward. The Taliban military commanders were clearly giving their political negotiators no flexibility to negotiate, and had every intention of winning what they wanted on the battlefield.

It was increasingly clear that the gap between the negotiating positions of the two sides was unbridgeable. The Taliban focused on extracting concessions rather than addressing the substance of a peace deal. They were only interested in getting their prisoners released and the UN sanctions on Taliban leaders lifted. Their goal was to retake power on their terms. The Taliban insisted that President Ghani had to step down as a precondition for there to be a negotiated settlement and a new government. There would be no ceasefire until a new government had assumed power.

Ghani, however, continued to insist that as the elected President of Afghanistan he would step down only when new elections were held and a new leader chosen. That was fine as a position of principle, but no longer bore any relation to the real world. In reality, the Taliban's demands would mean a Taliban government or a Taliban-dominated government, which in turn meant the Government of Afghanistan accepting the Taliban's terms. So: fight and talk.

A member of the Afghan Government told me that President Ghani did not seem to understand the severity of the situation. He only wanted to hear what he wanted to hear. Those advisers closest to him, happy to oblige, were not telling him the reality of the situation – if they themselves understood it.

The same member of the government told me that Afghan traders were pleased with how the Taliban were running the border crossings they had captured. The Taliban only charged a single, fixed customs fee, unlike government officials who charge variable tariffs according to what the market would bear, with demands for additional 'fees' (i.e. bribes) on top.

Wednesday 21 July

We were about to get an opportunity for some plain speaking on where things were headed. Hamidullah Mohib, Ghani's national security adviser, was due to visit London later in the week. I checked in with Stephen Lovegrove, the UK national security adviser, to brief him ahead of his meeting with his Afghan counterpart. We talked through the situation on the ground and the key messages for Stephen to get across to Mohib: the urgency and gravity of the situation, and the need for everyone to come together around a survival strategy for the summer. I offered Stephen a prediction: 'This is your summer crisis.'

Summing up at the end of a week of intensive discussions with the Afghan Government, I commented to a colleague in London that the Arg, the Presidential Palace, increasingly felt like a strange parallel universe, detached from the realities of the country at whose heart it sat and from where that country was in theory governed. There no longer seemed to be a working transmission belt between decisions and their execution.

The Eid rocket attack should have shattered any remaining illusions. My hunch was that the Afghan Government had a couple of weeks, at best, to get a grip before the situation become irreversible. There was little reason to believe that they would be able to do so.

The date for final completion of the US and NATO military withdrawal was six weeks away.

Thursday 22 July

National Security Adviser Hamidullah Mohib was in London for several days of meetings. His talking points with senior UK officials showed that some of the issues

I had raised with him in our preparatory discussion had landed. He spoke of the risk of a cascading collapse – where failures lead to bigger failures in an accelerating sequence. And he acknowledged that the Afghan Government's feeble strategic communications were reinforcing a sense of defeatism. But, unsurprisingly, he was vague about the government's plans for wresting the initiative back from the Taliban.

Later in the week Mohib paid a visit to Nawaz Sharif, the former Prime Minister of Pakistan, now in exile in the UK, posting a picture of the meeting on social media. This infuriated the Government of Pakistan. To complete the effect, Mohib then took to the UK media, where he was once again heavily critical of the Pakistan Government and military. I had no clue as to why Mohib thought this was an appropriate thing to do, at a time when we were urging the Pakistan Government and military to use what influence they had with the Taliban to persuade them to seek a political settlement with the Government of Afghanistan.

The weekly stocktake with senior colleagues in London was sobering. I warned that we would likely see a serious inflection point in the next 10 to 14 days. The situation was now deteriorating further and faster than anyone had expected. The Afghan defence and security forces were underperforming on all fronts, their capabilities undermined by poor strategy and weak leadership.

The decline could be slowed with better strategy, including effective mobilisation of the People's Uprising Forces; by more effective strategic communications to win the battle of hearts and minds; and above all, by unity of purpose among the political leaders. But there was no sign of any of that happening. In reality, the government and the defence and security forces were fast approaching the point of no return. Maybe they were already there. Analysts in Kabul were concerned that the Taliban might go for the jugular and launch an assault to take Kabul itself.

I warned London that the likely scale of a US evacuation, if and when it came, would create serious risks for us if we were still in place in the Green Zone. The US Embassy was still huge, and the talk was of an evacuation of Afghan nationals in the tens of thousands. It could make the fall of Saigon look tame by comparison. Our people could be making their way through Kabul to the airport amidst fighting, with no helicopters, in civilian armoured vehicles, with only modest UK military back-up. We would not be able to rely on support from anyone else. The Americans would be focused on getting themselves out. In such circumstances the Afghan army would in all likelihood have ceased to exist.

This meant that we could soon be faced with big, difficult judgement calls against tight deadlines. Did we want to get ahead of a US decision to evacuate its people? If so, by how much? Were we prepared to accept the risk of triggering the collapse of the Afghan Government and the exodus of a large part of the Western international presence in order to be in greater control of our own destiny?

I invited the Indian Ambassador, Rudrendra Tandon, over to lunch. He gave me an in-depth teach-in on the complexities of the Afghanistan–India–Pakistan triangle, heavily coloured by India's visceral suspicion of Pakistan. Later that afternoon the German Deputy Ambassador came over to the residence for a long talk about where we thought things were heading. He had a healthy scepticism about how things were going in Afghanistan – and a healthy capacity for beer. The outgoing German Ambassador had left Kabul a few weeks after I arrived, and his replacement was not due to arrive for some time. This put the deputy ambassador in a difficult position, with a major crisis quickly building up. Seniority counts when trying to get your capital to pay attention. I gave the German a detailed and very frank assessment of how I saw the situation, to use as he saw fit with Berlin. Germany is an important ally of the UK, not only on Afghanistan.

Rumours swirled endlessly around the Green Zone about which embassy was on the point of leaving. I heard from a European colleague that France was edging towards the exit. David Martinon, my excellent French colleague, did not confirm this but neither did he go out of his way to deny it. He did send his chef home, a few weeks before mine was resettled under ARAP. That was possibly a bigger deal for David than for me. One morning not long after, my residence housekeeper announced that he was being evacuated under the ARAP scheme later that day. We took a quick selfie by the flag inside the front door of the residence and I wished him good luck. After that, I resorted to collecting takeaways from the canteen. Immediately, the kitchen staff spotted me and asked for selfies, laughing and calling out to their colleagues to come and join us. A moment of lightness amidst the gathering storm.

FRIDAY 23 JULY

The aircon in my office at the residence stopped working. Not good, in the height of the Kabul summer. I set up my battered laptop on an ironing board in the sitting room, cranked up the aircon in that room and called in the maintenance people. To my surprise, they fixed it quickly. I had been prepared for a different response: no spare parts – or, quite possibly, no maintenance people.

Canada announced that it would evacuate a wide range of Afghans who had worked for its armed forces and embassy.

SATURDAY 24 JULY

I contacted Foreign Minister Hanif Atmar to try to unblock flight clearances for a sequence of ARAP charter flights in the coming days. I had raised this with Atmar a few days previously. He had told me then that the Ministry of Foreign Affairs had given its approval. But now the Afghan Civil Aviation Authority insisted that they were still waiting for approval from the Ministry of Foreign Affairs. In other words, the bureaucracy was stuck – its default state – and needed a shove. I knew that Atmar had bigger problems on his plate, but I needed to get those planes moving without delay. I apologised to him for taking up his time with what should be a routine administrative issue. He responded with his usual good grace, and fixed the problem quickly. He found it as frustrating as I did that nothing happened without constant badgering.

Another routine administrative issue reared its head, this time on our side. We needed a better correspondence-tracking system in London, to keep tabs on the growing number of representations received about evacuation and resettlement cases. And we needed better tracking and responses to campaigns by the special interest groups which were starting to build up on social media. I raised this with FCDO, Ministry of Defence and Home Office colleagues in London, commenting: 'This may quickly become a hot potato.'

The Afghan Government announced that it would divert all discretionary expenditure towards the military effort. This was a big development and an important signal; the decision subordinated all government activity to the task of military survival. There was probably no realistic alternative, given the situation on the battlefield. But this was bound to make an already dire humanitarian situation even worse. The population was enduring a cocktail of escalating conflict, drought and Covid. There was a $400 million hole in government finances. The United Nations had appealed for $1.3 billion to fund a Humanitarian Response Plan. It was proving hard to raise the money from international donors, and only 37 per cent of the requirement was funded.

SUNDAY 25 JULY

Together with Meha, my political officer, I met Shaharzad Akbar, the Chair of the Afghanistan Independent Human Rights Commission. Modest in her demeanour but a forthright campaigner, Shaharzad is courage and integrity personified. She made a powerful case for an international fact-finding mission to support accountability for war crimes. The purpose was not just to describe the situation, which was awful and getting worse, but to influence the Taliban and government forces in the prosecution of the war.

We talked at length about how to get the Taliban to moderate their behaviour for the 'day after' – to get them to understand that the international community's attitude towards them if and when they entered power would depend on how they behaved now. If the Taliban's fighters committed war crimes and atrocities, the leaders would be held to account and there would be no path to international legitimacy.

Shaharzad was clear that the Taliban had not changed their views on women. Nor were they seeking a negotiated settlement. She pressed hard on the obligation to resettle human rights defenders, journalists and civil society activists.

Shaharzad and her family managed to get out of Afghanistan on the day the republic fell. She continues her work, from exile in the UK, on behalf of less fortunate Afghans, with the courage and tenacity that I remember from our meeting in Kabul weeks before the fall of the republic.

I continued my round of meetings with ambassadors of Afghanistan's big neighbours, going to see China's Ambassador Wang Yu. I was accompanied by Ingrid, our newly arrived political officer, bright and quickly finding her feet. We arrived at the Chinese Embassy's heavily fortified entrance. After a short delay the big metal gates swung open, letting us into the vehicle airlock. Disconcertingly, the People's Liberation Army guards assumed firing positions, crouching behind thick metal shields. I don't *think* they were aiming at us. Even more disconcertingly, before allowing us to pass through the second vehicle gate and onto the embassy compound, they insisted on spraying the outside of the car with some kind of liquid. I presume disinfectant. Maybe they thought we were harbouring some worrying new infectious diseases.

The meeting took place on plastic garden chairs in the garden – one of Kabul's oases of tranquillity behind the blast walls. Wang was accompanied by half a dozen staffers, several of them evidently with deep, detailed knowledge of Afghanistan. The ambassador listened more than he spoke, but was engaged and evidently pleased that we had made the effort to consult. Once again, there was broad agreement on what we were seeing and what it meant: A Taliban military victory would be a problem for the international community. Wang identified the terrorist threat, together with regional stability, as China's primary interest. China has a border with Afghanistan at the far end of the Wakhan Corridor, a long finger of land that projects eastwards from the rest of the country, between Pakistan and Tajikistan. Like us, Wang and his colleagues were thinking through their contingency plans should the situation deteriorate sharply.

On our outward journey we passed a heavily armed column of Afghan military travelling in the opposite direction. A dozen or more vehicles, bristling with guns, with at the front and rear a Technical – a pick-up truck with a large gun mounted on the flat bed. Nothing unusual in that. Except that as it passed, we noticed among the weaponry on the rear Technical a fine selection of tall garden plants, swaying elegantly as the pick-up bounced along Kabul's rutted streets. In pots, with supporting canes. Maybe they had just been to the garden centre.

My old friend and colleague Jane Marriott contacted me from Nairobi, where she was high commissioner (the title for an ambassador in a Commonwealth country). I had visited her embassy in Sana'a a few years previously when she was ambassador to Yemen, and had been involved in a difficult decision to pull her and her staff out when the situation became too hot to handle. Jane is brilliant and fearless in equal measure. And collegiate: the very best of the FCDO. She could see what was coming, and offered to talk over what we would have to do when it came to evacuating the embassy. She had done three evacuations. The offer was very welcome, and I replied: 'You're either psychic or can see the writing on the wall!'

We had a long discussion a few days later. One thing Jane said sticks in my mind to this day. 'You won't be able to help everyone who needs help. Get ready for the guilt.'

That evening I attended a dinner hosted by the Swedish Ambassador for a visiting senior official from Stockholm and a selection of European colleagues. The evening was cool and pleasant, with the TV antennae mountain in the background. I was asked to brief them on the security situation and outlook. I offered few grounds for optimism. Months later, my friend Judith Gough, the UK Ambassador in Stockholm, passed on to me the verdict from her hosts: 'We should have listened to Ambassador Bristow.'

MONDAY 26 JULY

Alexei Venediktov, Editor in Chief of *Echo of Moscow* radio station, contacted me asking if I would give an interview on the unfolding situation in Afghanistan. He is an old friend and Russia's top political commentator. Almost everyone who is anyone in Russia followed *Echo*, or appeared on it: a great opportunity to influence decision makers in a key country where I was well known from my time as Ambassador to Russia. I forwarded the request to London for clearance, recommending that I should do this. No response. Eventually I decided to turn the request down, out of courtesy to Venediktov, rather than keep him hanging on for an answer that never came.

Echo was forced to close in the days following Russia's invasion of Ukraine in February 2022. The radio station had been one of the great icons of Gorbachev's glasnost, and its closure was a sad indictment of Russia's failed experiment with a more open society since the dissolution of the Soviet Union.

One of my staff reported back from a NATO coordination meeting that Stefano Pontecorvo, the NATO Senior Civilian Representative, had told the meeting that the UK Embassy was 'on a crisis footing' and was evacuating its Afghan Country Based Staff 'down to zero by the end of the week'. It was not true – and even if it had been, it was not for anyone else to announce. It risked setting a very damaging rumour running, and we were the benchmark for many Western embassies. We took corrective action. Stefano was contrite, calling me to apologise and putting round a correction.

Even so, the underlying problem was becoming more acute with each passing day. We had to face the ongoing dilemma that if the UK Embassy closed, the decision would probably trigger a chain reaction as others pulled their much smaller embassies out. That would damage the Afghan Government that we were all trying to support, and cause major discord with our US allies. If the Americans closed their embassy, that would make our decision for us, and all other Western embassies. Our evacuation planning was developing at speed. But for our plans to make sense, we needed to know what the USA planned to do if a major crisis developed.

It was not clear to us what state the US planning was in. A further drawdown of US Embassy staff was in progress, but even when completed that would leave the Americans with several thousand staff in Kabul. That seemed to me to be detached from the reality of the situation. What we knew of US planning for a Non-combatant Evacuation Operation (NEO) envisaged huge numbers of people being airlifted out. The figures seemed to get bigger with each telling. One report that reached me put it at 160,000. It was hard to see how that would be possible in the circumstances in which it would become necessary. It was not hard to see the impact an operation on such a scale would have on our own ability to evacuate people. Kabul airport had limited facilities even when they were working. If an evacuation became necessary, nothing would be working as normal.

The February 2022 minority report of the Senate Committee on Foreign Relations heavily criticised the Biden Administration's lack of preparation, stating that 'The Administration waited until less than a day before Kabul fell to make senior leadership decisions on organizing and executing a withdrawal'. [23]

In the afternoon I went over to the Sapedar Palace, the official residence of Dr Abdullah, President Ghani's long-time rival, now head of the High Council for National Reconciliation. He was just back from the latest round of peace talks with the Taliban in Doha, where he had led the republic's delegation. He too confirmed that there had been no progress; the Taliban negotiators refused point-blank to discuss the substance of a political settlement, and were evasive even on the date and venue of the next meeting. Instead, they pushed for yet more concessions, including substantial prisoner releases, arguing that the republic should see this as a confidence-building measure. Confidence in what? Everyone knew perfectly well that the Taliban would not reciprocate with concessions of their own. And that released prisoners generally went straight from prison to the battlefield, further weakening the republic's position and strengthening that of the militants within the Taliban movement.

The situation on the ground was emboldening the Taliban and shifting their calculus in the wrong direction. Greater unity on the side of the republic was now critical to its survival. As agreed with Chief of Defence Staff Nick Carter, who was also in regular touch with the republic leaders, I majored on unity and leadership (subtext: *we are not seeing much of either*) and the need to take difficult decisions. I also picked up on recent unhelpful public statements about Pakistan by senior Afghan officials. We needed Pakistan to take political risks in using its leverage with the Taliban, and public slanging matches were not likely to encourage them to do that. Quarrels should take place behind closed doors. Leaders in Kabul needed to be statesmanlike and create space for Pakistan's leaders to do likewise.

Abdullah looked rueful and appeared to agree. He was clearly frustrated, angry and worried, both by the Taliban's behaviour and by the lack of grip on the republic side. He said he would be seeing Ghani shortly after our meeting, and would take these points up with him.

I commented to colleagues in London that Doha was clearly not going to deliver a political settlement unless something major changed. We needed the republic's leaders to create the facts on the ground that would deliver that change. There was no cohesion within the élite, and it was now very unlikely that this could be fixed in the time available.

Tuesday 27 July

I patched in by video conference to a meeting with colleagues in London, and warned that there was now a high likelihood we would have to close the embassy during August or September. We should look now at staffing needs in both London and Kabul: what people we would need, where, when a big crisis hit us.

My close protection team were unsettled. They had picked up rumours that we were going to close the Archipelago – the row of villas on 15th Street which included the residence – and move to Pod Land, the shipping containers on the Egyptian site. That would have a big impact on them because of the need to rethink my security arrangements, which were built around the residence and could not be moved elsewhere overnight. I talked the head of the team through where I thought things were heading.

Over at the UN compound, the major donors met to plan our approach to a big donor coordination meeting with the government, which would take place the next day. The Joint Coordination and Monitoring Board was a mid-year stocktake of the government's progress in meeting the conditions set by the major international donors in return for our support. The main meeting, with President Ghani and senior politicians, would be televised to the nation. It was therefore a big moment, particularly in the current circumstances, and we all needed to use it to get the right messages across given the NATO military withdrawal and the escalating crisis in the country. I agreed our approach with Edwin, the very capable member of the development team leading our preparations for the event.

The preparatory meeting was in two parts. First, a pre-meeting with only the donors and international organisations present. Then, a coordination meeting with Fazel Fazly and Deputy Finance Minister Kabiri.

In the donors' pre-meeting, all agreed that the republic was approaching a tipping point and that our fundamental objectives as donors were at serious risk. I argued that we should take a two-pronged approach. In private, we needed to get across some tough messages about the urgency of the situation and the need for very rapid action. Our key message in private should be: the republic is in an existential crisis; everything we have worked together for 20 years is on the line; what is your plan to address that; how can we help? The televised main meeting, the next day, needed to demonstrate to the wider public the international community's support for the republic at such a critical time. But it also needed President Ghani and his government to demonstrate that the republic was worth fighting for and that they were on top of the situation.

Unfortunately, while Fazly tried to come across as smooth and urbane, speaking platitudes about government reform and digitisation of public services, he did not seem to have thought about what the key messages for the public should be, with the survival of the republic on the line.

Time for a reality check. I interrupted Fazly and set out in plain terms what was at stake. The question was: how was the republic going to survive through the next three to six months? The republic and the international community needed to give a convincing answer to that question, and would not get another chance to do so. We should all use the televised meeting to communicate to the public why the survival of the republic mattered and what the plan was to ensure this happened. This was not a meeting of technocrats but a fight for the hearts and minds of Afghans. The government needed to show that life would be better under the republic than under the Taliban – particularly for women and girls. We should use the occasion as an opportunity for the kind of public communication that had been totally lacking so far. Others piled in, making similar points. Fazly agreed to brief President Ghani accordingly.

In the evening, the United Nations hosted a dinner in the garden of the UN compound. To lighten the mood, Ramiz Alakbarov valiantly took on the role of Master of Ceremonies. He played the role effortlessly, helped by an imposing physical presence and an easy, good-humoured style despite the tension in the evening air. He invited people to stand up and speak about their hopes and fears for Afghanistan. There were some emotionally charged responses from people who had invested large parts of their lives in the country. As dusk fell and we batted away the predatory insects, there was a sense that we were entering the twilight in more ways than one. Several senior Afghan officials pulled me aside and quietly registered their interest in evacuation for themselves and their families when the time came.

Wednesday 28 July

The Joint Coordination and Monitoring Board took place at the Char Chinar Palace. President Ghani and senior members of the government sat on a raised platform. Other participants sat at a long U-shaped table with the United Nations at one end, ambassadors down one side, and senior republic politicians on the other. With the television cameras rolling, we made our set-piece speeches along the lines we had choreographed the previous day.

Formally, the purpose of the meeting was to present the impressively named Cumulative Progress Report on the Afghanistan Partnership Framework Commitments and Key Principles; and to set strategic priorities and prepare for a Senior Officials' Meeting in November. Despite the mangled English of the Cumulative Progress Report, the meaning was more or less clear. A loosely translated summary would be: some progress but not enough. None of this will matter if you lose the war.

Ghani's speech was lengthy and in places strangely disconnected from the world outside the Char Chinar. Ghani has a reedy voice and an underwhelming stage presence. His speech, again, was more like a university lecture than a major political speech at a historic turning point. It included a substantial digression on the republic's plans for introducing digital governance. Digital governance was doubtless important – but should it really have been top of the agenda in the final weeks of a fight to the finish with the Taliban, which the republic was clearly losing?

The tone suddenly changed. Ghani launched into a political message for the benefit of the phalanx of TV cameras. He referred to the Taliban being directed by 'a General Staff', calling on the United Nations to investigate this and hold those responsible to account. Later he spoke of those who sought 'hegemony', and 'see chaos as beneficial'. (He did not need to name names; no one, starting with Pakistan, would have any difficulty working that one out.)

What? I kept my best poker face, staring expressionlessly at a bearded gentleman in shalwar kameez on the other side of the table.

Abdullah, sitting next to Ghani, also kept a poker face as he stared into the middle distance. Vice President Saleh, sitting on Ghani's other side, looked fierce. When Saleh's turn came to speak, he went one further and described the Taliban's military campaign as a Pakistani invasion. For good measure, he laid into the foreign ambassadors lined up in front of him for withdrawing their Afghan staff, thus undermining confidence in the republic.

The UN Head of Delegation Deborah Lyons, as co-host, made an impassioned and inspired speech – in many respects the speech that President Ghani should have made. She spelled out with crystal clarity and carefully controlled emotion what was at stake for Afghans. We went round the table, one ambassador after another giving their set-piece speech. As I had suggested the day before, every single one made prominent reference to the advancement of women and girls during the previous 20 years. I spoke on behalf of Australia and Canada as well as the UK, citing the 42 per cent reduction in maternal mortality and 47 per cent reduction in infant mortality since 2001, when the Taliban had been forced from power. The purpose of using these numbers was to spell out for the wider audience watching on TV what a Taliban victory would mean for them, their wives and their daughters.

Back in the office, I tried to get overturned a decision in the FCDO that we could not proceed with this year's Chevening Scholarships for Afghans. The Chevening Scholarships are the UK Government's scheme for bringing some of the brightest and best from around the world to study in the UK, usually for a one-year Master's. After that, they are expected to return to their home country and put what they have learned to good use. Each year we sent two dozen Afghan scholars.

The 2021 scholars had already been selected and notified. They were due to go to the UK in the coming weeks but would need a substantial amount of administration in Kabul before they could travel. The decision not to proceed was taken in London on the basis that the scheme did not meet the cut for prioritisation. That was clearly correct in terms of what was and was not essential for our increasingly heavily pressed staff in Kabul to do. My concern, though, was that the decision was politically indefensible, and we would end up having to reverse it. Better to grip it up front and find a way to make it happen, doing as much of the work as possible in London or elsewhere in the region.

Meanwhile Katrina, whose numerous roles included that of consul general, alerted me to a difficult consular case that was starting to loom large. A few months previously a former British soldier known as the Milkman of Kabul had been arrested for selling alcohol. He was now in a Kabul prison. Whatever the rights and wrongs of the case, a prisoner on an alcohol charge was a complication that no one would need on their plate in an escalating crisis. If the Taliban seized power his prospects would not be good. We agreed that we should raise his case with the Afghan Government and persuade them to release him quietly. We would take charge of him and get him out of the country.

In the UK, a large group of retired senior British government officials and military officers had written an open letter to the newspapers, which was published on 28 July, urging the British Government to widen the criteria for resettling former interpreters. For a generation of soldiers and officials who had worked in Afghanistan, the issue was often deeply personal; a military interpreter is someone who lives, works and fights alongside you in the most intense experience of your life. For civilians, too, working in such a difficult environment is more than a job; the friendships and mutual loyalty which you grow with colleagues in the most difficult posts can last a lifetime. The authors of the letter highlighted Afghans whose applications had been rejected because they were deemed not to have worked in an exposed role, or had been contracted through private companies, or had been sacked from their job. About 35 per cent of military interpreters had been dismissed, often for minor infractions and without right of appeal. The authors of the letter urged that only those sacked because they presented a national security risk should be ineligible for resettling.

In a cross-Whitehall ARAP coordination meeting the following day, I warned that we were in an accelerating crisis and that we could be in a very different place by the end of August, four weeks from now. We should move forward as quickly as possible on ARAP relocations. I also argued that we should be proactive in briefing the UK media on what we were doing to deliver the ARAP policy launched at the end of April, to counter the growing chorus of criticism that we were not doing enough.

THURSDAY 29 JULY

After a day of to-and-fro on the Chevening scholars, I reluctantly accepted defeat. It would not be possible to run the Chevening scheme this year. With crisis piling up on crisis, and with rapidly reducing staff numbers in Kabul, we had to prioritise ruthlessly; candidates for the ARAP scheme had the strongest claim on us, and processing them had to take precedence. We did not have the capacity in Kabul to do the paperwork and pre-departure support for the Chevening scholars in August and September, ahead of the start of the new academic year, unless we put off other urgent and important work.

I wrote to the scholars to tell them the bad news. The responses, from the scholars themselves, previous Chevening alumni, and their supporters in the UK, were not long in coming. These were articulate, well-connected people, and they knew how to press their case. Within days of the fall of Kabul, faced with a growing chorus of protest in the UK media, parliament and universities, the government took the decision to stand by the offers for the 2021–22 academic year and evacuate the Chevening scholars under Operation Pitting.

FRIDAY 30 JULY

Fighting off a bug, I spent the weekend holed up in the residence, catching up on my reading. It included Theo Farrell's history of the UK's military campaign in Afghanistan – *Unwinnable: Britain's War in Afghanistan, 2001–2014*.

Following Eid, and the attack on the government in the very heart of Kabul, the Taliban piled the pressure on the government and armed forces. They now turned their attention to the major cities. In Kabul, the analysts were openly discussing the possibility that a major city could fall this week.

The situation in Kandahar was very bad. Meanwhile a big crisis was brewing in Herat – Afghanistan's third-largest city, in the northwest of the country. There was fighting at the airport, temporarily grounding all flights in and out. The UN compound was attacked, killing several Afghan nationals. The Taliban claimed that the United Nations had been caught in the crossfire. Several British nationals were trapped. In Kabul, the team worked through our limited range of options for extracting them, in the meantime advising them to lie low. Ismail Khan, a veteran warlord, politician and former mujahideen commander in past struggles against the Soviet Union and later the Taliban, took control of the defence of the city in the absence of effective military support from the government, mobilising another People's Uprising Force to help fight off the Taliban assault.

Dan Blanchford and Brigadier Tom raised with me their concern that we should carry out an ordered departure from Kabul under our control and on our own timing rather than wait for a crisis to break over us. We talked through our options. For now, our political direction from ministers in London was to stay and deliver what we were here to do. We would need to be ready to call time when the circumstances dictated, and to get our people out safely. But we faced an ever-sharpening dilemma: doing so too late or inadequately prepared would greatly magnify the risks; doing so too early risked triggering the collapse of the Afghan Government, which we wished to avoid. In addition, it risked serious political embarrassment for the UK if we did so while the USA, our closest ally and the lead partner in the coalition supporting Afghanistan, was still committed to staying. For this reason, we needed to be very careful in how we talked about our contingency planning, even with close and trusted partners outside the embassy.

Saturday 31 July

Following the open letter of 28 July from the retired military and officials a growing head of steam was building up in the British media about the slow pace of resettlement of interpreters under ARAP. Meanwhile the number of ARAP relocations to the UK was steadily building. The small Ministry of Defence ARAP team in Kabul was rotated, bringing in fresh people. The new team were hard-working and stayed the course throughout the fall of Kabul and the evacuation.

Sunday 1 August

At the weekly breakfast club over at the UN headquarters, the main topic of discussion was the Taliban's attack on the UN office in Herat. Several people put forward possible reasons why the Taliban had chosen to attack the representatives of the international community. Was it payback for recent UN reports that had heavily criticised the behaviour of the Taliban? Or maybe that was just how things were with the Taliban?

Ismail Khan was the hero of the hour for pushing back the Taliban's advance in Herat. The airport was now back in operation. But there were rumours that a ceasefire agreement was being touted, which would involve Herat taking itself out of the fight and surrendering to the Taliban.

The situation in Kandahar was still very bad, with attacks on the airport over the weekend. The loss of Kandahar would be a major blow. A state of emergency had been declared in Kandahar, Helmand and Herat provinces.

As for the Afghan Government, there were signs that any remaining clarity and unity of purpose were breaking down. Abdullah and other ex-Northern Alliance leaders were calling for extensive changes to the regional political leadership. There were rumours that Mohammed Masoom Stanekzai could replace Hamidullah Mohib as National Security Adviser. Stanekzai, now the republic's chief negotiator with the Taliban, was a former Minister of Defence and chief of the National Directorate of Security (NDS), the internal security agency. He had resigned in 2019 over allegations of extra-judicial killings by NDS forces during a night raid.

A colleague told me that Ghani was highly critical of the international community stripping out key staff from the government and offering them relocation out of Afghanistan. According to this source, Ghani had named the UK as one of the main offenders. I could not help noting, however, that many of Ghani's senior officials already had UK or other Western passports and had their own escape routes organised.

Later that day I called on National Security Adviser Mohib. The meeting was difficult and tense. There were no raised voices, but there was a sense of desperation in the air. Mohib repeated to me the accusation that we were evacuating people who were needed by the security forces to hold off the Taliban advance. He was very concerned that if Kandahar fell to the Taliban it was essentially game over. He fished hard for advice on what to do. I offered the same as we had offered countless times before. The republic's senior figures (everyone, immediately) had to get behind a coherent military strategy to save the republic from total collapse; and everyone had to do a much better job, quickly, of demonstrating why the republic was worth fighting for.

But we were now well past the point at which advice alone, however good or well meant, would change anything.

I heard that the USA was about to announce a refugee programme for Afghans not covered by its Special Immigration Visa (SIV) programme, such as civil society activists who had received US government grants. Inevitably, this would increase the pressure on our own government to widen the net for those eligible to come to the UK.

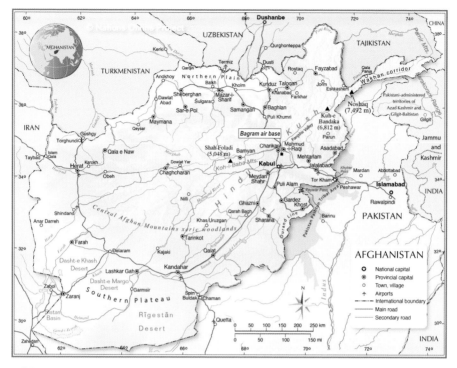

Afghanistan and the region.

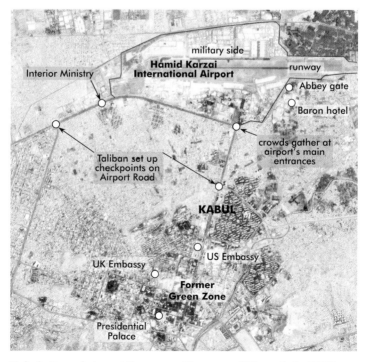

Kabul city and airport (base map Courtesy of Planet Labs PBC).

Dubai airport departures,
14 June 2021.

The Emir's Pavilion, Kuti-e
Baghtscha, 18 July 2021.

The Emir's Pavilion – Kuti-e Baghtscha.

Presenting credentials to President Ashraf Ghani, 21 June 2021.

The start of Operation Pitting. Inside the front gate of the Baron Hotel.

The street outside the Baron Hotel.

Observation post at the Baron Hotel front entrance. The airfield is the other side of the wire.

The container chevron outside the Baron Hotel from the Observation Post.

Lt Col David Middleton, Commanding Officer of 2 Para.

Lt Col Dave Middleton, 2 Para, and his team, Baron Hotel.

The canal. (UK Ministry of Defence © Crown Copyright (2024)

The canal – an open sewer. Identifying people called forward for evacuation.
(UK Ministry of Defence © Crown Copyright (2024)

Outside the Baron Hotel. (UK Ministry of Defence © Crown Copyright (2024)

The Baron Hotel, evacuation handling centre, Operation Pitting.

The garden of the Baron Hotel.

Gate control.

With temperatures in the 30s, dehydration was a constant risk.

Families with small children were at especial risk.

"We train these young
men and women
for combat. This is
much harder."

Service dog and handler.

Briefing the media. Stuart Ramsay, *Sky News*, in the Baron Hotel.

Kim Sengupta, *The Independent*, with Andy McCoubrey in the centre.

Moments of kindness amidst fear and violence.

Afghan girl in a party dress,
fleeing the Taliban.

The 10,000th evacuee of Operation
Pitting. Behind each number
a person with a name.

Women and girls paid the biggest price following the Taliban takeover.

Waiting to board a C-17. (UK Ministry of Defence © Crown Copyright (2024)

On the ramp. Some had taken days to get here.

(UK Ministry of Defence © Crown Copyright (2024)

The flight to safety.

Brigadier Dan Blanchford, Commanding Officer of Operation Pitting.

My close protection team in the garden of the Baron Hotel.

[Opposite] Inside a C-17 evacuation flight.

[Above] The end of Operation
Pitting, 28 August 2021.

[Right] Last view of Kabul,
28 August 2021. (UK Ministry of
Defence © Crown Copyright (2024)

[Below] Round the clock flight
operations. (UK Ministry of Defence
© Crown Copyright (2024)

I went to see US Ambassador Ross Wilson in his vast, heavily fortified embassy, to find out what I could about how the Americans were reading the situation and what were their plans for the coming weeks. Our analysis of the situation was not significantly different. But I did not come away with a clear sense of what the Americans intended to do about it.

Lyse Doucet dropped by for afternoon tea. Lyse is one of the most impressive, knowledgeable and likeable journalists I have ever met. And quietly courageous: she and her team had visited Afghanistan many times before, and she has continued to do so since the Taliban takeover. We talked long into the afternoon. I suspect I learned rather more from the conversation than she did.

Towards the end of the day, I summarised events for the key policy and military people back in London. The word in Kabul was that the strategic southern city of Lashkar Gah could fall to the Taliban in the next 24 hours. Whether or not that happened, it felt as if some very assertive interventions were needed to steady the nerve of the Afghan leadership and to stop the Taliban's momentum. Generalities about political unity were not going to help change things on the ground. We were at the point where the fall of a major city like Kandahar or Lashkar Gah, or a surrender deal, maybe, in Herat, would tip the Afghan Government into panic and paralysis. The collapse of the republic, if it came, would be less a consequence of lack of fighting power and more one of morale and confidence. Loss of a key provincial capital could be the trigger.

The UK and US governments publicly accused the Taliban of war crimes, following massacres of civilians in the border crossing town of Spin Boldak. The purpose was not just to say something in response to mass murder, but to deter future crimes by reminding the Taliban that the international community were monitoring their actions and that actions have consequences. I doubted that the Taliban cared in slightest. But we had to say it.

Monday 2 August

Around midday we issued a diplomatic telegram updating seniors in London on the direction of events.

Afghanistan: Security: The Gloves are Off

Summary

The Eid lull in fighting is over. The Taliban have launched assaults on at least four major population centres and threaten many more. Afghan security forces will not be able to hold them back everywhere. We are entering a new, dangerous phase of the conflict.

The conflict in Afghanistan is entering a new phase. Following a lull in violence over Eid, the Taliban have launched offensives on at least four provincial capitals. In doing so, and in publicly claiming to have taken territory within capitals, they are breaching their own moratorium on attacking major population centres. Lashkar Gah, Kandahar, and Herat are in the most danger, but in total 17 provincial capitals are currently isolated by the Taliban.

The city under the greatest immediate threat is Lashkar Gah in Helmand. The Taliban have taken a number of districts in the city and most districts are contested. … and on the current trajectory we assess it is likely to fall during the week. If this were to happen, it would damage the Republic and could help the Taliban build momentum towards Kandahar. The UK legacy in Helmand may add fuel to the public debate in the UK over relocating those who have worked for us during the last two decades in Afghanistan.

Kandahar is the big concern. Afghanistan's second city is where the Taliban has its roots. Its fall would be a huge blow for the Afghan government and the Republic. There has been intense fighting in and around the city for more than a week and despite US air strikes in support of Afghan troops the situation is precarious. Yesterday morning Taliban forces fired rockets at the city's international airport.

Heavy fighting has also taken place in Herat and Taloqan in Takhar. In Herat, the UN compound was attacked over the weekend. Local militia have been heavily involved in the defence of the city. The threat of airstrikes appeared to reduce the pressure on the city's defenders over the weekend, but at the time of despatch Herat was the most stable of the three.

Comment

We are facing a new reality in Afghanistan. Absent a major turnaround, it looks likely that the Taliban will soon control at least one major population centre, with more maybe to follow. If that happens the impact on already fragile political unity, military and public confidence and sentiment will be significant.

For now, Kabul remains insulated from the intense fighting occurring elsewhere in the country. This is very unlikely to last indefinitely – the Taliban are positioning to put the capital under intense security and economic pressure when they see fit to do so. Our focus is on supporting the Republic, delivering top priority HMG business in particular CT [counterterrorism], pressing ahead with the relocation scheme for our CBS [Afghan country-based staff], and contingency planning.[24]

BRISTOW

Later that afternoon I attended a meeting between the Minister of Interior and the major international donors, at the European Union Delegation offices. The UK was one of the biggest donors to the Law and Order Trust Fund for Afghanistan (LOTFA), covering the salaries of the hard-pressed police. With the police now effectively a branch of the armed forces fighting the Taliban, it was a good time to assure the Interior Minister of our continued support and funding. It was also a good time to signal our support to a wider audience: my intervention in the donors' meeting was also our press release. It was a hot, sleepy afternoon under a large canopy in the garden. The Interior Minister gave us a good amount of his time and was grateful for the support. But he knew the republic was in deep trouble, and he did not look like a man with a plan that was going to recover the situation.

President Ghani spoke in the Afghan Parliament to present a new military strategy. He criticised the speed of the US withdrawal, which he said was responsible for the current situation. But he claimed that the situation would be 'under control within six months'. If he really believed this, he was the only person who did.[25]

Tuesday 3 August

I wrote to the FCDO that we should now base our planning for the summer on our reasonable worst case scenario: that the republic would lose one or more major cities in August, maybe Lashkar Gah and Kandahar, and that this was looking increasingly likely to happen within the next seven days. If it did, then our reasonable worst case would become our default scenario, with what were previously nightmare scenarios becoming reasonable worst case. The republic would be unlikely to recover if it lost Kandahar, which could in turn set off a cascading crisis as the republic's losses mounted and its ability to do anything about them evaporated. From my viewpoint today, we might then end up with the Taliban tightening the noose on Kabul through a military and economic blockade, and probably also through a campaign of targeted violence within Kabul to destabilise it.

I added that the atrocities being reported in Spin Boldak and elsewhere looked like vengeful, untargeted and extreme violence. We would be unwise to assume that if the Taliban saw military victory within grasp they would exercise restraint. Why would they do that? What evidence was there that they had done so to date?

What this meant for us, I concluded, was that we should plan on the basis that we would probably have to conduct an evacuation in the second half of August or early September.

The Afghan Government was refusing to allow Afghans to leave without valid passports. Many of the Afghans who qualified for resettlement under ARAP had out-of-date passports or no passport, and there were reports of long queues at passport offices, as well as demands for kickbacks to move applications forward. We needed to crack this problem urgently. Several other Western embassies reported similar problems as they sought to relocate Afghans who were at risk because of their association with Westerners.

The pressure on British diplomatic staff of dealing with increasingly distressed Afghan colleagues was becoming worrying. These were people who had worked alongside us, including through a year of Covid lockdowns. It was hard to tell people to be patient as their applications for relocation worked their way through the system. It was even harder to tell people you knew and had worked with that they and their families did not qualify for relocation.

I dialled into a meeting of senior Ministry of Defence, Home Office and FCDO officials in London responsible for delivering ARAP. I warned once again that we were looking at an accelerating crisis. Now we needed to think through how we would continue to evacuate those people we planned to evacuate if the embassy had to close during August. We still needed greater clarity, agreed with ministers, on who was in scope and who was not for the flexible ARAP Category 4.

Mid-evening, a big explosion shook the windows of the residence, a long rumbling sound as it echoed off walls around the city. It took a second or so to realise what it was. I was already in the safe room pulling on body armour when the close protection team came to check that I was okay and lock down. Soon after, reports started coming in of a major attack on Defence Minister Bismillah Khan's house, a few blocks away, just outside the walls of the Green Zone. The initial car bomb explosion had been followed by secondary explosions and a prolonged gunfight between the attackers and Afghan rapid reaction forces. Katrina, in the Operations Room watching the attack unfold on the video feeds from the Blimp, kept me updated as the mayhem unfolded. The house caught fire and was, in Katrina's elegant Scottish turn of phrase, 'properly damaged'.

Fortunately, the Taliban's intelligence was imperfect and BK had not been at home. The Afghan Ministry of Defence quickly got out a statement that he was safe. Even so, it was a substantial propaganda coup for the Taliban that they were able to mount a large-scale attack on a second such sensitive and strategically vital target in the middle of Kabul.

Our first task, as always, was to account for all our staff. And to offer what reassurance was possible to people locked down alone in their pods. Especially to recent arrivals. It was tough to arrive in a place where things were going bad so quickly. Doubly so to be facing a major security incident in your first few days.

We were released from lockdown late in the evening. But it would still be some hours before the incident would be declared to have ended. I decided to do the ironing. No point in trying to sleep: too much adrenalin. And too high a likelihood that we would be locking down again that night. I sent a message round to staff to check that people were coping. Several asked if I would mind doing their ironing too.

WEDNESDAY 4 AUGUST

Jean Arnault, the UN Secretary General's Special Representative for Afghanistan, briefed the UN Security Council that the Doha peace talks had stopped; the Taliban, seeing an open path to a military victory, had no incentive to negotiate.

I went to see the Iranian Ambassador, Bahador Aminian. As we went into his reception room I noticed a replica of the Scroll of Cyrus in a display case. The scroll is one of the most important artifacts of Persian culture and is displayed in the British Museum in London. I recounted to Aminian a story that I once heard Neil MacGregor, the former Director of the British Museum, tell about taking the original on a kind of state visit to Iran during a time of heightened tension between Iran and the UK. It was a creative and highly effective act of cultural diplomacy, reaching past the serious political disagreements to something deeper and lasting.

Aminian is quietly spoken with good, articulate English. At our meeting he struck me as an intelligent and subtle man, thinking aloud with me about what was likely to happen next, and steering clear of standard talking points. He was glad of the meeting, and we talked for a long time. The Iranians were for obvious reasons happy that US military forces would no longer be in Afghanistan and benefited from the visible US strategic failure that this represented. The Iranians had a complex relationship with the Taliban. But they were also clearly worried about the prospects of a Taliban Emirate on their border, and understood all too well the challenges this would present to Iran – for example refugees, instability, persecution of the Hazara (Shia) community in Afghanistan. We agreed to keep in touch.

Mohammed Umer Daudzai, Afghanistan's Special Envoy to Pakistan and the Region, dropped by for a chat. He wanted to talk through last-ditch attempts to pull the Taliban into talks about power sharing. The Taliban were not playing ball. Meanwhile the fractious relationship between Afghanistan and Pakistan was impeding efforts to find a way forward. I offered what advice and support I could. It was not much.

Speaking to Indian media, Daudzai described the US military withdrawal as irresponsible.

Johnny Mercer contacted me about his former army interpreter. Mercer had been an army officer who served several tours in Afghanistan. He had gone on to take a close interest in the welfare of military veterans, serving as Minister for Veterans' Affairs. He had stayed in touch with his Afghan interpreter, as so many soldiers had done, and had set the man up with a job and the prospect of a new life in the UK.

The interpreter qualified for resettlement. But he had no passport, and the system for issuing passports was broken. There were now long queues at the passport office, and demands for extravagant backhanders to move applications forward. So the interpreter decided to go back to his hometown to try his luck at the local passport office. I promised Mercer that we would do what we could. The embassy team had been pursuing a number of similar cases, but the relevant ministries were barely functioning any longer. Mercer was unfailingly polite and helpful as we struggled to move this and similar cases forward, despite the anguish he clearly felt for his former colleague.

Other embassies had the same problem. None had found a solution. We needed to find a workaround, quickly.

That evening I hosted a dinner in the residence garden with a small group of Afghan officials in charge of border controls and security at the airport. The main purpose was to try to work out a pragmatic solution for people whom we had cleared for travel under ARAP but who did not have valid passports. Besides, with the airport looming large in everyone's contingency planning, these officials were people we needed to know better: people whom we could call on when we encountered problems that needed to be fixed. A bright young diplomat represented the Ministry of Foreign Affairs. A few weeks later he emailed me asking for help getting out of Afghanistan.

The pressure continued to mount over who should be eligible for refuge in the UK. A group of UK broadcasters and newspaper editors wrote an open letter to the Prime Minister and Foreign Secretary appealing for an urgent special visa programme for Afghan journalists, translators and support staff who had worked with British media organisations over the previous 20 years and whose lives were at risk from the Taliban. They noted the UK's championing of media freedom. They cited the Taliban's campaign of targeted killings of journalists, and the closure of media outlets in those areas of Afghanistan where they were in control. They gave as examples the murder in July of Danish Siddiqui, whose body had been mutilated by the Taliban, and of Helmand-based reporter Elyas Dayee in 2020. Earlier in the week the Americans had agreed to give Afghan journalists and media people with US links access to their refugee programme.

Bowing to the inevitable, our Foreign Secretary agreed to offer refuge to journalists sponsored by the major news media.

Alex Pinfield, my deputy, arrived back in Kabul after a badly needed short break. One of us had to be in Kabul at all times. While he was away, we closed the villa in which he lived with several colleagues, moving its occupants to Pod Land, deeper into the embassy compound and behind another security wall on the Egyptian site.

Thursday 5 August

The weekly meeting of senior officials in London took stock of the attack on BK's house. I briefed them on the Afghan army's response. The view of our military analysts was that the army had dealt with this major attack effectively, killing the attackers and regaining control, but they would have been stretched to deal with a simultaneous attack on a second target. If the Taliban had succeeded in killing the defence minister, the consequences would have been far reaching. And following shortly after the Eid rocket attack which had come close to wiping out the government, the attack on BK's house was a propaganda coup for the Taliban, in that they were able to mount such a spectacular attack against the republic's most senior figures and against well-guarded sites. The Taliban were fighting to win; the republic was in a critical situation; the peace process was clearly going nowhere.

In renewed discussions as to whether the Taliban had changed their spots in the 20 years they had been out of power, I said once again that I saw no evidence to support that view, and plenty to suggest otherwise. Their barbaric behaviour in Spin Boldak, which included killings of civilians and systematic human rights abuses, exposed as an illusion the idea that today's Taliban were different from when they had been in power previously. The success of the military campaign meant that the most violent and intransigent of the Taliban were in charge. Whatever the range of views within the Taliban movement, it was clear that the Taliban were seeking power through military victory and not a negotiated power-sharing deal. I warned that there was now a serious risk of the Taliban intensifying its attacks within Kabul city to cause the republic to collapse from within. With that in mind, we needed to move as quickly as possible to resettle people under the ARAP scheme.

The attack on the Defence Minister's house also meant that our own dilemma over whether and when to close the embassy was becoming pressing. The ramifications of the decision were wide and long-lasting. The British Embassy was second in size and complexity only to that of the USA. We knew that a decision for us to withdraw, even to the airport, would trigger a chain reaction as other nations took this as their signal to leave. That vote of no confidence could be a mortal blow to the republic we were all trying to support.

Move too early and we would risk bringing the whole edifice down. At the very least we would risk opprobrium from our US ally, even though we had been the first country to stand in support of it after the 9/11 attacks. Move too late, and we could put our people at unacceptably high risk of being killed or taken hostage by the Taliban, by ISKP or by other extremists. At the very least we would be trying to get our people out through the middle of a US evacuation perhaps ten times the size of ours. There would be enormous pressure on the airport and its surroundings.

In my mind I kept coming back to the prospect of an awful Saigon-style scramble to get everyone out. The scale of the US and international presence in Afghanistan, the extreme nature of the Taliban rule, and the sheer number of Afghans who had worked with us over the previous 20 years, guaranteed that the fall of the republic, if and when it came, would be apocalyptic, even if the airport and the Green Zone were not under direct Taliban attack.

Even that was a big assumption. We just did not know what the Taliban's plans would be when they made their attempt to take Kabul. They had not fully honoured the commitments they had made to the Americans in the Doha Agreement. We had little knowledge of how decisions were made within the Taliban movement. And we knew little about the USA's evacuation plans for its embassy or for those Afghans who had worked closely with the Americans. My suspicion was that that was because such plans were not yet fully developed.

In the afternoon, I held a very difficult and emotional meeting with a dozen of our Afghan staff who had been refused places on the ARAP scheme. Some had been turned down on the grounds that they were not directly employed by the embassy but were contractors working for private companies. Others on the grounds that their jobs were not high profile enough to expose them to serious risk of Taliban reprisals. They had written to me asking for a meeting. I decided that at the very least I should hear what they had to say and do what I could to make their case with London.

We sat in a circle in the embassy garden next to the war memorial, with one of the men translating for those who needed it. I invited each one of them to have their say, one at a time. They all had strong points to make. The women spoke first, coherently and at length. One of them, an older woman, was confident and spoke with natural authority, not deferring at all to the men. There was fear and anger in the air, and some tears were wiped away, but tempered with the Afghans' natural courtesy and dignity.

All were very worried about their own and their families' safety, especially those with daughters. The Taliban would not be interested in their job description or contractual status but in their association with the British Embassy, which was widely known in their communities. Those with daughters feared that they would be forcibly 'married' (that is, sexually enslaved) to Taliban fighters. The longest-serving had been with the embassy for 19 years. It was impossible for me to look them in the eye and tell them I thought the decisions to refuse their applications for resettlement were justified. So I undertook to have their cases re-examined on the basis of what they had told me.

With concerns growing about the worsening security outlook, I agreed a plan with senior colleagues in London and Kabul to reduce further the number of UK-based staff in the embassy at any one time, by changing working patterns and doing more work remotely where possible.

Throughout the first ten days of August, the team in Kabul progressively closed sections of the embassy compound, clearing buildings and equipment as they went. Any British staff whose presence in Kabul was not absolutely necessary were sent out of Afghanistan or their arrival put on hold. The embassy was reduced in size, again, to a core team.

As the republic's military options narrowed, its Western supporters discussed with increasing urgency and pessimism how best to advise and help them. For the republic, it was now a question of doing whatever it took just to survive through to the winter. One last-resort scenario was that the Afghan Government might hold onto a rump state based on Kabul and maybe a couple more cities. That would mean giving up on other cities and swathes of the country, to concentrate on the defence of Kabul.

There were divided views on whether it would come to that. Sami Sadat, the charismatic general in charge of the resistance in Helmand, had said he was confident of holding Lashkar Gah. But there was no longer a clear consensus that even this was the right strategy, given the rate at which the Afghan Government was burning through its most capable forces. The implications of losing Helmand to the Taliban were awful. For us, after all the lives lost and the costs sunk in our efforts to hold and pacify Helmand. And for the republic: at its heart, a coalition of political leaders and others with regional, ethnic, economic, tribal and factional interests. Part-colleagues, part-rivals.

FRIDAY 6 AUGUST

Time for me to take a short break. The working pattern in Kabul – six weeks on, two weeks off – was to allow people to recover from the pressures of seven-day working weeks in a conflict zone. The fatigue and stress of working in such an environment creep up on you insidiously. Over time this can lead to serious mental and physical health problems. More immediately, it can lead to bad decisions made by exhausted and burned-out people who have lost their sense of perspective and can no longer think straight or exercise good judgement.

I had learned this the hard way some years previously when running the London crisis centre during a series of major terrorist attacks overseas. It is bad leadership to soldier on, or allow others to do so, beyond the point where exhaustion sets in. In a crisis, what you need above all is people who can think clearly and take good decisions. And to have a deputy who you know will be able to do so if you are not there. You do not get to choose when a crisis will happen. I was very fortunate to have outstanding deputies, both in Kabul and in Moscow.

Alex Pinfield, my deputy in Kabul, had arrived there a few months before me. He and I coordinated our absences so that at least one of us was always in Kabul. I had thought long and hard about whether to go back to the UK, leaving the decision to the last possible moment. But eight weeks into a six-week rotation of shattering intensity, with the prospect of a long hot summer ahead, I decided that it made better sense for me to take at least a few days out than to press on. It would also be a good opportunity to hold the sort of discussions in London that are better done face to face than on a screen.

Before heading to the airport, I wrote to London about the growing pressure to accommodate more people in ARAP Category 4, the provision to offer resettlement to a limited number of special cases considered on their merits: people who had worked for us, or had been employed by contractors to work for us, or who had worked alongside us contributing to the UK's military or national security objectives and were at risk of Taliban reprisals. It was obvious that we would soon be facing intense pressure to evacuate a wide range of people, going beyond the criteria set out in ARAP and previous schemes for military interpreters. If we were going to go down this route, I argued once again, far better to address the question early and proactively than late and reacting to pressure.

Before leaving, I packed up most of my personal belongings in case the embassy needed to move me out of the residence and into a pod while I was away.

As I passed through the airport VIP room, a group of airport facilitators asked to speak to me and handed over a letter seeking evacuation. They had worked with us and others for many years, helping us move senior people through the airport safely and discreetly. I took a photograph of the letter and sent it to embassy colleagues from the VIP waiting room.

On the plane, the man in the next seat looked relieved to be leaving Kabul. Heavily built, with tattoos and a buzz cut, I guessed he was in the private security business and had spent a lot of time in places like this. He polished off several stiff drinks before we were airborne and drank with application until we landed in Dubai. I stuck to orange juice, as I usually do on planes. Neither of us said much.

While I was in the air, there were some serious developments. The Taliban captured the city of Zaranj, the capital of Nimruz province, next to the Iranian border in the southwest of Afghanistan. The city is a regional hub. The nearby border crossing into Iran is an important trade and migration route – and, in August 2021, it was the last land border crossing still under Afghan Government control.

Above all, though, Zaranj mattered because it was the first provincial capital to fall to the Taliban. Its fall turned out to be the beginning of the end. Over the nine days that followed, all the other provincial capitals fell as government forces collapsed.

In Kabul, the head of the Government Media and Information Centre and presidential spokesman Dawa Khan Menapal, a key figure in the government, was assassinated. I had not even had time to get to know him. The Taliban claimed responsibility.

In London, the FCDO changed its travel advice to: 'Leave immediately.'

Saturday 7 August

On arrival at London's Heathrow Airport I found it a nightmare of Covid restrictions. Most travellers headed by bus straight from the airport into obligatory 'managed quarantine' in hotels. Kabul embassy staff had a special dispensation, reflecting the fact that if staff had to spend their decompression time in a quarantine hotel before heading straight back to Afghanistan it would be impossible to keep the operation going. After a few hours of standing in queues I was eventually spat out by the system into a deserted car park at Terminal 4. Fiona was there to collect me.

I picked up the email as we drove into London. Events in Afghanistan were gathering pace, and it was clear that I would be heading back to Kabul within a very few days. In the meantime, some difficult decisions needed to be made about the embassy and its staff. These decisions were best worked through face to face with colleagues in London.

Sunday 8 August

The crisis accelerated with each passing day. The cascading collapse of the republic that we had feared was happening before our eyes. It was clear that the Afghan National Defence and Security Forces were no longer viable: collapsing or collapsed. I talked through with Nigel Casey where we stood on the triggers for a decision to close the embassy. We would probably need to put some big, difficult decisions to ministers in the coming days.

In Kabul, Alex sent a diplomatic cable towards the end of the working day summarising the situation for a wide and senior audience in the FCDO, across government, and in our global diplomatic network:

Afghanistan: The Cities Begin to Fall

Summary

Five provincial capitals fall to the Taliban, and more losses could be on the way. Attacks in Kabul rise.

In the last 48 hours the Taliban have taken control of Zaranj on the border with Iran, and Sheberghan, Kunduz, Taloqan and Sar-e-Pul in the North. If they are held they will become the first provincial capitals to be administered by the Taliban since the military campaign that toppled their regime in 2001.

Zaranj, the capital of Nimroz in the south west of Afghanistan, is small, but it is a major border crossing with Iran. The town reportedly fell without a shot being fired. Sheberghan, the capital of Jowzjan in the north, was the stronghold of former Vice-President Dostum. His militia contested the Taliban advances, but it was not enough. As with the compound of the late General Raziq in Kandahar, images of Taliban fighters posing inside the luxurious Dostum residence symbolise the watershed moment for the country.

The northern cities of Kunduz, Taloqan and Sar-e-Pul fell amidst heavy fighting today. Kunduz has been taken temporarily by the Taliban a number of times in the past. Taliban forces are targeting local prisons and releasing inmates, bolstering their ranks with loyalists and grateful new recruits alike.

Kabul does not seem to be under imminent threat of Taliban capture, but they are pre-positioning and stepping up attacks. The Taliban claimed a complex car bomb attack on the residence of the Defence Minister on 2 August, 500m from the British Embassy. High profile targeted killings continue in the city, including the head of the Government's Media and Information Centre.

But in the absence of a credible overall strategy, air strikes alone will not be enough to halt the Taliban's advance.

Comment

The battle is rapidly slipping away from the Government, irretrievably unless there is a turnaround which at least slows down Taliban momentum.

The Taliban look set to continue their successful strategy of pressing on multiple fronts at once and making it difficult for the ANDSF [Afghan National Defence and Security Forces] to regroup and consolidate. Herat, Lashkar Gah, and Kandahar, amongst others, are still at risk.

We have changed our Travel Advice to urge British nationals to leave now by commercial means and we are proactively contacting them to reinforce the message.

PINFIELD

That evening I compared notes with Brigadier Tom, back in Kabul, on the significance of the weekend's military and political losses. During the day the fifth provincial capital had fallen to the Taliban – only two days after the fall of Zaranj, the first to go. The analysts in Kabul thought that another five capitals might fall within the next 24 to 48 hours. It was starting to look like the end for the Afghan state, opening the way for a Taliban military victory. Heavy fighting continued in Kandahar and Lashkar Gah. I was concerned that the loss of either city, but Kandahar in particular, might precipitate a sudden and total collapse of the Afghan army and the republic. We agreed to be in touch first thing the following morning.

I contacted Alex to update him on discussions in London. Depending on developments overnight, we would probably have to take the decision to close the embassy site in the Green Zone. I asked Alex to pull together a handful of senior staff to do what should be done now, to get ahead of such a decision. In particular, to carry out elements of the closure plan that could be implemented immediately before a decision to close, buying us time later, but which would be reversible if the situation stabilised. We agreed that this was not for wider discussion with staff – particularly the Afghan staff – unless and until we had a decision and a clear plan to communicate to them.

I asked Alex to push the Afghan Government again about getting the Milkman of Kabul released. We had discussed this case repeatedly with the authorities but drawn a blank. In normal circumstances an embassy will try to ensure that a British citizen in a foreign prison is properly treated and has a fair trial. But these were not normal circumstances, and we needed to leave no stone unturned to get him out of prison and out of the country; we might not have much time left to do so. Alex and the team came up with a plan to press senior government officials for early release on humanitarian grounds.

Monday 9 August

The early morning headlines from Kabul were grim. The Afghan army and security forces were collapsing. We were seeing increased Taliban activity throughout Kabul province and in the city itself. Targeted killings of government officials in Kabul were in full spate. Overnight, the Taliban had launched an offensive on Pul-e Khumri and Baghlan. They had seized control of Highway 1, the main transport route between most of the major cities. Mazar-e Sharif was cut off. Within hours, Mazar-e Sharif, Balkh, Aibak and Samangan were under attack. There were reports of widespread Afghan army surrenders in the north.

Brigadier Dan Blanchford and his advance team deployed to Kabul, pressing Go on the months of detailed planning for Operation Pitting, the plan that we had all hoped would never be needed.

TUESDAY 10 AUGUST

I contacted Alex first thing. We worked our way through our checklists. Near the top of the list was making progress on people being allowed to leave without passports – a key blockage that we needed to overcome to speed up the ARAP relocations.

It was clear that the Ministry of Defence's ARAP team in Kabul, although working as fast as they could, were under-resourced for the size of the task they now faced. I asked Alex to put all available embassy staff onto processing ARAP applications unless there was a compelling reason for them to be doing something else.

Early that afternoon, I summarised for Alex a long discussion I'd had with colleagues in London. It was clear that we would have to start the evacuation of the embassy within the coming days. The advice from the military was that they would not be able to assure the safety of our staff beyond the end of August.

The plan taking shape was for a two-stage departure. The first stage involved reducing even further the number of staff in Kabul and relocating those who were to remain to Taipan, our military base at the airport. We would close the embassy compound in the Green Zone, removing or destroying sensitive equipment and papers. All remaining staff in Kabul airport would work flat out on evacuating British Nationals and ARAP candidates in whatever time we had left, using a combination of scheduled airlines, charter flights organised by the Foreign Office, and military flights if it came to that. We would need to take decisions on whether it would be possible to set up an Evacuation Handling Centre at the Baron Hotel, and on a Plan B if that was not possible, depending on the facts on the ground.

The second stage, to be held very closely among those with a strict need to know, would involve the extraction of all remaining staff from the airport if and when that became necessary. That would almost certainly be a high-risk military operation, in circumstances where the republic had collapsed, security had completely broken down, and we had to get everyone out quickly.

This plan would need to be signed off by ministers, both in principle and when the time came to execute it. In particular by the Foreign Secretary, who was legally responsible for the embassy and its staff.

I gave a similar update to Brigadier Tom in Kabul, to ensure that civilian and military colleagues at the sharp end in Kabul were seeing the same picture. And also to ensure that our decision making in London was informed by the reality on the ground, and by what we were seeing of US plans. As far as I could tell, US evacuation planning was still not yet fully formed.

It was time for me to get back to Kabul. There are some jobs you cannot delegate. I booked a flight and the obligatory pre-flight Covid test, which would take a day to process. It was a bright, sunny afternoon. I went for a walk in Richmond Park with Fiona and the dog, to clear our minds for what was to come.

That evening, Brigadier Tom updated me on the fighting. Farah City, in the west, had fallen to the Taliban during the afternoon. Pul-e Khumri, not far north of Kabul, had fallen a few hours later, following the withdrawal of the Afghan army – the seventh and eighth provincial capitals lost. Mazar-e Sharif was on the brink and likely to fall in the next 48 hours. The Taliban were preparing to attack Bagram and Maidan Shar, only 45 km from Kabul. President Ghani was making last, desperate changes to the military leadership.

I heard from contacts in Kabul that the thinking in Washington was turning to a possible evacuation of the US Embassy. Some staff were being relocated from the Green Zone to the airport. But the US Embassy still dwarfed ours. It all looked desperately late.

Wednesday 11 August

In London, the mood among officials – and my advice – was that it was time to press Go on the first stage of the evacuation plan. If we wanted to avoid getting stuck in the middle of a very dangerous situation, we should move quickly. If we were not in control of events, events would quickly be in control of us. The consequences of that happening could be dire, for the people concerned and for the UK Government: deaths, serious injuries, staff trapped or taken hostage. The recommendation went to the Foreign Secretary to close the embassy in the Green Zone and relocate a smaller team to the fall-back location at Taipan, our military base at the airport. The closure and destruction plan would have to be shortened from a week to five days, given the speed and severity of developments on the battlefield.

Last-ditch talks were under way in Doha between the Afghan Government and the Taliban Political Commission, with US Special Representative for Afghanistan Reconciliation Zalmay Khalilzad trying to bring the two sides to some sort of agreement. The talks were not going well. I heard a report that Mullah Baradar, the Taliban's political leader who had signed the Doha Agreement back in early 2020, was now avoiding giving a straight answer to whether the Taliban would stand by their assurances under the agreement not to attack Western interests. Even if they did stand by their word, that might not mean much in the fog of war. Representatives of the international community gathered in Doha made it clear that they would not recognise a regime that took control of Afghanistan by military force.

The bad news was coming thick and fast. The northeastern capital of Faizabad had fallen to the Taliban the previous night, meaning that nine provincial capitals had now been lost. Mazar-e Sharif was surrounded, and was expected to be taken within 24 to 48 hours. Faryab, in the northwest, was also expected to fall quickly. The 217th Army Corps, responsible for the defence of Kunduz and a number of other towns, collapsed, and its headquarters were overrun. The analysts thought that the northwest province of Badghis was likely to capitulate soon. In Herat, the charismatic leader Ismail Kahn, who had saved the day only weeks earlier, was reported to be negotiating a handover of the city to the Taliban.

In Kandahar, the Taliban overran the prison and released more than 900 prisoners. Many of them were Taliban and, as anticipated, would be heading straight for the fighting, for revenge and for their share of the victory spoils. The Taliban were preparing to attack Bagram Airfield and the Parwan Detention Facility next door. This prison contained thousands of Taliban and ISKP fighters, many of them inherited by the Afghan Government from the US and other allies' detention operations. All of those fighters would be freed within days.

In Lashkar Gah, a week of heavy fighting between government forces and the Taliban culminated in a massive car bomb outside the police headquarters. Ghazni, on the road from Kandahar to Kabul, was under sustained attack.

The Taliban were making their move on parts of Kabul province. Brigadier Tom described to me the mood in Kabul city: 'Grim with a sense of foreboding.'

President Ghani sacked Defence Minister Bismillah Khan and Army Chief of Staff General Wali Mohammad Ahmadzai. They had only been in their posts since June. It was hard for me to see how making changes in these two critical roles could rescue the situation. Maybe, though, there were other things going on behind the scenes. A few days later, BK called for Ghani to be arrested for betraying Afghanistan.

The government was disintegrating. The previous day, Finance Minister Khalid Payenda had resigned while on an 'official visit' to the USA, after a public falling-out with Ghani. Payenda stayed in the USA, finding work as a taxi driver in Washington DC and as an academic.

THURSDAY 12 AUGUST

Alex Pinfield contacted me early in the morning as I was setting off back to Kabul. He had a meeting in a few hours with Fazel Fazly, President Ghani's close adviser. We agreed that Alex should tell Fazly of our plans to close the embassy in the Green Zone and relocate to the airport. The news would be public within a matter of hours. Better that Ghani should hear it from us first.

The flight from London to Dubai was packed. While I was in the air, Herat, Kandahar, Lashkar Gah, Ghazni and Badghis were lost to the Taliban. Ismail Khan had surrendered Herat to them. In Ghazni, the governor and police chief had done a deal with them, handing over the city in exchange for safe passage. I spent the layover in a transit hotel in Dubai airport, catching up on events, making and taking calls through the night.

The US State Department spokesman announced that while the American Embassy in Kabul would reduce to a core diplomatic presence over the next few weeks, 3,000 additional troops would be deployed in the coming days, to secure the airport and the US Embassy, and to help with the evacuation of embassy staff, US nationals and applicants for Special Immigrant Visas. Pressed repeatedly by journalists on whether the US Embassy would stay at its current site or relocate to the airport, the spokesman said that it would continue to operate from its current location in the Green Zone.

The following day, the Pentagon announced the deployment of the 3,000 troops, in addition to the 650 already in Kabul to protect the US Embassy, and a reserve force of 3,500 to Kuwait in the coming week, in anticipation of an airlift from Kabul. The reserve force sent to Kuwait included elements of the 82nd Airborne Division, the USA's rapid reaction force, ready to deploy anywhere in the world at short notice. The Pentagon spokesman was pressed on why the Taliban continued to advance despite US air strikes in support of the Afghan army. Washington continued to insist that the Afghans had the capabilities, including modern weaponry, to hold back the Taliban's advance.

Friday 13 August

The morning flight to Kabul from Dubai was surreal. The big Boeing 777 was nearly empty. I studied the other passengers intently. Several of them studied me right back. Across the aisle a few rows away sat a group of three young men in beards and traditional clothing, laughing and joking. A few rows ahead, a couple of single young men, similarly dressed but scowling. One sat a couple of seats behind me. Taliban, I guessed. I did not ask. There were a couple of families with young children. I felt like asking them what on earth they thought they were doing, travelling back to Afghanistan just as the Taliban were on the point of taking control, but I resisted the temptation.

I noticed from the map on the in-flight entertainment that we did not take the direct route over Kandahar. Instead, the plane flew a less direct route over Pakistan, turning west over Jalalabad.

In Doha, the Taliban rejected a ceasefire and power-sharing deal offered by the Government of Afghanistan. Rumours began to spread – or be spread – about Ghani's resignation and about the locations and intentions of the senior Afghan Government leaders.

As the Taliban closed in on Kabul, a meeting in London chaired by Prime Minister Boris Johnson agreed to Foreign Secretary Dominic Raab's proposal to reduce the British Embassy in Kabul to a core team of 20 people and relocate it to the airport by 15 August. If the situation deteriorated further, all remaining embassy staff would be evacuated from the country. Operation Pitting was launched, to evacuate those who wanted to leave Afghanistan by the end of August. The Ministry of Defence announced the deployment of 600 troops to Afghanistan over the coming days.

The instructions for dialling into the meeting by video conference reached me after the meeting had finished. No matter. I had already fed in my advice: to move the embassy to Taipan, our military base on the airfield. There was no other realistic option.

I landed in Kabul early afternoon and transferred to Taipan. I contacted Alex and Katrina, who were still at the embassy in the Green Zone, leading the closure team. They asked me to hold where I was for now, in Taipan. The move across town was too risky, and would put further pressure on the already very stretched close protection teams, who were fully committed with the closure of the embassy and moving people from the embassy to the airport. I would not after all get to be the person who closed and locked the doors of the British Embassy Kabul after 20 years of operations.

Taipan was a UK military facility inside the airport perimeter, just south of the runway and next to the main taxiway, close to the civilian terminal. It was surrounded by high concrete walls and watchtowers. The approach road was off the main road from the airport to the city, behind layers of fortifications, concrete switchbacks and high metal gates. To one side of Taipan were aircraft hangars. To the other, a much larger, and heavily fortified, US facility. From the Taipan compound a heavy metal gate opened directly onto the aircraft hard standings and taxiways parallel to the main runway, allowing us to move freely onto and around the airfield.

The conditions were basic but serviceable: a jumble of utilitarian military buildings, separated by high concrete blast walls. Nigel Casey, the Afghanistan Director in London, had summarised it accurately if unsympathetically when, months earlier, he and I discussed its merits and limitations as a possible fallback embassy: 'You've got showers, you've got telly – what are you complaining about?' The soldiers were friendly and accommodating.

I set up shop in a spartan office on the first floor of the main building, next to a kitchen with limitless supplies of instant coffee and a rapidly overflowing dustbin. A couple of small windows let in some daylight. The first challenge was to get online. This was surprisingly difficult. We plugged in wires to random wall sockets. No luck. In the end someone handed out scratch cards for a military welfare wifi network. That seemed to work, though it often meant chasing an erratic signal around the building.

Within a day, with space under increasing pressure, that room filled up with sleeping soldiers. I decamped to a smaller, windowless office with two rows of trestle tables and harsh strip lighting. Body armour and helmet were permanently at the ready, on a chair nearby. I worked out of an Ikea backpack – just the right size for a laptop, phones, chargers and notebooks.

In the background, the gunfire was incessant. It was impossible to tell whose gunfire it was, or what it meant. The military and close protection teams would judge if I needed to move. Amidst the clatter and popping of small calibre weapons, there was the occasional slower and much deeper note of heavier calibre weapons being fired. From time to time there were great crashes from the roof above, as the soldiers dismantled and destroyed sensitive equipment in preparation for a quick departure when the time came.

We took meals in a low canteen, past a high blast wall and across a concrete service road. On a large TV screen, the global news channels relayed the unfolding events in Kabul in a constant loop. A small picture of the Queen hung on the wall. On the final day Claire – one of my close protection team – and I climbed on a table and unscrewed it from the wall with a kitchen knife to ensure that it did not get overlooked as the military cleared the base.

London ran past me an offer of six Home Office Border Force officers who could be ready to travel to Kabul in the next few days, to help with document checking and establishing who was entitled to evacuation. First, though, they had to undergo the obligatory Hostile Environment training for working in a conflict zone. I asked for them to be sent out as soon as possible. They would prove to be indispensable members of the Operation Pitting team.

There were further exchanges with London on the eligibility of staff and contractors for evacuation. We were now under intense pressure to widen the eligibility criteria, from all sides. I repeated my mantra: better to do so early and proactively than late and defensively. But we were still approaching the problem as if we had time to collect biometrics (fingerprint data), refer applicants back to the Home Office for security screening, and put recommendations about individuals to Ministers for decision. I told London that we would shortly be in a completely different environment, in which decisions would have to be taken on the spot – in minutes, not hours or days.

I contacted Foreign Minister Hanif Atmar to set up a call between him and the Duty Minister, Lord Goldsmith. The political issue was for Lord Goldsmith to offer Atmar what solidarity we could. The practical issue was for Lord Goldsmith to ask Atmar to overrule the Afghan bureaucracy and allow our current and former Afghan staff to leave the country without passports. The Afghan bureaucracy was still not letting people leave without them, and as many of our Afghan staff still did not have passports they now had no way of getting them. We also needed to make urgent progress on getting our prisoner released – the Milkman of Kabul. Hanif Atmar offered a phone call with our minister that evening or next day.

Early the next morning Atmar and I exchanged further messages. I set out the issue in a couple of sentences, together with a proposed fix, so that he would have time to arrange things on his side and would be able to agree on the spot when the call with Lord Goldsmith happened. Atmar promised to find a solution and offered 3:00 pm Kabul time for the call. A while later, however, the call fell through: Atmar was called away to a crisis meeting of the Afghan Government.

Later that day, as we closed the embassy and withdrew our staff and guards to the airport, Atmar contacted me to ask if we could keep our security presence at the Wazir Akbar Khan gate to the Green Zone until alternative arrangements could be made. His residence was just a few steps down the road from the embassy, which by now was all but shut down. I had to tell him that that would not be possible: we had to withdraw our people while we still could. It felt bad, but we had no alternative.

The Foreign Office Press Office asked about my availability for media interviews; requests were coming in all the time. I said that I was willing to give interviews, but the requests would need to be cleared with the Foreign Secretary's SpAds, who so far had turned down every media request that we had put to them. London would have to sort that one out for themselves.

Late that afternoon I heard from Johnny Mercer that his former army interpreter had made it back to Kabul. He was cleared to travel to the UK but still did not have an Afghan passport. I agreed with Mercer to try to get him onto a plane if he could get himself to the airport. Official channels in Kabul were now meaningless.

SATURDAY 14 AUGUST

I checked in with Brigadier Dan Blanchford, the senior military officer running Operation Pitting, the military evacuation. Dan was as ever calm, measured, clear in his advice. The evacuation window looked like being 17 to 21 August. Our first priority would be to evacuate UK passport holders. The onward evacuation chain was, however, not yet in place, as the Temporary Safe Location in Dubai – key to our ability to move large numbers of people quickly – was not yet up and running. The 3,000-strong US military reinforcements were starting to arrive but would not be fully in place for several days. It was a similar picture for the 600-strong UK military contingent announced the previous day.

In Kabul events were racing ahead. President Ghani told US Secretary of State Blinken that he was ready to step down to enable a political settlement. Karzai and Matin Bek, Ghani's chief of staff, would go to Doha to negotiate a power-sharing arrangement with the Taliban. US Special Representative for Afghanistan Reconciliation Khalilzad sought assurances from the Taliban that they would not enter Kabul by force. For their part, the Taliban declared that they would not enter Kabul while a power-sharing agreement was being negotiated, although in reality small numbers of Taliban fighters were already entering the city. The US plan was to try to secure an interim agreement with the Taliban, allowing time for a peaceful transfer of power and for those who needed to evacuate to do so.

Matin Bek later told the BBC that 'we had a small window' to achieve an agreement, but this was scuppered by Ghani fleeing the country the following day.

Plans were being drawn up to secure Kabul, with General Sami Sadat, one of the most effective and impressive Afghan commanders, in charge. A few days later I sat down to drink tea with him as he was being extracted from Kabul, battered and bruised but still defiant.

That morning Admiral Vasely, the US military commander in Afghanistan, gave a briefing for allies. He set out his assessment that the Taliban would launch an attack on Kabul within the next 24 to 48 hours. He judged that of the 40,000 Afghan soldiers in Kabul, only 500 would be prepared to fight if the Taliban attacked the city. Vasely warned that we did not yet have enough US and other allied forces in place to defend the airport if the Taliban chose to mount a determined assault on it. The US forces being deployed into Kabul would not arrive in sufficient strength to defend Kabul airport for the next 24 to 48 hours.

At the height of the evacuation, a week or so later, there would be 6,000 US soldiers, over 1,000 British troops, and large numbers of Turkish and other forces in Kabul to secure the airport. But that was several days away. A day is a long time when the situation is changing for the worse with every passing hour.

So this was the moment of truth. If the Taliban attacked in the next couple of days, while we were still 'combat light', as one of my military colleagues put it, Kabul city, and the airport itself, could not be reliably defended. The airport was both our fallback location and the only viable way into and out of Afghanistan.

The decision to close the embassy complex in the Green Zone had already been taken, and the closure plan was under way, but even in its accelerated form, this was scheduled to take the best part of a week. We no longer had a week. We had only a matter of hours.

But speeding up the evacuation from the Green Zone was only part of the problem. There was an even bigger question. Was our fallback location at the airport still viable? The senior US commander in Afghanistan was telling us that if the Taliban decided to launch an assault on the airport before the substantial forces now on their way were in place, we would be in trouble.

I patched into a meeting of senior officials at 10:00 am London time. I advised them that unless the military could give positive assurance that the US, UK and other allied forces could hold the airport securely, the decision to keep civilian staff in Kabul would be the wrong one. The meeting adjourned until midday, and then reconvened in order to agree the advice that would go to the Foreign Secretary.

As all around us collapsed we needed to avoid getting trapped inside a fortress, with no way out, putting at risk the lives of both our civilians and military. Unlike the US, we did not have a 650-strong contingent of US Marines already stationed in Kabul to defend our embassy and its staff. Unlike the US we did not have attack helicopters or heavy lift helicopters in Kabul. Nor did we have military armoured vehicles. We had civilian armoured Land Cruisers – not the same thing at all if you needed to drive through a war zone to the airport or to the Pakistan border. In the planning discussions with Dan and his team in April and June we had talked through the extreme scenario in which our military would be fighting their way from the airport into Kabul, to the Green Zone to rescue civilian staff, and back out to the airport again. We had decided that that was a sure recipe for disaster; we had to ensure that we never found ourselves in that position. No one needed to be told that if the chips were really down we would not be the Americans' first priority, any more than other embassies' staff would be our own first priority.

People talk and write breezily of the fog of war. The reality is that you are trying to make decisions – potentially life and death decisions – based on the information you have, your knowledge (or lack of it) of what others might do next, and your best judgement about where things might stand hours and days into the future. You may by then be wishing you had done certain things while you still had the chance: options that are available now but will no longer be available in a few hours.

Or things might brighten up. You don't know. The thing about hindsight is that it's only available after the event. What you're trying to do in the moment is to apply hindsight up front. Senior people far from the action might have the bigger picture – or they might not know enough about the situation on the ground. Wherever you are, it's essential to look at what's actually happening, which may be very different from what you want to happen.

The shutdown of the embassy and withdrawal of all remaining diplomatic staff was accelerated and brought forward to the evening of 14 August. Foreign Secretary Dominic Raab agreed that we should evacuate as many British citizens and eligible others as we could in the time available, and withdraw all civilian staff from the airport to Dubai until the airport was secure enough to enable a team to return to support the evacuation. The military planned to hold their positions in Kabul airport in a defensive posture, to keep options open.

I asked the Foreign Office in London to pursue urgently with the Home Office and Ministry of Defence all remaining options to evacuate ARAP applicants, particularly the serving Afghan staff and their families who had not yet been relocated to the UK. We had to move quickly; this weekend might be the last opportunity for people to leave the country before the Taliban took over. I asked that anyone whose data was already enrolled and who was awaiting the completion of checks should be flown to the UK and their processing completed there. Anyone who got themselves to a third country should be allowed to continue their application from outside Afghanistan.

Above all, we needed decisions in principle which we could apply on the run in Kabul without the need to check back with London on each individual case. There would be no time to do that. There was no longer any point in asking the Afghan Government for permission for people to travel without passports. There was no longer a functioning Afghan Government.

There were reports of the Taliban massing in the vicinity of Kabul. In London, colleagues contacted the Taliban Political Commission in Doha, warning them off any action against our evacuation or against the military forces deployed to carry it out. The Taliban's response was less than reassuring. I thought it worth our sending the message to the Taliban Political Commission, but felt it unlikely that it would have much sway; the Taliban Political Commission were political negotiators in Doha, far from the military action, and with little if any influence over the Taliban's fighters or their commanders on the ground in Kabul, for whom military victory was now within grasp.

In Doha, US CENTCOM commander General McKenzie met Baradar, the Taliban political leader, and warned him that if the Taliban interfered with the US evacuation there would be severe consequences. It was clear, however, that the USA had neither the intention nor the capability to secure Kabul itself.[26]

I contacted Katrina over at the embassy with the closure team, still clearing the site of sensitive papers and equipment. She assured me that all staff were okay, working their way through the large, complex site, running on adrenalin and copious amounts of cake. I asked her to press on, finish the job as quickly as possible and get the team over to Taipan before nightfall.

The embassy closure team worked through the day and into the evening. With 130 buildings spread across three sites, there was a set order in which the emergency closure plan had to be carried out, with the most sensitive papers and equipment to be removed or destroyed at the top of the list. The team worked quickly and methodically through the compound, focusing on the main office building. They also disposed of anything that could offer the Taliban – or any other hostile actor – a propaganda victory. Pictures of the Queen, flags, the official wine store. All had to be removed or destroyed. Later, there were inaccurate stories in the media that the Taliban had captured a picture of the Queen. All of ours were accounted for. But inevitably mistakes were made, as we were to find out when we heard that some personal papers had been found, unburned, by the Taliban when they entered the embassy.

As darkness closed in and the security situation became untenable, the team were instructed to finish their work and make their way to Taipan. A five-day closure plan had been compressed into two days, and then into nine hours.

The team arrived in batches, grey and shaking with exhaustion after nerve-racking journeys across a city which was by now under no one's control and gridlocked. With them, bags of kit that could not be left behind or destroyed. Jason, the embassy security manager, seemed to be everywhere: calmly, methodically keeping track of who was where, what time each person would be leaving, on which flight.

The recreation room at Taipan turned into an informal muster point and clearing house. A nondescript windowless shed with rows of plastic sofas, a pool table and a large screen TV, it was now the nerve centre of the embassy evacuation. The sofas were quickly monopolised by exhausted people. Then the floors. Some would live there for days. One person failed to notice a low-mounted air-conditioning unit carefully positioned at head height near the door, and gashed his scalp. It was all too easy to do, especially after dark in an unlit compound. The medics patched him up. *Note to self: remember that aircon unit. Especially at night.*

As darkness fell, the people due to leave on the first military flight were called forward. The roads outside the recreation room and down to the gate leading onto the airfield hard standing filled up with people, including a large contingent of the embassy guard force. It was hard to recognise people by the light of torches and mobile phones. Weapons had to be accounted for and checked in. Bags with personal belongings piled up on pallets: you might see them again in a few days or weeks, or you might not. Those leaving filed through a gate in the wall, onto the airfield and onto a nearby military transport plane. The plane took off for Dubai at 8:30 pm, bound for Minhad military air base in the UAE. It would return around daybreak to pick up a second group, including the embassy closure team.

I texted Fiona to say that things were moving very quickly and that plans might change at zero notice. I would update whenever I could, from wherever I happened to be.

Late that night I texted Alex, who had just arrived in the UAE, leading the first group of staff to be evacuated: 'Welcome to Minhad!' I updated him on the developments in Kabul and the discussions going on with London about what should happen next. We agreed to keep a team of volunteers in Dubai for now to help with evacuations and to be ready to come back to Kabul quickly when it was possible to do so. Over the next few days, the volunteers from the embassy waiting in Dubai to return to Kabul were bolstered by a Rapid Deployment Team from London and the Home Office Border Force team.

While the first flight was in the air, a big argument broke out in London among ministers and their advisers about the Foreign Secretary's decision to evacuate the embassy. Admiral Vasely's assessment had prompted Dominic Raab to take the decision to evacuate all civilian staff. As Foreign Secretary, he held the legal and political responsibility for the safety of the embassy staff; if our people were killed, injured or taken hostage, he would be legally and politically accountable for the decision to keep them in Kabul. This was not a hypothetical question. In 2012 US Ambassador Chris Stevens and several of his colleagues had been killed during a terrorist attack on the US diplomatic mission in Benghazi, Libya. The deaths had led to serious criticism of the US State Department and of Hillary Clinton, who was Secretary of State at the time. As had the Iran hostage crisis for Jimmy Carter's Administration in 1979, when 52 US diplomats had been captured by revolutionaries in Tehran and held for 444 days. Eight US servicemen and one Iranian civilian had died in a botched rescue operation.

In London, some seniors saw it differently, believing that there was no reason to think that the Taliban would attack allied forces. A senior official called me from London to ask my views and advice. I set out the risks and uncertainties, and my recommendations, as dispassionately as I could.

Events were unfolding at lightning speed, and hard facts were in short supply. There were many more questions than answers. The Afghan Government and armed forces had collapsed in the face of a determined Taliban military onslaught. We did not know what the Taliban leadership or its fighters intended to do next. Their behaviour, as they overran Afghan towns and cities, had been violent and vengeful. Would there be street-to-street fighting in Kabul? Would the Taliban leadership be willing and able to exercise full control over their fighters – in particular, over those who had just been released from prison, and might want to make their mark or take revenge? We did not know. With the Taliban massing around Kabul and with military victory within grasp – victory over the Afghan Government and, in their eyes, the US-led coalition – it was a leap of faith to believe that they would exercise restraint.

Meanwhile what we could be certain of was that ISKP's and al-Qaeda's intentions towards us were anything but good. Thousands of ISKP fighters had just been let out of the prisons.

Would we be fighting our way out of Kabul – the nightmare scenario that we had identified months earlier and had planned to avoid at all costs? At every stage the situation had changed faster and worse than anyone had predicted. The US military commander in Kabul had told us that there were not yet enough troops in place to hold the airport should the Taliban attack. Our window to extract people relatively safely could be very short – maybe hours.

We did not know whether the USA still intended to run a Non-combatant Evacuation Operation, or whether we would be able to do so ourselves. Up to this point the Americans' plans had been remarkably undeveloped, at least to our knowledge.

Late that night the same official in London called me back and asked me to stay. I understood the political imperatives and agreed to do so, on the basis that it was my decision. In such a situation the right thing to do is to use your judgement, not blindly follow orders from people with far less knowledge of the situation on the ground. The people in London were simply too far away from the ground truth, and the situation on the ground too dynamic, for it to be any other way.

I was asked to find volunteers from the embassy team to stay. I could not ask other civilian staff to stay, though the small ARAP team of Ministry of Defence civilians did so.

Anonymous sources in London later briefed the press that I was ordered off a plane in an angry confrontation with the military commanders on the ground in

Kabul. The story was fabricated, as its sources well know. The military commanders in Kabul were people of integrity, who gave me their best advice and support at all times under the most extreme stress. I have never worked with finer people.

It looked to me that the priority of some in London was to spare ministers and their close advisers – military as well as civilian – personal and political embarrassment. Like everyone else, the UK Government had been caught out by the speed of events. Personal rivalries and animosities played a big part in the infighting that erupted. The advice, assessment and welfare of the people on the ground was of secondary importance.

In the weeks that followed, the FCDO were accused of over-optimism in the late stages of the Afghanistan campaign. If that was true of the FCDO, it was not only them. During the last weeks and months of the republic, some very senior people in Whitehall made heroically optimistic assumptions about what would happen next and what the Taliban would do next, based on little evidence and a lot of wishful thinking. That was a pattern that had been repeated again and again during the 20-year Afghanistan campaign, too often leading to tragic outcomes.

In Kabul, Jason, the head of security at the embassy, was in a back room of the recreation hut, working on the rosters for the second and final flight, taking out all remaining embassy staff. I told him that I would be staying. He frowned, clearly unhappy at the decision. He bit his tongue, and said: 'I'll arrange a close protection team.'

My close protection team, all ex-military, stepped forward without the slightest hesitation, as did Jason himself, saying that as long as I was staying they were too. You don't often have the privilege of working alongside colleagues who will do that.

I told Fiona that I would be staying in Kabul for the time being. She replied immediately: 'Needless to say, you should stay until the job is done.' A few days later, with the British media reporting that I was still in the airport issuing visas to Afghans, she pulled my leg about my now being the Foreign Office's most senior visa clerk: 'I'm telling people that you're embracing your new career as a visa writer.'

The military hunkered down in a defensive posture. We needed to get through the next few days and keep open the possibility of an evacuation of British nationals and Afghans, once enough US and UK forces could be brought in to secure the airport and make that possible. It was impossible to predict when, or even whether, that might happen. Or what our options would be if it proved impossible to get enough soldiers in to secure the airport.

Through the evening and into the night Brigadier Tom and I compared notes on developments on the battlefield, and what they meant for the wider picture. In rapid succession, two more cities fell to the Taliban: Mazar-e Sharif, Afghanistan's fourth largest city, and Jalalabad, the gateway to Afghanistan's main border crossing into Pakistan. Maidan Shar surrendered. Zarifa Ghafari, the Mayor of Maidan Shar, one of Afghanistan's few female mayors and a prominent women's rights advocate, escaped to Kabul airport hidden in the footwell of a car. Only Kabul remained under government control.

Then came unconfirmed reports that the maximum security prison at Pul-e Charkhi had been overrun and the inmates released. This huge wheel-shaped facility was very close to Kabul: planes flew over it on final approach to Kabul airport. It contained thousands of hardened Taliban and other fighters. I texted Tom: 'Do we know how many Tb [Taliban] in Pul-e Charkhi?' (That is, how many would now be heading straight for the battlefield.) '7200 inmates, 3186 are Tb.'

And besides them, a large number of ISKP fighters, violent extremists with their own agenda.

Late into the night, we followed as best we could developments at the US Embassy. They had left the decision to evacuate very late and were now carrying out a crash closure. I heard stories of the closure teams going from room to room, digging out staff who were in denial or in blind panic, and putting them into helicopters and vehicles.

The size of the task was colossal. In addition to the staff of the enormous US Embassy, their SIV programme looked to be a gigantic undertaking, and it was not clear how, where or whether any of this work would be done once the US Embassy relocated to the airport. This mattered deeply to us, because we were all going to be dependent on that single, one-runway airport with limited infrastructure, in a remote country. With no government and in the middle of a war zone.

Part 4: The Fall of Kabul

Sunday 15 August

The Americans announced that they would double the size of the US military deployment at Kabul airport, to 6,000 troops.

Negotiations were under way in Doha to agree terms for a transfer of power in order to spare Kabul and its inhabitants from street fighting. The Taliban in Doha said that they did not want to enter Kabul until a formal transfer of power had taken place. They talked of a 100-strong *shura* (council) to govern the country in the short term and to allow foreign forces to leave peacefully. Although the discussions in Doha continued, they were rapidly overtaken by events.

I asked US Ambassador Ross Wilson whether there was any confidence that the Taliban Political Commission in Doha reflected the intentions of Taliban commanders and fighters on the ground – in other words, would an agreement made by the politicians in Doha be binding on the fighters in Afghanistan? I already knew the answer before Ross replied: 'You've identified a big issue.'

The final act was soon to come. In my first sitrep (situation report) of the day I stated that five of the seven Afghan National Army Corps had collapsed. The Taliban were massing their forces in the vicinity of Kabul. They were already in the southern and eastern districts of Kabul, contradicting assurances given by the Taliban in Doha.

As Taliban forces converged on Kabul from all directions, so too were thousands of people seeking to flee the Taliban. Many of them slept rough in Kabul's parks. The city was gridlocked. There were long queues at the banks as people tried to withdraw dollars. Scheduled civilian flights were still operating, and huge crowds gathered at the airport as people tried to get on planes – any plane, as long as it was out of Afghanistan. Things quickly broke down into anarchy. The Taliban later claimed that they were forced to enter Kabul to put a stop to the killing and looting.

President Ghani was still in the palace, where his staff posted videos of him pulling the levers of power. But the levers were attached to nothing, and his government was melting away. The Ministers of Defence and Interior had been sacked a few days previously and could no longer be reached. Vice President Saleh had left for the Panjshir Valley, from where he would lead the armed resistance to the Taliban. A group of senior Afghan politicians made their way to the airport to fly to Islamabad, putting their hopes in the Pakistan Government to broker a last-minute agreement with the Taliban. Or maybe just to save themselves. Even now, there were divisions within the government, with Ghani reported to fear that this group of senior politicians were planning to cut him out of any future political settlement.

I joined calls with US, UN and other international colleagues. Someone asked what the US Government's plans were: how long should we expect the US military presence to last? The American response to the group was telling. 'Don't ask how long it will last; if you want to leave, do so today or tomorrow.'

I did a quick stocktake of the status of other embassies ahead of a call with London. At that time, France, Germany and Italy were en route to the US Embassy South Compound, the former Resolute Support Mission HQ next to the main US Embassy in the Green Zone, for onward evacuation to the airport by the Americans. The Indian Embassy were leaving as soon as they could get their people out. Wang Yu, the Chinese Ambassador, was staying put for now. Stefano Pontecorvo, the NATO Senior Civilian Representative, was reported to be planning to relocate to Doha. A dozen Japanese diplomats were trying to move to the airport, but communications with them had been lost.

The daily Emirates flight from Dubai took off at its normal mid-morning time, scheduled to arrive in Kabul at 2:30 pm. But in the two hours or so that it was in the air, the situation in Kabul changed. It was no longer possible to land at Kabul airport. The pilot turned the huge plane back towards Dubai. Afghanistan was cut off from the outside world.

At midday, Dan Blanchford reported that the Taliban leadership were expected to make a strategic pause, possibly responding to the deterrent effect of a US 'show of force' – noisy, demonstrative passes over the city by military jets. The Afghan army had deserted the airport checkpoints. Dan, setting out the risks to our own operations, noted a military assessment that not all Taliban fighters were fully under control of the leadership. Our own 600-strong UK military contingent would take another day or two to arrive in full.

Alex Pinfield messaged me from Minhad airbase in Dubai to say that the second Royal Air Force flight from Kabul had just landed, carrying the remaining civilian staff from the embassy. He had agreed with London to keep a team from the Kabul embassy in the UAE for now, and planned to set up a small office in the Abu Dhabi embassy for the next couple of days. The embassy had much better communications links back to London than the military transit facility at Minhad. He was deeply troubled that I was still in Kabul, and urged me to leave.

In the early afternoon I received reports that President Ghani was about to flee the palace and that three helicopters were being prepared. They took off with Ghani and a few of his closest officials around 2:30 pm. A few hours later the media reported that President Ghani, Hamidullah Mohib and Fazel Fazly had reached Uzbekistan. The planeload of ministers headed for Pakistan had taken off as well.

According to an interview with the US journalist Kathy Gannon published on 15 December 2021, former President Hamid Karzai had 'invited' the Taliban to enter Kabul to secure the city, 'to protect the population so that the country, the city doesn't fall into chaos'.[27]

I messaged London: 'Tb are through the palace gate.' Shortly afterwards, pictures appeared on social media of the Taliban gathered around Ghani's desk in the Presidential Palace, from which he had broadcast to the nation a few hours before. Kabul had fallen. The Taliban had taken Kabul.

The Taliban announced a general amnesty for all Afghan Government officials and urged them to return to work. Mullah Yaqoob, the deputy leader and military chief of the Taliban, issued a recorded message telling Taliban fighters not to enter private houses or confiscate cars. But within days, reports would emerge of the Taliban fighters going door to door to find collaborators.

With the President and other leading members of the government gone, most of the remaining Afghan National Defence and Security Forces laid down their weapons and went home.

The Green Zone was no more. The evacuation of the US Embassy was in full flow. Helicopters were photographed lifting off from the US Embassy compound. In them there was standing room only: the seats had been ripped out to make room for more people. The city streets were gridlocked. Brigadier Tom reported in with news that the clearance of the US Embassy would be completed overnight. No news on what sort of operation, if any, the Americans planned to set up at the airport.

Around mid-afternoon we heard news of the Japanese diplomats. The Japanese Ambassador, who was out of the country, called me to say that they were trapped in a security company's compound outside the airport. He asked if we could provide helicopters to bring them onto the airfield. We had none: I suggested he try the Americans. Eventually, however, our military helped to arrange secure passage for the diplomats onto the airfield. They turned up later that afternoon at Taipan in a minibus. We took them in, and they camped down in the recreation room until we could fly them out. They were among my most appreciative guests, bowing and thanking me profusely every time I saw them. The stress was clearly overwhelming. All were exhausted and some were overcome with emotion. Getting them out safely was clearly a top priority for the Japanese Government. In the days that followed, the requests for status reports came to me every few hours, day and night. We put the diplomats onto a plane at dawn on 17 August.

During the afternoon Brigadier Tom and I kept up a running dialogue on the security situation as we tried to answer key questions. How long would our position remain tenable? What were the prospects of us being able to run any sort of evacuation? What were our options if the situation worsened? Tom's advice was, as ever, dispassionate and professional: 'I think we need to think in 6-hour blocks. … A lot more cbt [combat] power in this evening, so increasingly able to effectively defend.' Far more useful than anything I received from anyone in London.

Alex and I also talked through the next 24 hours, to ensure we were giving accurate and consistent information to people in London about what we would be able to achieve in Kabul.

Late in the afternoon, there were reports of small arms fire against the civilian terminal on the southern side of the airport. It is quite close to Taipan. There were constant breaches of the airfield perimeter. The situation was slipping out of control. Our focus shifted from evacuations to defence of the airfield.

The Turkish Ambassador called to say that he would be evacuating all his staff that evening. As it turned out, he and a small team stayed on, working out of the military north terminal.

We received a message that the Milkman of Kabul was at one of the airport gates, attempting to get in. He had walked out of prison with nothing but the clothes he was wearing and had no identification documents of any kind. The email contained a picture of a dishevelled man, with the laconic description: 'looks like an Afghan'. We identified him, got him into the airport, and put him on a plane.

Overnight, a flight departed with some 200 British Nationals, Afghan staff and others on board. An ARAP flight was due to leave the next day.

A colleague reported that such was the haste of the US evacuation that the US Air Force were bringing people out of Kabul and 'just dumping them on the runway in Doha'.

Late evening, I heard from a reliable source that when Ambassador Ross Wilson arrived at the airport, he did so with not one but two close protection teams. The second was for the US Embassy flag. It was not hard to understand why: no one wanted more pictures of triumphant militants burning US flags. We had all seen that film before, and knew the effect it had in the US as well as inflaming anti-US opinion in volatile parts of the world. I had our own flag for safekeeping.

We had heard a suggestion that all US Embassy staff might leave Kabul overnight or the following day. If true, it would clearly have major implications for us. I asked the team to get as much clarity as possible about the Americans' intentions.

Late into the night and into the next day I exchanged messages with Foreign Minister Hanif Atmar as he searched for an evacuation route for himself and others in the government. I was still waiting for clearance from London to evacuate him when he contacted me in the small hours to say that he was boarding a plane. I wished him luck. And then his phone went dead for some hours. He had succeeded in leaving Afghanistan on a Turkish rescue flight shortly before the chaos on the airfield forced the suspension of all flights in and out.

Over the days that followed there was a tsunami of requests for urgent evacuation. Our priority was to evacuate those with the strongest claim on us: British nationals and their families, and those accepted onto the ARAP scheme. We were directed to use any spare capacity to evacuate others who ministers in London decided were the highest priority.

And so began an endless process of trying to move forward difficult and high-profile cases. A consortium of UK media organisations had written to the Prime Minister on 4 August and again on 18 August seeking evacuation for the Afghan journalists who had worked for them. NGOs pressed for sanctuary for human rights defenders and civil society activists who had worked with or been funded by the UK. There were campaigns on behalf of judges who had put terrorists and corrupt officials behind bars. Some of them were women, their gender a death sentence if those they had locked away were freed from prison. There were advocates for groups of women and girls, whose rights and safety were incontestably at risk under Taliban rule. There were vocal lobbies on behalf of Chevening scholars. Footballers. Skateboarders. Musicians.

Many of the appeals for help came in the form of messages and replies to posts on social media. I asked London to monitor social media, including mine, to pick up cases we had not been aware of and those who might not have contacted us direct. We did not have the capacity to do this in Kabul.

As the requests poured in for vulnerable groups to be evacuated, the pressure intensified. Home Secretary Priti Patel announced that she would use her discretion to permit certain categories of people exceptional leave to enter the UK outside the immigration rules: LOTR (leave outside the rules). This made it possible to consider for evacuation family members of British nationals who would not otherwise meet the immigration rules. Many had never lived in the UK, and many had not qualified to do so previously. It also allowed greater scope to evacuate vulnerable groups who would not otherwise qualify for entry to the UK – journalists, civil society activists, judges and lawyers, LGBT+ people.

On 18 August the government would announce the Afghanistan Citizens Resettlement Scheme, another route for Afghans seeking refuge in the UK, for up to 20,000 people over five years. The scheme opened in January 2022.

The World Food Programme warned that Afghanistan stood on the brink of a humanitarian catastrophe.

MONDAY 16 AUGUST

One of the many emails in my inbox was about Nowzad, an animal sanctuary in Kabul set up and run by Pen Farthing, a former Royal Marine who had served in Afghanistan. Several members of the embassy staff had adopted animals from the sanctuary in the past, and Nowzad and its supporters were seeking help to evacuate Afghan female vets. Over the days that followed, a campaign began to build, to evacuate both vets and the animals they looked after. There was no time to engage with this in Kabul. London would need to decide whether the vets met our criteria for evacuation, and how to handle the growing campaign to save the dogs and cats. Dan and I quickly agreed that rescuing dogs and cats was outside our remit. Our job was to evacuate people.

But now a much bigger problem was unfolding, which would call into question whether anyone at all would be getting out of Afghanistan from now on.

Without Afghan security forces to guard the airport gates or the perimeter, or enough US, UK and other forces to do so, the civilian terminal, the airfield and then the runway itself were being overrun by thousands of desperate people. With not enough soldiers to guard the fences, they were pouring onto the airfield from all sides. There were confrontations as terrified Afghans refused to budge unless they were put on planes out of Kabul. During the morning the situation spiralled out of control. The world's media were full of pictures of people climbing on buildings, standing on collapsed airbridges, standing inside and on top of civilian airliners. I watched from the Taipan operations room the images of people on the airfield and the chaos in Kabul city.

Around midday I picked up a message from the American Embassy, stating that the US military would be restricting airborne access to the airport to US planes only. I asked Ministry of Defence colleagues to find out what lay behind this. Was it accurate? What was going on? If it applied to us, it would leave us with total dependency on the Americans and little control over our own evacuation.

The situation worsened. US attack helicopters flew up and down the runway feet above the concrete, trying to drive the crowds clear so that planes could land and take off. A huge US C-17 transport plane was mobbed as it taxied and tried to take off. People clung to the sides as it moved. Some were still clinging on as the aircraft took off and climbed high into the sky. They fell to their deaths on the runway. The awful images flashed around the world.

That afternoon the airport was closed to all air traffic. We had lost control of the airfield and its single runway.

With planes unable to land, it was impossible to bring in the thousands of US and UK troops still needed to secure the airfield. And with planes unable to take off, there was no way out of Kabul for anyone. Everything depended on the military forces already in Kabul regaining control of the runway so that flight operations could resume. Without that, we were out of options.

A worried senior military colleague messaged me: 'Absolutely the right decision to have got the Embassy staff out when you did.'

I took a call from Lord Tariq Ahmad, the Minister of State for Afghanistan at the FCDO. I had worked with him before: a thoughtful, knowledgeable, and considerate minister. We talked about the immediate problem and also about the need to think beyond the immediate crisis: to start planning now for the large-scale humanitarian crisis that would surely follow.

Under mounting pressure over the unfolding disaster in Kabul, President Biden addressed the nation from the White House. He set out the reasons for the decision to withdraw U.S. troops. His words speak for themselves:

> I stand squarely behind my decision. After 20 years, I've learned the hard way that there was never a good time to withdraw US forces.
>
> Afghanistan political leaders gave up and fled the country. The Afghan military collapsed, sometimes without trying to fight.
>
> American troops cannot and should not be fighting in a war and dying in a war that Afghan forces are not willing to fight for themselves.
>
> We gave them every chance to determine their future. What we could not provide them was the will to fight for that future.

Biden recalled his discussions with President Ghani and Abdullah in the White House back in June:

> We talked about how Afghanistan should prepare to fight their civil wars after the US military departed, to clean up the corruption in government so the government could function for the Afghan people. We talked extensively about the need for Afghan leaders to unite politically. They failed to do any of that.
>
> I also urged them to engage in diplomacy, to seek a political settlement with the Taliban. This advice was flatly refused. Mr Ghani insisted the Afghan forces would fight, but obviously he was wrong.
>
> I will not repeat the mistakes we've made in the past – the mistake of staying and fighting indefinitely in a conflict that is not in the national interests of the United States, of doubling down on a civil war in a foreign country, of attempting to remake a country through the endless military deployments of US forces.
>
> I am now the fourth American President to preside over war in Afghanistan ... I will not pass this responsibility on to a fifth President.[28]

TUESDAY 17 AUGUST

It was a long and sleepless night, punctuated by constant gunfire and the beat of helicopter rotors as the military struggled to clear the runway. In the middle of the night, amidst growing concern about the course of events, the close protection team hustled me off to a more secure part of the Taipan compound. There were tense moments as we were moving around the compound in pitch darkness. For much of the night I watched our soldiers going out onto the airfield, and later coming back into Taipan, as they sought to regain control. The stakes could not be higher, and the situation was on a knife edge. The strain on the soldiers was all too visible.

The military did an incredible job against impossible odds. Flights recommenced in the early morning. A C-17 is a big four-engine jet plane. It makes a lot of noise on landing and take-off, especially when you are a few hundred metres from the runway. I had managed to doze off, but I have never been happier about a broken night.

A little later I checked in with military colleagues on the north side of the airport: 'You guys okay over there?'

'Deprived of sleep. The clearance operation on the airfield last night was high stakes ... I had about 2 hours of wondering whether it was going to end badly. As it stands it's enabled us to secure the airfield and runway, get flights in with combat power ... to resolve the security perimeter issues. Shaping okay so far today.'

I replied: 'Hats off to you guys.'

But I also needed to ask a straight question: Did we lose anyone, and did we kill anyone?

No, to both.

Some time afterwards, stories began to emerge of Afghan military units firing on civilians and running vehicles into crowds of people out on the airfield that night.

Later that morning I discussed the situation with the military and with Jason, who had also stayed in Kabul with me. The big inflow of combat forces was under way: thousands more US and UK troops to secure the airfield and support an evacuation. Suddenly and unexpectedly, things were feeling a lot more positive than on the previous day. We might just be able to make this work. All agreed that we should seize the moment and get the evacuation going as soon as possible. I messaged Lesley Craig, the Head of Afghanistan Department, who had covered the overnight shift in London:

> We are good to go. Overnight the US/UK mil established control of the airport perimeter and cleared the field. Planes are now arriving and departing. Top priority is to complete the troop inflow but that should not stand in the way of getting the RDTs [Rapid Deployment

Teams] in. Baron Hotel is secured and Tb are/are cooperating over this. Mil here are keen that we press ahead and get the evacuation system up and running while the tide is in our favour.

Dan CJFO [Commander Joint Forces Operations] and [Brigadier] Tom concur. Let's get motoring.

I texted Alex in Abu Dhabi to update him on the situation in Kabul and on plans to move ahead with the evacuation. He and others were planning to fly back into Kabul, so they needed to know what they would be getting themselves into. I trusted Alex to tell it straight to our people, and to himself.

The situation here is still precarious but a lot better than yesterday. We now have control of the airfield; planes are landing and taking off. The issue is getting the balance right between having neither too many people at risk or [sic] too few people to get the job done in what will almost certainly be a short window .... But volunteers only, and be prepared for pretty basic life support. The canteen is still running.

Later, Alex contacted me to say that in addition to the Rapid Deployment Team from London already in the UAE, he, Andy and Katrina had also volunteered to come in on the first available flight. Others would help run the Temporary Safe Location in Dubai – a key part of the evacuation chain. Also coming to Kabul was Martin Longden, a senior diplomat who had previously served in Kabul as deputy ambassador. This was welcome news: some of our very best people, who knew first-hand the situation in Kabul.

It was particularly good that Andy, the embassy's development director, would be coming to Kabul. A highly experienced man, previously an official for the Department for International Development, Andy would strengthen our ability to plan ahead for the humanitarian response that would surely be needed after the evacuation.

When you are in the middle of a crisis it is easy to become transfixed by the most immediate and pressing questions that come at you like water from a fire hose. But it is also important to keep some head space to think beyond today and look ahead to where things might be a few weeks on. The unfolding humanitarian disaster was one part of that picture. Another was the prospect of civil war involving any or all of the remnants of the republic, Taliban factions and re-emergent warlords. Brigadier Tom and I did what we could to keep this bigger picture on the radar screens of senior political and military people back in London, beyond the logistics and the media pressures of the evacuation.

The Taliban themselves were apparently coming to terms with the new situation. Around midday, I heard that an Ariana (Afghanistan's national airline) aircraft was being prepared to fly to Doha to collect the Taliban Political Commission. It appeared that they intended to fly back into Kandahar, where the Taliban had their roots. There was speculation that they might declare the city Afghanistan's capital.

Doubtless there would be jockeying going on behind the scenes as the military factions and the Doha-based politicians sought to establish primacy. My money was on the most violent and hardline men coming out on top in any internal power struggle. When you are a military leader who has won a ruthless 20-year military campaign, why would you compromise with others who have not been involved in the fighting?

Later that day, before the Rapid Deployment Team assembled in Dubai took off for Kabul, I gave them a video briefing, together with security, welfare and crisis management colleagues from London. I wanted to tell them as clearly as I could what the situation was that they would be coming into. And to tell them that there was no pressure to come to Kabul, nor was there any pressure to stay if, once in Kabul, they changed their mind. If anyone wished to leave at any stage, they could do so without having to justify their decision to me or anyone else.

Alex and I talked through messages for those of our Afghan staff still in Kabul, hunkered down in fear of their lives. As Kabul had fallen on 15 August we had received anguished and heart-breaking messages from many of them, asking what the plan was for them. The only thing they would be interested in would be whether and how we planned to get them out of Afghanistan. I asked Alex to agree with London what our message to them should be, and to press London for a decision to contact them as soon as possible – ideally within the next few hours. This would need to be agreed between FCDO and the Ministry of Defence, the lead department for ARAP.

Brigadier Tom contacted me to say that there was a dangerous situation at the French Embassy, where staff were trapped and unable to reach the airport. It turned out that this was Ambassador David Martinon and his team; I had heard, wrongly, that they had already left Kabul. Tom was trying to help them agree safe passage with the local Taliban commander. Fortunately, David and his small team made it to the airport and set up their evacuation hub, staying to the end. I called him later that day. He and his colleagues were smart, resourceful and courageous people.

Meanwhile over 400 contracted guards, many of them from our embassy guard force, were stuck in their employer's compound, the Taliban refusing to allow them to leave. The situation was becoming increasingly tense. The Taliban were being truculent and aggressive, and demanding large amounts of money to release them.

Some rare good news. The Australians contacted me to say that an Australian military team were on their way, with several military transport aircraft at their disposal. They hoped to work alongside us, evacuating Australian and New Zealand nationals. This was very welcome news. The Australians are highly capable allies, and they made a big difference.

We started receiving messages from colleagues in European embassies, asking us for help getting their Afghan staff out of Kabul. Later, as word got around that our system worked, the requests to use the Baron to filter and process people onto evacuation flights multiplied. We were as helpful as we could be without putting our own operations at risk.

I had an important document to write: the diplomatic despatch recording the momentous events of the last few days. Andrew from the embassy political team, now in exile, produced an excellent first draft. The final product would need to be in my own voice and would be a historical document, in due course for the public record. Above all, it needed to acknowledge the national and human scale of the moment for Afghanistan, but also for our country and for a generation of soldiers, diplomats and others who had invested so much, and many cases paid so high a price, in support of the mission. I sat in my windowless office in Taipan and finished it in one take. The despatch was issued just before midday Kabul time:

Afghanistan: The Fall of Kabul and Return of the Taliban

Summary

The Taliban capture Kabul as the Government collapses. B[ritish] E[mbassy] Kabul relocates to our military facility at the airport, to conduct consular evacuation and relocation of Afghans who have worked with us over the years. Security environment very challenging but US, UK and Turkish forces now have control of the airport and flights are moving. Taliban are not contesting the evacuation operation.

After 20 years, the Taliban are back in control of Afghanistan. The Government of the Islamic Republic of Afghanistan has collapsed, and President Ghani has fled. The only part of Kabul outside of Taliban hands is the airport, which is being run by the US with large UK and Turkish contingents. The large Afghan flag that topped the hill next to our Embassy for years has been lowered. It took only nine days from the fall of the first provincial capital to a complete Taliban victory.

With the Taliban closing in on Kabul from all directions, we closed our Embassy and relocated a handful of core staff to our military facility at the airport, under the protection of 16 Air Assault Brigade and other UK military elements. Our focus is on ensuring the safe departure of our staff, British nationals, and Afghans who are eligible for resettlement under ARAP.

While the city itself is reported to be relatively calm, the situation at the airport has been very challenging with large numbers of desperate civilians on the airfield, preventing flights from landing or taking off for much of yesterday. Global media have shown the distressing scenes. Overnight, US, UK and Turkish military brought the situation under control and flight operations have restarted. This allows us to bring in the large numbers of military needed to secure the airport and our Evacuation Handling Centre, which will be fully up and running in the next 24 hours with the arrival of an RDT and Home Office staff.

The Taliban are not contesting the evacuation and in some respects are being cooperative. My judgement is that, having secured their strategic aims, it is not in their interests to pick a fight with the 82nd Airborne or the Parachute Regiment now. But the situation remains very precarious.

What happens next?

Karzai, Abdullah and Hekmatyar are among those who remain, and they are making efforts to support the transition to a functioning Taliban government.

The eyes of much of the world will be on the Taliban's behaviour towards women, minorities, and those who have worked with the West since the fall of their last administration in 2001. Despite public statements guaranteeing the safety and freedoms of Afghan citizens, early indications from areas that have fallen under Taliban control are not encouraging.

Our immediate task is to repatriate our nationals and ensure the relocation of those Afghans who are in danger due to their association with our work here in the last 20 years. After that, the focus will rapidly shift to the humanitarian consequences of the conflict, compounded by Covid and drought. That is the autumn crisis.

As we navigate the immediate and looming crises, it is important that [redacted].

It's also a big and difficult moment for many of our people. Afghanistan has played a big part in the lives of many staff across Whitehall, and many have been deeply affected by developments. Above all, this is a difficult moment for our military colleagues who have paid a high price in the Afghanistan campaign. But watching them and our civilian staff in action over the last days and weeks, it is also a moment to recognise the courage, skill and resourcefulness of our defence, development and diplomatic people.

BRISTOW [29]

The media showed pictures reported to be of 640 Afghans packed into a US C-17. The number was later revised upwards to 823: the Americans had not counted several hundred small children held in their parents' arms.

The international diplomacy was going into overdrive. In New York on 16 August an emergency meeting of the UN Security Council had called for the immediate cessation of hostilities and the establishment, through negotiations, of a new government that was united, inclusive and representative, with the full, equal and meaningful participation of women. The Security Council called for unfettered humanitarian access, and demanded that neither the Taliban nor anyone else should support terrorists operating from Afghanistan's territory. The UK would host a virtual meeting of G7 Foreign and Development Ministers on 19 August, calling on the Taliban to guarantee safe passage to foreign nationals and Afghans who wanted to leave. NATO Foreign Ministers would meet on 20 August. G7 leaders would meet, also virtually, on 24 August.

As far as we could tell, the Taliban studiously ignored all but a few of the international community's demands.

WEDNESDAY 18 AUGUST

The Rapid Deployment Team arrived in Kabul in the small hours. I met them in the Baron Hotel a few hours later as we set up our evacuation processing operation, initially in a large bar-restaurant area next to a walled garden. Dan Blanchford and I held an impromptu video conference with the Prime Minister, my battered laptop propped up on the bar. Miraculously, the hotel wifi was still working. We told London that the Evacuation Handling Centre was open and operating. The Prime Minister would need to be able to report this to Parliament later that day. In the background, a medic was patching up an early casualty – a soldier who had tripped and injured himself.

In a side room, I had a quick meeting with Dan Blanchford's combat media team, Ben Shread and James Langan – two soldiers whose job was to capture images of the events as they unfolded. They would win well-deserved awards for their work in Kabul, demonstrating to the UK public what their armed forces, diplomats and civil servants were doing on their behalf. The worldwide media were desperate for content from inside the airport, and the FCDO had asked me to make a 30-second video for social media, to put a face and a voice to the evacuation effort. Could Ben and James do it? They explained apologetically that if they filmed it for me they would have to clear the results through the military chain of command. I could not agree to that. In any case, the news cycle is inexorable and we needed to get something out quickly. They gave me some useful tips.

Andy McCoubrey and I went into the hotel garden with a smartphone and some memory joggers written in marker pen on a couple of sheets of A4. Andy held the phone, and one of my close protection team held the crib sheet. The video was viewed over a million times and picked up by the main TV news bulletins. A global media firestorm was brewing. Later that day I did a short, pooled TV interview from one of the quieter alleyways between the residential blocks of the Baron Hotel.

It is difficult to do full justice to the work done over the ten days of the main evacuation by the team in the Baron Hotel – the diplomats from the embassy and the Rapid Deployment Team, the Border Force people and the soldiers. The Baron is a resort hotel spread across a large, complex site a short distance from the airport terminal. During Operation Pitting it came to resemble a giant refugee camp inside the walls. Outside was far, far worse.

Imagine that you are sitting at a desk in the middle of that refugee camp. In front of you is an Afghan family, who have taken maybe several days to reach the point where they are now facing a British official. They may or may not speak good – or any – English. Most family groups include small children, and many have aged, infirm parents with them. Many of them have been beaten and abused by the Taliban before they have reached the Baron.

They present you with a plastic folder of documents. First questions: are the documents genuine, and do they belong to the people in front of you? Many applicants, though, do not have the right documents. Others do have documents but of such poor quality that it's hard to tell whether they are genuine or forgeries. Some, though, are obvious forgeries: photocopies with the names changed. Are the family members accompanying the lead applicant genuinely immediate family members? Are the children (unlikely to have any documents at all) that person's children, or those of a relative or friend? Or is something else going on? Are the children being trafficked, with or without the consent of their families?

What to do about an unmarried daughter who you think is over 18 and therefore not within the UK definition of 'immediate family'? In Afghanistan, an unmarried daughter of any age is a dependent until she marries. Life under the Taliban will not be good to her. Aged and infirm parents? Do they fit within a reasonable definition of the criteria?

What about the unaccompanied children who have been separated from their families, or have been thrust over the walls and the razor wire by their parents, or have somehow made it into the Baron on their own?

What are you going to do if any one of these questions is in doubt? Interpret the rules favourably? Give them the choice of travelling without some members of their party? Send them back out into the Kabul streets to take their chances with the Taliban? All the while keeping an eye out for people who have no valid claim – some of whom, bizarrely, have travelled from Pakistan or Central Asia into this hell on earth to take their chances of a new life in the UK.

If you take too long to deliberate, the system will quickly back up, and fewer people will get their chance to leave. For some, that could mean the difference between life and death.

If you have worked at the embassy, you almost certainly know some of the people seeking evacuation. It is especially tough when you have to tell people who last week were your colleagues that they do not qualify. Toughest of all is when you have to tell someone that they are cleared to travel but others in their party are not.

If you are working on the evacuation, in Kabul or London or elsewhere, you probably have strong feelings about what has happened and whether we are evacuating the people who most need our help. All the time you are receiving emails from well-meaning people, requesting or in some cases demanding that you prioritise an individual, a woman, a child, a group. Sometimes in emotionally charged language, reflecting the guilt and helplessness and outrage felt by the person contacting you. Do you prioritise that case? How do you even find the individuals in question, in a mass of desperate people, many of them equally or more deserving, stretching back as far as you can see in all directions?

You work like a dog day after day – 18-hour days, in stifling heat, with gunfire in the background and in increasingly unsanitary conditions. Katrina described the work in the Baron as 'like having a giant sand timer in the room'. Except that you do not know exactly when the sand will run out. If you take time to eat or sleep, you do so worrying that while you're eating or sleeping the clock is running down and someone might not get their chance of a flight to safety. You might pick up the stomach bug that is going around, or feel under the weather. You will certainly wonder what you are doing here and whether you want to be here, in the dead of night as the thoughts chase each other round and round. Forget about Covid precautions: no time for that. Remember to call home once a day, if you still have words and the wifi is working.

In London, a lot of work went into agreeing who were the priority cases to be called forward for evacuation. But there was a big difference between those considered a priority in London and the reality of the situation in Kabul. In some exceptionally difficult or high-priority cases, special arrangements were made to help people through the crowds or, in a small number of cases, to bring them in through the back gate of the Baron or through Taipan. But this was fraught with risk both for the individuals involved and for the whole operation.

For the most part people were processed in the order in which they presented themselves at the Baron. You tried not to think about how those who made it to the front of the queue had got there, and whether that was at the expense of more deserving people still outside. The crowds of people outside the gates of the Baron or the airport were violent and lawless. There were stories of some people paying substantial sums of money to private operators who promised to get them through the crowds and up the queue by any means.

And always people – ordinary, desperate people, fathers and mothers, babies and small children, teenagers and young women, frail grandparents. All hoping against hope that they would soon be on one of those planes. And dreading what would happen next if they were not.

These were real people, not numbers, and their fate lay in our hands. Playing God is not an experience to be recommended.

The people doing this work ranged from experienced diplomats to 25-year-olds fresh out of university. Border Force officers whose day job was staffing the immigration desks at Heathrow. Young soldiers not long out of school, and grizzled NCOs with decades of service. Soldiers and civilians working as one team in circumstances for which nothing in their previous lives or training could have prepared them. Trying day and night to help Afghans, most of them ordinary people themselves thrust into a nightmare world they had no control over.

All who worked on Operation Pitting in Kabul would receive the Afghanistan Operational Service Medal. But no one did it for medals or personal recognition.

That afternoon, Brigadier Tom alerted me to the US State Department's notice calling for US citizens and permanent residents and their families to register for evacuation. The mother of all evacuations was about to begin. Jason accurately summarised the situation with a laconic grin: 'It'll be a f*****g nightmare.'

My days were split between Taipan, the Baron Hotel and, on the north side of the runway, the military terminal. Travelling from Taipan to the Baron involved driving along the airport taxiways and hard standings in front of the civil terminal, and past lines of wrecked planes and helicopters. At the East Gate, run by Turkish and Azerbaijani forces, we took a sharp right turn onto the broken and dusty road running outside the perimeter of the airport. From there it was a slower, bumpy ride through checkpoints and crowds of people, to the gate of the Baron. On the right, we passed the Abbey Gate, the heart of the American evacuation. On the left, improvised barriers and razor wire fences. On the far side of those fences, the concrete 'canal' – an open sewer waist-deep in black, stinking liquid. People gathered either side of the canal, or in it, holding up papers, flags, placards, trying to attract the attention of the soldiers and any passing official.

The roads between the airfield perimeter and the Baron came to resemble a vast refugee camp. People found refuge from the sun under awnings, in concrete blast shelters, or in the shade of T-walls and buildings, wherever they could. Soldiers and officials worked the crowds to identify people who might be eligible for evacuation. Those fortunate enough to be selected for processing weaved their way through the crowds, in family groups or sometimes more substantial crocodiles. Vehicles could only pass along the roads at a crawl and with care. Sometimes the crush of people made the roads all but impassable, severely hampering the evacuation effort.

Abandoned and wrecked vehicles littered the roadsides, adding to the sense of unfolding apocalypse. Some looked as if they had been shot at or blown up. We still had use of the embassy CAVs – civilian armoured vehicles – and the UK military had flown in a number of additional vehicles. As the days and nights wore on, the array of vehicles in use to support different countries' evacuation operations became ever more exotic. It looked like anything available had been pressed into service. 'Availability' was a matter of interpretation. Only a fool would leave a vehicle unattended with the keys in the ignition. It became normal to see ownership advertised by means of '2 Para' or similar daubed onto the sides of vehicles. Long dribbles of paint diminished the artistic appeal. There was a rumour that the armoured vehicle used by the commanding officer of the 82nd Airborne had gone missing and that he would like it back.

In London, Parliament was recalled for an emergency debate. The speeches reflected the widespread shock and anger at the speed and finality with which the 20-year campaign in Afghanistan had collapsed. There were bitter recriminations: over the US decision to withdraw and the manner of its execution, over the UK's failure to influence US decisions, over why we had not seen the collapse coming or done anything to prevent it, over the government's alleged failure to plan or prepare for such a moment, over the cuts to the aid budget, including for Afghanistan. There was less discussion of the failures of policy and strategy over the 20 years that had led to this. In Parliament and in the media, some of those who had been responsible for UK policy and strategy carefully sought to distance themselves from what was happening. There were calls for a wider public inquiry.

Underlying this was a sense of grief, that so many lives, so much national treasure, so much effort over such a sustained period had delivered so little. Of humiliation, that our inability or unwillingness to act independently of the USA had been so graphically exposed. And of guilt over those who would be left behind.

As the blame game erupted in Washington, London and elsewhere, in Kabul we had no choice but to play the hand we had been dealt. I just hoped that we would be able to shield our people from the worst of it and keep everyone's minds focused on the job in hand.

The Foreign Secretary Dominic Raab announced the doubling of aid to Afghanistan to £286 million this year. This reversed a sharp cut in the UK's bilateral aid to Afghanistan only months before, a consequence of the reduction in the aid and development budget from 0.7 per cent of GNI to 0.5 per cent.

A UK tabloid newspaper ran a story that in the days before the fall of Kabul Foreign Secretary Dominic Raab had been 'too busy' to call Foreign Minister Atmar for help over the evacuation of interpreters and others, and had delegated the call to a junior minister. It emerged (that is, a rival had briefed the press) that Raab was on holiday in Crete as Kabul fell. It then turned out that the most senior officials in the Foreign Office, the Ministry of Defence and the Home Office, as well as the National Security Adviser, were also all on holiday. Inexplicably, when the news broke not all returned immediately to their desks. A media-briefing war erupted over allegations of a lack of grip and leadership in London.

As the scale of the crisis overwhelmed the Foreign Office and Whitehall's ability to manage its consequences, the focus turned to the inadequacies of the London bureaucracy.

In Kabul, the runway lighting broke down. Imagine what it's like to be at the controls of a gigantic and heavily loaded military transport plane landing or taking off at night with no runway lights and with the Taliban in charge on the other side of the airfield perimeter. Yet the aircrews kept the flights operating through the night.

Late that evening I heard from Jason that the Taliban had agreed to allow the trapped embassy contract guards to leave. So far so good. But they were not yet on our base and not yet on a plane.

Foreign Minister Hanif Atmar, now outside Afghanistan, contacted me about a deputy interior minister who had made it to the airport with his family. His son was a UK citizen and was cleared to fly, but the deputy minister was not. Atmar asked us to keep him under our protection at the Baron until he could be evacuated. If he went back out into Kabul his life would be at serious risk. Alex and the military found him and pushed his application through the system. The family were on a plane 36 hours later. Alex told me that he received a hug from the minister as he left the Baron to board the plane.

Early that evening, a youngish Afghan man came up to me in the Baron, in the bar that was now the centre of operations. 'You don't know me, but you're the British Ambassador, right?' The man introduced himself as Johnny Mercer's interpreter. He had made it to the Baron, against all the odds. He was cleared to travel and ready to leave. We took a quick selfie on my phone, and he was on his way. I sent the picture to Johnny Mercer: 'I think you know this guy!' Some time later I heard that he was in the UK, in a job, building a new life.

THURSDAY 19 AUGUST

Some bad news to start the day. The situation between the Abbey Gate and the front gate of the Baron Hotel had deteriorated to the point where it was not safe to open the Baron gate. The problem was not so much the number of people eligible for evacuation to the UK, but the vast press of people in the street looking to find any way out of Kabul, most of them trying to get to the Abbey Gate and into the US system. Things were getting out of hand. People were being crushed to death. US and UK forces battled to retain control of the crowds and the gates. What would happen if the crowds tried to storm the Baron's gates did not bear thinking about. We could not afford to lose control of those gates under any circumstances.

The Abbey Gate was one of the main entrance points to the airfield, several hundred metres from the main gate of the Baron Hotel. It was also one of the main US processing points, where people were screened for eligibility to enter the airfield and be put into the US evacuation system. Between the Abbey Gate and the Baron Hotel was the dusty road bounded by the airport wall, razor wire and the sewage canal. Huge numbers of people squeezed into this area, seeking to get into the US, UK, and European countries' evacuation systems. Over the next week, the street outside the Baron as far as the Abbey Gate developed into a gigantic and chaotic sorting centre, where those running the multitude of national evacuation operations tried to identify and screen the people they needed to evacuate. Each time I went out onto the street I encountered a strange multinational and multilingual world of soldiers, gendarmes, paramilitaries, border forces, and people of unknown affiliation working the crowds.

I called US Ambassador Ross Wilson to underline as clearly as possible the importance of fixing the crowd control issue. Without this, we would not be able to deliver our joint objective of getting eligible and vulnerable people out. I asked Ross to direct his people to work with us to implement crowd control fixes.

The evacuation paused overnight to fix the crowd control problems. The military engineers came up with an ingenious solution. This consisted of a chevron of shipping containers placed in the street outside the front gate of the Baron Hotel, which would allow for better segregation of UK evacuees from those seeking to get into the US or others' systems – or, in many cases, trying to get onto any plane to anywhere. It would also help reduce the risk of crushing in the crowds, and give our soldiers a better chance of keeping control of the approaches to the Baron entrance.

Inside the Baron, there were bureaucratic bottlenecks to be addressed. The Home Office security checks on ARAP candidates were still taking up to 48 hours. We needed to get this down to minutes, or the hotel compound would back up with people awaiting a decision from London. I discussed the issue with very senior officials in London. If we were to get the job done, we needed a combination of people on the spot empowered to make decisions, and more capacity in the Home Office to determine complex cases in real time. We needed to increase the flow rate dramatically. To achieve that, referral times needed to be drastically reduced, to zero where possible. The operation in Kabul might have to be cut short at any moment. It was now or never.

The second Rapid Deployment Team arrived in Kabul mid-morning. Some very welcome faces, including more Border Force people. Their flight had been longer than expected: a first attempt to land had had to be aborted. I gave them an impromptu briefing and pep talk, huddled in a blast shelter in the military terminal.

Within the Taliban different groupings appeared to be competing for primacy. Stories started to emerge of Taliban fighters going from house to house searching for people who had worked with international forces. Retribution was on the agenda. Taliban spokesmen denied this. They denied that people were fleeing Afghanistan in fear of their lives, calling them 'economic migrants'. And they denied beating people, both at their checkpoints and in the crowds at the airport.

The large contingent of embassy contract guards, mostly Indian and Nepalese, were still stuck at the security firm's site close to the airfield. Despite the previous assurances, the Taliban were still not allowing them to move, on the basis that US air strikes near the airport made it too dangerous for them to do so. This was nonsense. But the situation was becoming dangerous, with large numbers of angry and frustrated military people on both sides. We needed to get this resolved.

Meanwhile, each day I spent some time talking with the troops on the gates, and with their NCOs and commanding officers. Most were young people, many of them the same age as my sons. Working on the gates was tough and visibly draining, emotionally as well as physically, as the soldiers tried to marshal endless crowds of distressed and increasingly desperate people. Sometimes the job amounted to riot control with shields, helmets and body armour. The soldiers were frequently doing this right next to Taliban fighters, some of whom would certainly have fought with and killed British soldiers in Helmand, and would not hesitate to do so again if circumstances changed.

One British soldier stood out: a native-speaker Pashtun interpreter whose role included speaking directly with the Taliban as the military did what needed to be done, hour by hour and day by day, to keep the gates working. Up on the wall in a watchtower, he talked me through how the interactions with the Taliban worked and told me in a low voice who was who among the men outside with AK-47s and beards. From time to time those men brutalised the crowds with clubs and lengths of tubing. It was ugly to watch, and they clearly did not care that we were watching. Perhaps they even derived satisfaction from it.

Just inside the Baron Hotel gate, a medical team operated a clearing centre, offering first aid to people injured in the crush or overcome by heat and dehydration.

Alongside them, other teams – with women soldiers as well as men, to preserve as far as possible the dignity and propriety of Afghan women and girls – searched everyone entering the Baron for weapons.

When not on duty the soldiers rested in what shade they could find, growing more sunburnt and dirtier with each passing day. As I walked past with my close protection team, laden with body armour and helmets, backpacks and weapons, a shirtless teenage paratrooper slumped against a wall cheekily called out: 'How can you *not* be hot?' We grinned back at him: he had a point.

There was the question of my suspiciously well-ironed shirt. We had posted pictures in the press and on social media to give the public a sense of what was happening. I was trolled on social media by someone who thought a photo of me at the Baron gate was staged because my shirt looked ironed. Maybe I had a batman? I can now reveal the secret of the well-ironed shirt. If you wear a non-iron shirt for long enough in intense heat under body armour, the ironing takes care of itself. So does the laundry.

Another social media troll thought that the garden of the Baron, an oasis of green and relative calm if you chose the right camera angle, showed that things were less challenging than we were making out. Someone else pointed out the Hesco wall in shot behind me – a blast-resistant modular wall familiar to anyone who has worked in a war zone. The other side of the wall was now Taliban Land. A different camera angle would have shown groups of people scattered across the lawns, the footpaths and the roads, in impromptu encampments, or just in the open, staring listlessly into the middle distance or cradling their children or sleeping the sleep of the exhausted. It would have shown soldiers, all carrying weapons and many wearing body armour. It would have shown a sea of tired faces, lined with fear and dirt and tears. It would have shown mountains of rubbish and the occasional mound of human shit. It might even have shown the souvenir shop that bizarrely stayed open throughout the evacuation.

President Biden, in an interview with ABC News the previous day, had appeared to commit to keeping the troops in Kabul until every American who wanted to leave had been evacuated. The commitment extended to others who could and should be got out. But Biden did not state unequivocally that US forces would stay beyond 31 August.

FRIDAY 20 AUGUST

The UK's morning media was having a field day of recrimination and finger-pointing in the aftermath of the 18 August Parliamentary debate. Ahead of my first contact with London I checked in with Brigadier Tom. 'Any headlines for Whitehall start of business? They are busy eating each other in the morning press.'

Some welcome news from Dan Blanchford. The engineering works outside the Baron were nearing completion. Even so, in my morning update to London, I reported that the situation was still very difficult. The scale of the US call-forward of evacuees had created a gigantic surge of people converging on the airport, including at the front gate of the Baron, close to the Abbey Gate. There were still concerns that the airfield gates might be overrun. There had been near-rioting at the airport's civil aviation terminal the previous day, a short distance from the Baron.

There were reports that some US C-17s had left empty or near-empty. President Biden directed that every seat should be filled. The Americans widened their eligibility criteria to include 'Afghans at risk'. I asked what this meant. Apparently, not much more specific than women and children. It was not clear whether the problem was about to get more manageable or even less so. The entire US system started to back up – outside Afghanistan as well as in the airport. So during the morning the Americans paused flights for a few hours, to allow the processing of evacuees at their transit points outside Afghanistan to clear.

I commented to a colleague in London that it was 'make or break day for the Evacuation Handling Centre' at the Baron. The scale of the crowds, and growing security concerns, were putting ever-increasing pressure on every part of our system. I had to delay my moves around the airport because of the shortage of close protection teams needed to help move evacuees and staff between the Baron and the airfield. We had no helicopters, and all moves had to be by vehicle with security support. Remembering my trip over the Kabul rooftops with General Miller back in June, I reminded London of my request for my own Black Hawk helicopter. It was gallows humour, but with a serious point.

To get into the relative safety of the Baron Hotel, people first had to get through multiple Taliban checkpoints. There was little if any coordination between those checkpoints. In some, the men were more cooperative than others in letting people through their cordons. Many of them were violent, beating people with pipes and hoses.

As well as getting through the Taliban checkpoints, people trying to get into the Baron had to get through the vast crowds of other desperate people. There were stampedes, with people killed and injured in the crush. There were reports of women being raped in the free-for-all. Standing on the high wall at the front gate of the Baron, you saw a sea of people filling the dusty road into the middle distance. All were trying to get themselves out of Afghanistan. Our people were somewhere deep in that crowd – British nationals, our staff and others eligible for ARAP, other vulnerable groups eligible for evacuation.

Some in the UK had completely unrealistic expectations about the scope for identifying and pulling out of that crowd the people we were looking for. The soldiers did amazingly courageous and resourceful things to bring those at highest risk through the crowds to relative safety. But there was the ever-present risk that anyone who ventured into the crowd to find and help a potential evacuee might not be coming back.

The process of screening and processing people at the Baron settled into a rhythm of sorts. At the Baron's gate, the military identified those with a claim to be let in. Once inside, the potential evacuees faced a security check for weapons. There was first aid for those who needed it. Then began the process of establishing eligibility. The Baron complex is reached from its front gate by a long, dusty road with high walls and buildings along each side. The evacuation processing team set up first in a bar-restaurant, then moved to a suite of offices across the way that allowed a more rational workflow and greater volumes of people. The Border Force team worked the long queues, checking documents to weed out forgeries, identity theft, ineligible people and people traffickers – and advised the diplomats staffing the desks on the scope for discretion in applying the rules.

The applicants accepted for evacuation were then assigned to flights by the military, and were moved onto the airfield in vehicles through the airport gates. Final checks were carried out on the airfield, checking names against passenger manifests. The evacuees were boarded onto Royal Air Force planes – four-engine C-17, A400M and C-130 transport planes – and flown to Dubai.

For the hopefuls who needed further checks with London before a decision could be made, holding areas were set up at the Baron. At any given time there could be 1,000 or more people in the hotel complex awaiting a decision or evacuation.

Day or night, there were always lines and clusters of people waiting. Waiting to be processed; waiting for a decision; waiting to be moved onto the airfield. In the gardens, the roads and pathways, the car parks. In the shade of buildings, under tarpaulins, in the open. Parents with small children doing what they could to create the illusion of normality. Dan Blanchford's people in the UK shipped out colouring books and crayons, nappies, baby formula. As the days wore on, the conditions deteriorated, presenting health risks to everyone.

A deal was finally struck with the Taliban to allow our embassy contract guards to leave. We brought them into Taipan in a convoy of buses. The operation required the consent of our US neighbours, who controlled the approach roads and gates to both their and our military bases, adjacent as they were. Getting this movement over the line eventually required a personal appeal from me to US Ambassador Ross Wilson. The operation succeeded, but at the cost of much friction with parts of the American system. It didn't help that there was a growing sense that our operation was making theirs look bad.

I did what I could with Ross Wilson to put things back on the rails. Andy McCoubrey and the military did so too, with their contacts. We badly needed to continue to use Taipan to get out some of the highest-risk and highest-profile cases, including a number of Afghan judges and some of our own embassy staff. For that to happen we needed the Americans' cooperation. Over on the other side of the airfield, UK and US forces had to work together to manage the critically important stretch of road between the Baron Hotel and the Abbey Gate, as that was where the Americans screened many of their evacuees.

The inescapable facts were that the evacuation was a joint endeavour with the Americans, as the Afghanistan campaign had been from the very outset in 2001, and that the US presence vastly outnumbered ours. Working at cross-purposes or getting angry with each other would help no one and would be self-defeating.

There was nevertheless an increasingly pressing need for us to get clarity on when the USA would call time on the evacuation. The Americans had an understanding with the Taliban that the evacuation would run until the end of August. But it was clear that neither we nor anyone else would have completed the evacuation by then, however 'completion' was defined. No one knew what the Taliban's reaction would be if the international forces attempted to keep going beyond the end of the month. By some accounts the Taliban in Kabul seemed relaxed about it; by other accounts, anything but.

Our own departure timetable would need to be coordinated with that of the Americans; it was all too clear that the final days of the operation would be highly dangerous. We had quickly discounted any suggestion that the UK could run or lead a free-standing operation without the USA in the lead. We simply did not have the capabilities to do that, regardless of whether we were prepared to take on the risks involved.

The UK military in Kabul told me that they understood that the US military were working to a final departure overnight on 30–31 August. But that seemed far from settled. I asked if that was the Plan, or the Plan Until It Wasn't. But I received no clear answer. So we had no realistic option but to work on the basis that it was the former.

SATURDAY 21 AUGUST

The airport was seizing up, overwhelmed by the sheer numbers of people. The Americans alone had some 14,500 people on the airfield, waiting to be airlifted out of Kabul. At the gates and around the north terminal, everywhere you went and everywhere you looked, there were people: under awnings, in the open, in doorways. With children, elderly parents, heart-breaking luggage – whole lives packed into a battered case or a plastic supermarket bag.

The continuing problem was further down the US evacuation chain. Our system depended on the combination of the Evacuation Handling Centre in the Baron Hotel, and a Temporary Safe Location in Dubai – a transhipment point where, by agreement with the host government, we undertook to move people quickly onwards to the UK, on wide-bodied airliners. The US system was dealing with much larger numbers of people, but did not have the equivalent of our Temporary Safe Location, and was unwilling to take people directly to the continental USA for processing and clearance there. Instead, they sought holding arrangements with a range of countries – in the Gulf, in Europe and beyond. But these arrangements were already at capacity, causing the system to back up all the way to Kabul. This was proving to be a critical bottleneck for us as well as the Americans.

To manage the problem, the USA closed the airport gates to new arrivals while they cleared the backlog of people already in the evacuation chain. A British colleague commented to me that the Americans seemed 'transfixed' by the enormity of the problem.

At that day's NATO ambassadors' meeting we made a request for every country's representative to work with the Multi-National Coordination Centre – a clearing house for the various evacuation operations – to fill empty places on all departing NATO aircraft, helping clear the backlog of people on the airfield. And to raise with their capitals the need to increase capacity at the transit points in third countries, to reduce the huge bottlenecks in Kabul.

Access to our Evacuation Handling Centre in the Baron Hotel was restricted for much of the day. As I travelled across the airfield all the gates were jam-packed with exhausted, frustrated people, the crowds still stretching back as far as the eye could see. There had been multiple fatalities, including children, from crushing and heat. As we turned into the Baron, the Afghans at the front of the queue looked angry. There was shouting and waving of arms. Now, unlike on previous days, the security team advised me that it was not safe to go outside the Baron's gate on foot.

When I caught up with Dan Blanchford, over at his headquarters in the north terminal, he looked exhausted and frustrated. But intent, as always, on finding solutions for insoluble problems.

An email dropped into my inbox. One of many, many emails. I can still see this one, and it is still hard to write about. It was from a father in the UK, an Afghan-British national, whose wife and twin sons were stuck in the crowds trying to get to the Baron. It contained a photo of two tiny boys, two years old, in matching red shirts, asleep head to toe on the ground on a sheet of cardboard. They were somewhere way back in that crowd, in the blazing sun, surrounded by chaos, violence, anger and fear. They had been out there for days.

The awfulness of the situation welled up in a wave of anger and disgust at what was happening, our role in it and our helplessness. What was going to happen to those twins? How were they going to reach safety? Were they doomed to die out in that street? How many other small children were out there beyond any help, innocent victims of this mess? What use was all this military might and hardware – what use were *we* – if we could not answer such basic questions?

I took a couple of minutes to collect myself, then made some calls.

Over at the Baron that afternoon, I took a long walk around the car park with Alex. It was his birthday. Neither of us was having a good day. We talked through how we were going to get the team and ourselves through the rest of the operation.

That evening as my close protection team – all ex-military and used to dealing with bad situations – drove me back across the airfield to Taipan, they were very quiet.

When we reached Taipan I sent a terse, graphic description of the shocking scenes that were unfolding to a couple of very senior colleagues in London. No holding back. They needed to know what was happening, and to be ready for some very difficult questions. There would be ugly stories in the media. There would be political fallout, both for us and for our relations with the Americans, whose decisions had led to the consequences now playing out.

Months later, I finally steeled myself to ask what happened to those twins and their mother. They made it. They got out.

London asked if we would need a further Rapid Deployment Team. It would take a day or so to get them out to Kabul. I replied: definitely yes, as soon as they could get here. Ideally, people with consular experience in hostile environments – and more Home Office Border Force people to help with eligibility and document checks. The final days of the operation looked set to be very tough, and a huge test of the capacity and resilience of a Kabul team that was already exhausted and stretched far beyond any reasonable limits. With conditions at the Baron bad and deteriorating, we also needed to anticipate the near-certainty of illness reducing our capacity just when we needed all hands on deck. By some miracle we had not yet had any identified Covid cases. An outbreak could tip the whole operation over the edge.

Martin Longden reported to me that as the end of the evacuation period approached, the mood among the Afghans in the Evacuation Handling Centre seemed to be shifting. There was a sense of rising anger and desperation. I had seen it myself, too, in the faces and gestures of people waiting at the gate to be let in.

Martin and Alex were working with Dan on the plan for closing down the Evacuation Handling Centre when the time came. This needed to be done in a way that kept up the pace of evacuations for as long as possible but did not put staff or soldiers at greater risk than necessary in the final, most dangerous, hours of the operation. Above all we wanted to avoid a stampede of desperate people trying to get into the Baron when word got around that we were closing.

I received a message from Saad Mohseni, the owner of Tolo. He had three planeloads of journalists, human rights activists, and others at risk. They were seeking help gaining access to the airport. Into the system went the request, along with the thousands of other people trying to squeeze through half a dozen narrow, dangerous gates to safety and freedom.

Late in the evening meeting I went with Dan to see Cihad Erginay, the Turkish Ambassador, to talk through some ideas about how to increase the capacity of the airport. Before the fall of Kabul the Turks had been in detailed discussion with the Americans for months about taking on responsibility for the security of the airport after the NATO withdrawal. That plan had been overtaken by events. Even so, the Turks had detailed knowledge of how the airport worked; they had ambitions to stay after the completion of the evacuation; and they were, and are, a staunch and capable NATO ally. We wanted to know their thoughts on whether the civilian terminal could be re-opened during the evacuation phase, with the prospect of getting more people through, faster. We also wanted to explore their thinking on what would happen after the evacuation ended. A secure, functioning airport would be a prerequisite for any continued international presence, and for getting out those whom we had not been able to evacuate during Operation Pitting.

The temporary Turkish Embassy was on the other side of the runway, in the north terminal, the military side of the airport. We stumbled down alleyways in the gathering darkness, making plenty of noise and trying to not to surprise any trigger-happy sentries. The meeting took place in a kind of garden conservatory among the utility buildings and blast walls. We sat on large squishy sofas. There was even a Turkish tea waiter, polite and attentive in his waistcoat. It was a magnificently different approach from the spartan military encampment at Taipan. Cihad was looking dapper and, as ever, completely unfazed by the mad situation unfolding around us. We talked into the night, the planes roaring in the background.

A US travel advisory notice to the public popped out of the American system, advising of potential security threats at the airport gates. What was behind this? Was there a terrorist threat that we were not seeing? We investigated urgently with US contacts in Kabul and Washington. The Americans insisted that the purpose of the advisory notice was to manage the risk of crowd disturbances at the airport gates, which were now totally swamped.

Even so, the risk of a terrorist attack was firmly on everyone's mind. There was no shortage of violent extremists with the capability and intent to mount an attack. The Baron, close to the Abbey Gate, one of the main entry points where the USA processed people into their evacuation system, would be a prime target for anyone wanting to get the world's attention.

Sunday 22 August

With better crowd control and access to the Baron improving, it was full steam ahead. The Taliban were letting people through, albeit with their usual brutal crowd-control methods. In the space of 24 hours, 1,722 people flew out on UK Royal Air Force flights.

The UK and international media coverage was, though, as ugly as I had predicted, full of stories of people being crushed in the crowds and pictures of people handing their small children to soldiers from the melee. At least seven people had died in the crush. The *New York Times* ran a front page story that the US exit plan was 'unravelling'. Former prime minister Tony Blair, in the UK media, described the US withdrawal as 'imbecilic'. There were media stories of friction between UK and US forces in Kabul. Some of them I recognised.

I talked this through with colleagues in London and Kabul, arguing that it was clearly not in our interests to feed stories of political or operational difficulties with the Americans. Talking about friction between the UK and the USA would generate friction with the USA and would be self-defeating. We should avoid self-congratulatory claims that our system was working while theirs was not. It was not that simple. Without the US military to hold and operate the airport, we would be doing none of this.

Even so, from one of the many emails I received, requesting help: 'Thank you for all you are currently doing in Afghanistan, we hear the British soldiers are by far the best organised. You are saving lives.'

The Americans announced that they were planning to impose a 'pause' of 24 to 36 hours in letting more people into the airport, to clear the continuing backlogs on the airfield and put in place a more functional system. This could have major implications for us, making a difficult situation worse at the Baron and meaning that we would get fewer people out. Fortunately, however, we were able to continue our evacuation while the Americans got to grips with theirs.

I received a request from an American NGO, which had support from senior officials in the US Administration, to use the Baron to evacuate some high-priority individuals, bringing them in through the back gate. The NGO came to us because they were not able to get these people into the US system. The group consisted of 25 NGO staff and their families. It was a big ask; getting this number of people into the Baron would be anything but discreet. It would be bound to attract unwelcome attention – and would attract more requests from others to do the same.

Whenever these requests arose, we tried to be accommodating, yet we were always mindful of the risk of causing serious damage to our own operation. And of the inescapable fact that prioritising some people meant deprioritising others.

The back entrance of the Baron was a growing worry. It was in a sleepy residential street parallel to the main airport perimeter road. Two sets of big metal gates created an 'airlock' big enough for a large vehicle to enter and be checked before entering the main compound. The back entrance was usually under less pressure than the front gate, which fronted onto the airport perimeter road a short distance from the Abbey Gate; the back entrance, used sparingly and discreetly, offered an alternative way to bring small numbers of people in quickly. But it was also the main service entrance for the Baron, to bring in food and other supplies, and the Taliban could, if they wished, stop that happening. If word got round that the back gate was the best way to get into the evacuation system, prompting the Taliban to prevent access, it could quickly bring our whole operation down.

Each day I went up into the watchtower on the wall beside the back gate to get a first-hand view of what was happening in the street. Each time, my presence was quickly spotted, with a mixture of hostility from the Taliban and desperate waving of papers in plastic folders from people trying to escape.

Inside the Baron, the casework was becoming inexorably more complex and therefore slower. It was getting harder to identify and prioritise the people entitled to evacuation and at highest risk. The arrival that evening of the next Rapid Deployment Team and Border Force people would help a lot.

Katrina was one of the people in the Baron dealing with the most difficult cases. Down to earth and entirely dependable, Katrina had been the Consul General in the embassy. She had overseen its closure, and had been one of the last people to leave. She was one of the first volunteers to come back into Kabul during the night of the 17th.

From time to time unaccompanied minors turned up – children who had somehow made it into the Baron or been abandoned by their parents in the hope that they would be evacuated and somehow would make it to a new life.

One of them was a feral 11-year-old girl described as 'disruptive and difficult'. She had got into the Baron somehow, with no documentation. No one knew who she was or where she came from. Katrina, kind and big-hearted, looked after her and kept an eye on her while the UK social services were consulted on what action to take: do we bring her to the UK and put her into care, or do we leave her in Kabul? The girl was resourceful, managing to get herself onto one of the minibuses transporting people onto the airfield for evacuation. She was taken back to the Baron. And then, before anyone could work out what to do with her she was gone, disappearing suddenly back out into the chaos and violence of Kabul. Who knows what happened to her?

UNICEF's staff reported children being abandoned at the airport 'like shopping trolleys in a car park'.

The Americans were in discussion with the Taliban about establishing a new perimeter 1 km back from the airport, manned by the Taliban, with US-run transport hubs outside it, from which they would bus passengers into the terminal.

The Foreign Office media team in London warned me that a tabloid newspaper was writing a story asserting that I had been ordered to stay in Kabul while Foreign Secretary Dominic Raab was on holiday. This was obviously an attack on Dominic Raab. But it was not a great feeling to be pulled into it in this way, and it was taking up time and attention that I could not spare. Colleagues in the press office were shocked by what was going on. Although privately supportive, they had no success in persuading the newspaper not to run the story. They advised keeping a dignified silence.

The stories could only have come from someone in government in London choosing to brief their contacts in the press, and those journalists choosing not to question what they were being told. Always on the basis of unnamed 'sources' – people with an agenda, or working on behalf of others with an agenda, safe in their offices far away from Kabul.

Denial and destruction of our CAV fleet was now under way, in accordance with a sequence and timetable agreed previously with London. We needed to keep using these vehicles until the last possible moment. But it would not be practical to fly them out – and when the media showed pictures of a vehicle being shipped on an evacuation flight there was criticism. It was important, too, though, that we did not leave them behind for the Taliban, ISKP or any other violent extremists. An armoured Land Cruiser would form the basis for a virtually unstoppable car bomb.

My close protection team decided that destroying armoured Land Cruisers was a good way of dealing with stress, and undertook the task with gusto, leaving the wrecked vehicles on their sides outside Taipan. As the boneyard grew in size and cost, I sent a photo to Ed Hobart, the Foreign Office's security director in charge of the department that owned the vehicles, with the message 'Sorry!'

Very late in the evening, Martin Longden contacted me to let me know that most of the Foreign Office's Afghan Chevening scholars and their families were outside the back gate of the Baron. The crowds were dense and volatile. It was not clear if we could get the scholars safely into the Baron compound without provoking a violent and unstoppable surge of people trying to get through the gate as well. Eventually the soldiers controlling the gate managed to get some of them in, sending snatch squads out into the crowd to get them through the gate in small groups. Other members of the group were sent the long and hard way round to the front gate, where they were eventually picked out of the crowd. That depended on a small miracle of coordination with the British soldiers, carried on through the day and into the night. Even so, word quickly spread that there was an alternative route into the Baron, leading to severe pressure on the back gate.

Some of the Chevening scholars identified themselves by holding up improvised signs bearing the words 'Chevening Scholar'. They attracted the attention of a soldier who – not unreasonably in the circumstances – asked 'What the f*** is Chevening?' Whenever I recall those events I think of that soldier, who had probably never had the opportunity to go to university himself. Thank you, whoever you are.

Monday 23 August

The additional Rapid Deployment Team arrived: a mixture of Foreign Office and Border Force staff. I met them at the Baron. Like the others, just ordinary officials of the sort you might encounter writing a briefing paper or checking passports in an airport arrivals terminal. Except that they too had volunteered to come to Kabul to help with an evacuation that was becoming harder and more dangerous with each passing day. Most people would have sat that one out.

Their arrival brought the number of staff in the airport to 19 Foreign Office and 13 Border Force people, enabling us to run half a dozen desks round the clock. The number of evacuees being processed at the Baron jumped; a few days later over 2,000 people passed through the Baron in 24 hours, nearly doubling the number of people being processed onto Royal Air Force flights.

Mid-afternoon, I joined Lord Ahmad for a video conference with UK parliamentarians. I described what was happening in Kabul and the status of the evacuation. Although it had been billed as a private event for parliamentarians, and as off the record, the next day a more or less verbatim account of what I had said appeared in a national newspaper. I had said that that trying to hold Kabul's airport beyond 31 August would be fraught with risk. This apparently put me at odds with Boris Johnson's intention to lobby Biden at the G7 summit the next day to extend the evacuation beyond the end of the month.[30] I felt a moment of irritation, quickly overtaken by resigned indifference. There were bigger things to worry about.

The crowd control problems were worsening. There were reports of US forces using gunfire and teargas to control the masses of desperate, terrified people trying to find a way out of Afghanistan. During the previous night, shots had been fired in the airport. There were concerns that this might be a probing attack by ISKP, in preparation for a bigger attack.

'How long have we got?' That was the big question for the evacuation teams in Kabul as well as in and between NATO capitals.

The answer depended on the Americans and on the Taliban. In the daily NATO and EU coordination meetings there were lots of questions, both about the US timetable for completing the mission, and about whether the UK would be following it. I was repeatedly pressed for details of our plans for completing and closing down our evacuation. Just as with our plans for the embassy in the Green Zone before the fall of Kabul on 15 August, the UK was seen by the smaller European and other international missions as a bellwether.

And just as with the plans for closing the embassy, there was an art form in trying to be helpful without giving away information that had to be very tightly controlled. We had at all costs to avoid a rush on the Baron, putting at risk the lives of our soldiers and civilian staff, when word got around, as it surely would at some point, that we were closing. So I advised our European colleagues to take their lead from the Americans and to work closely with the US on their closedown plans, or expect to find themselves in a very difficult situation.

We started to receive persistent reports of ISKP planning a terrorist attack. But never with enough detail to form a clear picture: where, when, how? In the

Panjshir Valley, meanwhile, former Vice President Amrullah Saleh's Resistance Front continued to put up a fierce and brave fight against the Taliban. Seen from Kabul, though, there was no way that Saleh's people would change the outcome in Kabul and the rest of Afghanistan any time soon. Some US military analysts expressed concern that the ongoing fighting in Panjshir would force the Taliban to take its more capable people off the checkpoints around the airport, increasing the risk of random violence and arbitrary interference while also increasing the risks of an ISKP attack against both the evacuation and the Taliban.

My inbox, like everyone else's, was now completely swamped with last-minute appeals for help. On my official Foreign Office email account; on my personal accounts; on social media; on Skype; in texts; in WhatsApp messages. Messages were even sent to Fiona, back in the UK. Everyone, it seemed, could see that this operation had only a few days left to run.

There were not enough hours in the day to read all the messages or respond to them all individually. I relied on a rota of diligent and resilient Kabul embassy staff, now back in London, to pick up particularly difficult and urgent cases and try to get answers from the cross-Whitehall crisis response system in London. But that system was being rapidly overwhelmed by the scale of the crisis and the sheer volume of people. People in Afghanistan seeking help, and people outside Afghanistan who, with the best of intentions, were seeking to get help for people who had contacted them. I put out a series of messages on social media to signpost Afghans and others towards the right contact points in London.

Jason, as always on top of the next problem coming our way, was planning our closedown sequence with the military: who was to move where, when. The first stage was to move a handful of staff to a small basic logistics compound on the airfield, to complete final processing of any remaining evacuees when we closed the Evacuation Handling Centre in the Baron. That move was planned for after dark on 25–26 August. The closure of the Baron would be obfuscated to avoid last-minute panic and the risk of a stampede or confrontation; those already inside the Baron would continue to be processed, but those being let in would be reduced to a trickle and then stopped. Final closedown would happen over the following 24 hours. The last UK military to leave would do so under cover of darkness. Their departure from Kabul had to be agreed and coordinated with the much larger US presence. The US military would be the very last to leave the airport.

This had practical implications. From 23 August all staff were instructed to reduce their kit to a daysack only. Larger bags would be collected up, and would be shipped if and when possible. We should not necessarily expect to see them again (to my amazement, mine turned up at RAF Brize Norton, battered and dirty, at the end of Operation Pitting). Jason helpfully clarified the situation: 'work out how many pairs of socks and pants you need!' Answer: fewer than you might think; when clothes had outlived their usefulness they went in the dumpster. A daysack is not large. Mine had to include space for a laptop, phones, chargers and notebooks.

Tomorrow would be Jason's birthday. Organising a cake was not going to be possible. The catering staff had been evacuated and everyone was living on MREs: Meals Ready to Eat.

An MRE contains everything you need to keep you going in the field. The military version comes in a sealed plastic bag about the size of a supermarket carrier bag. It is geared towards the needs of a fit young soldier expending lots of energy, covering terrain under combat conditions with full kit. No one engaged in sedentary work could eat that many calories in 24 hours with impunity. The UK version comes in ten menu variants, some of which are virtually indistinguishable from each other. My favourite was the all-day breakfast, which bore some resemblance to an all-day breakfast. All the menus can be eaten hot or cold, depending on available facilities. A lot of science has gone into MREs. They are not fine dining, and are not meant to be. But they will keep you going and well fuelled.

Ours appeared the day before the kitchen staff disappeared: a tall pile of boxes sitting on a pallet in the roasting sun outside the canteen. They stayed there, simmering gently in the summer heat, during the days that followed. Apparently they do not need to be kept in a refrigerator. You rummaged around in the boxes to find your preferred menu. A lively barter trade took hold, with some items inexplicably unpopular. The close protection team delighted in showing an ambassador how to operate an MRE. First, find your spork …

With the kitchen staff gone, the soldiers explored the abandoned kitchens. First, out came the remaining stocks of fresh fruit. The apples and pears and oranges lasted minutes. Next, big catering trays of ice cream. I was not sure of the wisdom of eating ice cream under battlefield conditions in 35-degree heat. But when in Rome …. Finally, someone found huge catering-size tins of tuna chunks, and put these on the serving counter. I like to think of the soldiers tucking into outsize tins of tuna chunks alongside the MREs.

With the end of Operation Pitting in sight, thoughts were turning to the day after. What would happen to the people who needed to leave but had not managed to do so when Operation Pitting ended? What would we say about that? Whatever we said would have practical implications for the people left in a desperate situation, and political implications for the UK Government as it tried to manage the wider public messaging around the end of the 20-year campaign in Afghanistan.

Would we wish to retain some sort of diplomatic presence in Kabul, to engage with Afghanistan's new masters? To achieve what? And how? Who, if anyone, would be responsible for security in Kabul? For keeping the airport open and operating? What were we going to do about the stark prospects of a humanitarian catastrophe going into the winter? Would it be possible to work with the Taliban on this, given their repellent views and practices towards women and ethnic minorities?

The Prime Minister had appointed Simon Gass, Chair of the Joint Intelligence Committee and a former Ambassador to Afghanistan, as Special Representative for the Afghan Transition. He was in Doha talking to the Taliban Political Commission before travelling on to Kabul with the intention of meeting the Taliban in Afghanistan. It proved remarkably difficult for him to get the Taliban to engage, even once he arrived in Kabul a few days later.

CIA Director Bill Burns visited Kabul for secret talks with Taliban political leader Mullah Baradar. The media reported the visit the following day. Few details of the talks emerged, though a key subject of discussion was the deadline for ending the evacuation and withdrawal of foreign troops. The Taliban remained insistent that foreign forces had to leave by 31 August.

TUESDAY 24 AUGUST

My mobile phone rang at 4:30 am; a person I'd never heard of, on behalf of a US-based NGO, wanting to talk to me about evacuating a large group of human rights defenders. Some big names were supporting the effort. None of them appeared to have any connection with the UK. Nothing out of the ordinary so far – we had fielded multiple similar requests in recent days, and no night had passed without the phone ringing repeatedly. The NGO, said the caller, had chartered planes for the group and had already secured visa waivers from a European Union country that had no one on the ground in Kabul.

The caller was emotional and incoherent, and it took some time to get to the bottom of why he was cold-calling me in the middle of the night. Essentially, the NGO were not getting traction with the American system, so were trying any other avenue they could think of, and wanted us to organise the Kabul end of the evacuation. Later that day one of the organisers wrote to thank me for trying to help, saying: 'You have run the most efficient operation there is at the airport.'

To complicate matters, there seemed to be a second evacuation project running in parallel. For a day or so, it was not entirely clear whether this was one group or two similar-sounding groups. It turned out that it was two.

Such initiatives as these, with worthy intentions, soaked up scarce time and resources. The arrangements were not always as firm as they were claimed to be. There were false dawns as arrangements fell through: visa waivers did not exist; charter flights lacked the necessary war zone insurance; people turned up at the wrong gate, or gave up and went away before they could be helped. A lot of our time was taken up helping such groups get their people onto the airfield and linked up with their flights – time that we could have spent on processing other applicants.

A great deal of this went on, as individuals and groups in the West sought to help people they knew, or knew of, in Afghanistan and who fitted their criteria of people at highest risk and greatest need. There was duplication of effort and confusion as people tried every possible option to extract their candidates for evacuation. It was inevitable that some people were evacuated not because they had a stronger claim or were at higher risk than others who were not evacuated, but because they had more influential and persistent advocates.

Over at the Baron, I went up onto the walls at the front and back gates, as I did every morning to get a feel for the mood. At the front gate, I was warned before going up onto the wall that the atmosphere had changed and that I should not go beyond the top of the broken metal staircase. The Taliban, now standing or lounging incongruously in wheeled office chairs on top of the container chevron, were different. Different clothes, different weapons, different demeanour, different men. The slightly awkward mutual politeness of the first few days had been replaced by the swagger of battle-hardened fighters. A Talib standing on the chevron eyeballed me with a long, unblinking stare. In place of an AK-47 he was toting a modern US automatic weapon. The message was clear: 'This is ours now.' After a few minutes one of my close protection team whispered quietly in my ear: 'Sir, we should leave now.'

At the back gate it was a similar story. My presence was quickly and openly registered by the Taliban. Bearded men with sharp eyes spoke animatedly to their colleagues, pointing and staring. Meanwhile, like their predecessors, they were asserting their authority over the crowds with sticks and lengths of piping.

That evening I compared notes with Brigadier Tom. What we were seeing and hearing of the atmosphere in Kabul city and further afield was not good: 'dark, oppressive and violent'. This was the Taliban in their true colours. We were under no remaining illusion that the people in charge in Kabul represented a Taliban 2.0 with whom we could do business. We feared a vicious and brutal settling of scores once the international presence had left.

A US CODEL – Congressional Delegation – turned up in Kabul, unannounced and unexpected. Seth Moulton (a Democrat) and Peter Meijer (a Republican) had got themselves onto a military flight from Dubai and had come to see for themselves the scenes unfolding in Kabul airport. Their arrival took US State Department and military seniors in Kabul by surprise. Although my American colleagues kept largely to themselves their views on the additional burden of looking after their new guests, it was clearly something they could do without – a point made clear to the media in Washington by State Department, Pentagon and White House officials. The two Congressmen criticised the US Government for starting the evacuation late.

A text from a British colleague summarised the situation in one word: 'Mental'. I replied: 'What part of this isn't?' The CODEL's visit was in part about putting pressure on President Biden to extend the evacuation. There were reports that the President had demanded that all American citizens should be accounted for – an impossible task given that, like the UK, the US Government had no way of knowing how many of its citizens were in the country, and quite possibly no realistic way of getting out, in the time available, those that wished to leave. US decision making, increasingly driven by internal pressures of which we had little visibility in Kabul, was becoming ever harder to read, with potentially far-reaching impacts on our own operation.

As the political dogfight in Washington intensified, another CODEL turned back to the USA while in the air.

The G7 leaders met by video conference, chaired by the UK as presidency, and joined by the UN and NATO secretaries general. They set out their expectations of the Taliban in the Leaders' Statement:

> Any future Afghan government must adhere to Afghanistan's international obligations and commitment to protect against terrorism; safeguard the human rights of all Afghans, particularly women, children, and ethnic and religious minorities; uphold the rule of law; allow unhindered and unconditional humanitarian access; and counter human and drug trafficking effectively. We call on all parties in Afghanistan to work in good faith to establish an inclusive and representative government, including with the meaningful participation of women and minority groups.[31]

The 31 August deadline to complete the evacuation was a week away. The G7 political leaders discussed the possibility of extending it into September, with Prime Minister Johnson urging the US President to do so. But the White House made it clear that the USA planned to keep to the end August deadline for foreign forces to leave. There was media speculation of a growing UK–USA rift between political leaders over this. And there were calls from some politicians for the UK to work with NATO allies to come up with a plan to hold Kabul airport beyond the 31 August deadline, if necessary without the Americans.

From where I stood in Kabul, the discussion had an air of unreality. Although our presence in Kabul was impressive it still depended on the much larger number of US forces on the ground – at least six times the size of the UK contingent, itself the second largest after the Americans. And we depended on air cover and overhead imagery, from the US B-52s and drones operating overwatch missions from bases in the Middle East, and from the F/A-18s from the USS *Ronald Reagan* nuclear aircraft carrier in the Arabian Sea. The UK presence in Kabul depended on US forces. Our timetable depended on the US timetable.

Our American colleagues in Kabul were faced with the same question as us: how to get as many people out as possible in the limited time left. It was for the political leaders back home to decide how long that was: no point in arguing about it in Kabul.

Meanwhile the Taliban were consistent and clear that they would not agree to foreign military forces staying beyond 31 August. As more and more Afghans fled the country the Taliban were becoming increasingly uncooperative, demonstrating that they could and would prevent people reaching the airport.

But the evacuation, even as far as 31 August, depended on Taliban cooperation or at least non-interference. We could run an evacuation or we could face down the Taliban. We could not do both.

The Taliban spokesman, speaking to the media in Doha, warned:

> It's a red line. President Biden announced that on 31 August they would withdraw all their military forces. So if they extend it that means they are extending occupation while there is no need for that.

> If the US or UK were to seek additional time to continue evacuations – the answer is no. Or there would be consequences. It will create mistrust between us. If they are intent on continuing the occupation it will provoke a reaction.[32]

The Americans nevertheless explored with the Taliban in Kabul whether there was any scope for flexibility to extend by a few days. The response was stark. People who took part in the discussions described the Taliban representatives as shaking with anger as they reiterated that the coalition had to leave by 31 August.

Zabihullah Mujahid, the Taliban spokesman, announced that Afghans should not go to the airport, because of the chaotic situation. It was not clear whether this meant that the Taliban were prohibiting people from going to the airport or were stating that it was no longer possible to get into the airport. Either way, the announcement had no discernible impact on the numbers of people trying to get themselves onto planes.

Zabihullah called on the Americans to stop encouraging a brain drain from Afghanistan. And he claimed that the restrictions imposed by the Taliban on women leaving the house without a male chaperone, or on going to work, would be temporary. Those claims would later be shown to be worthless as the Taliban closed down girls' access to education, tried to force foreign aid agencies not to employ women, even closed down beauty parlours and shut businesses run by women, and with them social spaces for women. As a result women are now isolated in their homes, where some are subject to unlimited abuse – emotional, verbal and physical – from their male family members.

Later that evening I went over to the US military compound for a meeting with US Ambassador Ross Wilson and Tom West, Special Representative Khalilzad's deputy. I particularly needed to get the latest US advice on meeting the Taliban in Kabul, ahead of Simon Gass arriving. Both the security arrangements and the politics were going to present formidable difficulties.

We talked through our latest thinking on the evacuation and on the post-evacuation issues. It was increasingly apparent that when the Taliban said 'no foreign forces' were to remain in Afghanistan, they meant exactly that. And it was also becoming apparent that they had little idea of and not much interest in what it would take to run an airport, or a country, or – if we were to keep envoys in Kabul beyond the end of August – what foreign governments would want from them, including basic security requirements. I was reminded of the earlier description of a senior international official with extensive personal experience of dealing with the Taliban: 'Solidly uneducated people.'

Wilson was unable to shed much light on thinking and decision making in Washington about the future of the evacuation. He fished for insights into the debates inside Whitehall. He seemed to be particularly interested in the tone of the commentary about the USA, following the lurid media stories of tensions between London and Washington.

Outside in the pitch dark, someone drove into my heavily armoured Land Cruiser, putting a nasty scrape along the wing. The close protection team and I debated solemnly whether to complain or put in a damage claim to the Americans. My team may have been pulling my leg. We decided not to bother. This vehicle was designated for 'denial'. That is, in the closing stages of the evacuation it would be trashed.

I was becoming increasingly concerned about the humanitarian catastrophe that we could see beginning to unfold around us, and throughout the country. Vast numbers of displaced people – on top of a Covid wave, drought, and the effects of years of conflict – who would need humanitarian support. On top of that, no working government structures, a sharply diminished international presence, an insecure operating environment for relief workers, and a Taliban interim administration under international sanctions. Addressing the basic needs of the population was clearly going to be the top 'week after' priority.

The United Nations had previously set out its intention to 'stay and deliver' humanitarian support in the event of a Taliban takeover. But in the new situation it was not clear how it would do that. The World Health Organization had already been in touch with Simon Manley, our representative to the UN Agencies in Geneva, about getting vital supplies into Kabul. Another reason to persuade the Taliban to cooperate. No airport: no supplies.

One of my university professors from over 30 years ago contacted me trying to help the family of an Afghan scholar and poet who was now in Cambridge. He was apologetic, and realistic about the chances of success. We did what we could but ran out of time before we could bring them out ourselves. Many months later the family reached Albania.

Around this time, Operation Pitting reached a milestone that we had never dared to hope we would pass: our 10,000th evacuee. Her name was Uzma. A schoolgirl. She planned to finish school, and train to become a nurse. She smiled as she displayed the number, written in marker pen on her forearm. And then she was gone, onto a plane and on to a new life in the UK.

Every remaining hour of Operation Pitting had to be made to count. The military planners were working on compressing the UK departure timetable to maximise the amount of time available for the evacuation to continue. It would make the final departure scrappier and more expensive in terms of the equipment that would have to be left behind. The big question was whether we could do this without putting civilian staff and soldiers at greatly increased risk, particularly if the situation deteriorated sharply and we had to make a hurried exit.

There was heavy criticism in the media when a photo was published of an armoured Land Cruiser being freighted out in the back of a military plane, surrounded by evacuees. The accusation was that we were shipping cars in preference to people. The reality was that the planes had to arrive and depart in a tightly timed pattern to prevent the airfield seizing up. No people were left behind to make space for equipment: planes left full, or partly full, depending on how many people were available to evacuate when the plane had to leave.

I commiserated with Dan. It was a bitter blow to everyone in Kabul working crazy hours in dangerous and awful conditions, doing their best to do the right thing. We were both clear that we had to shield our people from the increasingly toxic media and political storm back home, and concentrate on getting the job done. The story added fuel to an increasingly bitter public row over attempts to evacuate the animals from the Nowzad animal sanctuary, and a wider blame game that senior people in London seemed only too happy to fuel, with no regard for the people in harm's way on the ground in Kabul.

Andy, who had been troubleshooting some of the more difficult cases, working at the gates with the military, messaged me: 'It's the beginning of the end now … frayed for us a bit today.'

London informed me that the Greek Ambassador in Islamabad would be arriving in Kabul to oversee Greece's evacuation efforts. It looked like he would arrive just in time to leave.

WEDNESDAY 25 AUGUST

The Taliban were becoming much more assertive with each day that passed. There were increasing reports of harsh crowd control and intimidation of civilians. I saw them beating many more people with piping and cabling. They tightened access to the airport for civilians to leave. The motivation was not entirely clear, but settling of scores: no question. Vindictiveness and exercise of power: certainly. Also their concern that the 'brain drain' of educated Afghans was gathering pace: but why on earth would anyone other than the Taliban wish to stay?

And on top of this, fear that ISKP might attack both the international forces and the Taliban. There were rumours that the mobile phone signal might be cut from tonight. It was a mystery to me that the mobile phones still worked at all. Maybe the Taliban too were relying on WhatsApp?

I travelled over to the north terminal for coordination meetings of the NATO and European Union ambassadors' groups. We picked our way through the makeshift barriers and a sea of trash to reach the offices. The strain was beginning to tell. One of my European colleagues, a highly competent and experienced senior diplomat, broke down as she described the intolerable pressure that she and her colleagues were under, both from the situation in Kabul and the political recriminations back home. I told her quietly that if it was of any help, we had all been in similarly dark places in recent days.

The Taliban were becoming ever more obstructive. The system of bus convoys coordinated by the US military's Multinational Coordination Centre to bring evacuees through the Taliban cordon and onto the airfield had quickly broken down, so people were facing eight-hour waits on buses to access the airport, and even then were not getting through. The conditions on the buses defied description. No water, no sanitation, intense heat, intimidation and worse. The Taliban were demanding lists of names of passengers, and pulling people off buses for real or imagined reasons.

In the middle of the day, everything paused as Taliban seniors did an inspection tour of the airport that they would soon own. It was hard to believe that any of those men had the first idea of what was involved in running an international airport. It was clear that they wanted to assert control of it as soon as the foreign military presence left, for both practical and symbolic reasons. I wondered too whether the Taliban feared that ISKP might try to seize it or force it to close down altogether. Either would be a major blow to the Taliban's prestige.

In the daily NATO meeting we were informed of a US military directive that all Western journalists were to leave Kabul and were being scheduled onto military flights. This was news to most of us. Several ambassadors noted that it would raise questions of media freedom. I asked what would happen if they refused. 'They can't.'

The risk of a terrorist attack on the airport was now looming large. We were seeing growing signs of ISKP planning an attack. The gates onto the airfield, and into the Baron, were a particular concern, given the dense crowds and the heavy military presence needed to keep order and keep the evacuation moving. The Americans closed two of the most exposed gates, increasing the already immense pressure on the Abbey Gate. That gate, close to the Baron, was now the most important bottleneck in the entire system.

The FCDO press office contacted me to tell me that *The Times* had a story about a slew of papers on staffing matters being found on the floor at the embassy. The FCDO had not been shown any of the documents, and we had only hazy details from Anthony Lloyd, the British journalist involved. I agreed to speak to him to find out as much as we could, so that we could take any necessary action to protect our staff, and to have a better sense of the story that was soon to break.

I spoke with Lloyd late evening and went through with him exactly what information was in the papers he had seen. His account of what he had seen was sketchy. He had not found the papers himself. He had been shown them by Taliban in the embassy, but not allowed to go through them in detail. He did not have copies of the papers, and did not know what was in them other than the few he had been shown. I walked him step by step through the layout of the embassy to determine where the papers were found and if there were any clues we could glean from that. He told me that he had noted down six names. He had himself tried ringing the names and numbers he had seen. Most had rung out; it later turned out that four of the six were already in the UK. One of them, whose name was in the papers and who was now in the UK, gave the journalist the names of three other individuals and their families who could be at risk. These names had not come from the papers seen by the journalist.

We worked late into the night trying to work out who might have been named in the papers the Taliban had shown to the journalist; who the people were whose names had been passed to us – London checking through staff and contractor records going back 15 years – how to contact them and get them out of Kabul if they were still there.

The immediate priority was to reach the three people identified by the person in the UK. Their names might be in the papers, or they might not: no way of knowing, and no time to quibble. London agreed that we should try to evacuate them. They were contacted and we identified a possible pick-up option. Andy and the military brought them in at dawn and they were processed onto planes.

A discussion was under way with London to work up options for keeping a small diplomatic presence in Kabul, in order to maintain contact with the Taliban. Reopening the embassy was out of the question. So was staying in Taipan once the military had left. That meant finding another diplomatic mission or international organisation to host a small UK presence. None of the options looked viable to me: too many unknowns, too risky. The Taliban were not by any means the biggest security risk. That was ISKP and al-Qaeda. The Taliban might not be able or willing to do much about the threat from either of them.

The situation at the Baron was deteriorating. The back gate – the last-resort option for bringing in small numbers of people at highest risk – had been closed because of the developing security threat. Redirecting people from the back to the front gate was easy to say but much harder to do. It involved them moving around a couple of city blocks, a distance of a mile or more, through crowds of desperate people also trying to get into the Baron or the Abbey Gate. All the while the Taliban were becoming increasingly restrictive and violent in their crowd control.

Through the afternoon there was a flurry of exchanges with Tom and Dan as we assessed new information about a possible terrorist threat to the airport gates. The threat was serious. But it did not relate to a specific gate or location. Throughout the next 24 hours we were faced with a dilemma: either call people forward for evacuation, with the possibility that they were walking towards a threat; or not call people forward for what could be their last chance to get out of Afghanistan. Later that evening the FCDO changed its travel advice, now instructing people *not* to travel to the airport.

Simon Gass arrived in Kabul, to try to make contact with the Taliban leadership. The priority was to secure safe passage for those British and Afghan nationals who wished to leave after the evacuation ended. After several days waiting for a call that never came, he left.

The Taliban had other things on their minds. As they formed an interim government they announced key appointments. Among them was former Guantanamo detainee Abdullah Ghulam Rasoul (Mullah Abdullah Zakir), who was named Minister of Defence. As he had been responsible for the deaths and injury of many British soldiers in Helmand, it would not be possible for us to have anything to do with him. And Sirajuddin Haqqani as Interior Minister: a terrorist with a $10m FBI bounty on his head. This was another clear sign that the Taliban 2.0 would not be in any way more moderate than its predecessors.

THURSDAY 26 AUGUST

Work carried on through the night to identify and extract people who could have been affected by the lost papers. Andy reported that the three families we had identified the previous day, a total of 11 people, had been brought in at 6:00 am. I could hear the children talking and laughing downstairs as they were processed for evacuation. I passed the news of this on to London and to Anthony Lloyd.

One of my staff suggested that the embassy's official social media accounts might contain names or pictures that could identify Afghans linked to the embassy. We closed them all, straight away. There was no time to check for any compromising material: just do it. The team set up new accounts, primarily for messaging people who needed evacuation. This spawned a new line in conspiracy theories: what were we seeking to hide?

An even bigger concern was looming ever larger: developing intelligence that an act of terrorism was being planned against the airport. You very rarely get a clear picture in advance that such and such will happen at a certain time at a given location, using the following plan of attack. A former colleague once described it as like flicking a flashlight on and off again in a dark room. What did you see in that brief moment? What did it mean? An attack on the Baron could be devastating for our staff and soldiers and for anyone else caught up in it. But if we closed the Evacuation Handling Centre that would be the end of the evacuation hopes for the many people in the system or waiting to get into it.

Throughout the day, the picture was darkening. It was increasingly clear that ISKP were planning an attack. But what kind of attack? Where and when? One nightmare scenario was a so-called complex attack, where a bomb blast against the gates of the Baron would open the way to marauding gunmen making their way through the compound, killing as many people as they could.

Jason worked flat out to come up with a plan to keep our staff safe and to enable the evacuation to continue to the last possible moment. We decided to bring forward our close-down plan for the Baron, which involved winding down the Evacuation Handling Centre there and transferring operations to a basic but serviceable complex of container offices on the airfield inside the airfield security cordon – the Hart facility, belonging to one of the security contractors providing services to the international presence in Afghanistan. The military would secure the Baron and then extract themselves under cover of darkness.

But a critical question remained. If we were going to close the Baron and move people to the Hart, was it safer to do it soon and risk moving by daylight, or wait until dark, as planned earlier, and risk getting caught up in an attack before then? Get it wrong either way, and we could lose people.

As I was about to leave Taipan for the Baron, a terse message from Brigadier Tom popped up on my phone: 'Attack IMMINENT.' Tell-tale signs of activity had been picked up. But still no indication of where, when, what kind of attack.

I put my move to the Baron on hold while we worked out what to do. Decision time. Should we move now, or wait? We settled on a plan to move the staff to the Hart. The remaining queue of applicants at the Baron would be moved there when the situation allowed. A quick conference call with Dan and Jason to ensure that all concurred, and we were ready.

The team wasted no time. The staff were told to stop what they were doing and move to vehicles which would take them through the airport perimeter to the fallback location at the Hart facility on the airfield.

The attack took place at 5:36 pm. A suicide bomber at the Abbey Gate detonated in the crowd by the canal. Early reports that there had been two explosions proved unfounded. US Army investigators later determined that the device was packed with ball bearings to maximise casualties. First reports suggested large numbers of casualties, including possibly scores of US service personnel. So far, no reports of UK casualties.

I learned of the attack from almost simultaneous messages from military colleagues. My flash report to London was necessarily terse:

> Attack at/near Baron. Multiple US casualties reported. No reported UK mil casualties. All FCDO and HO [Home Office] staff are at the Hart. More details when I have them.

The team from the Baron Hotel had passed the site of the explosion an hour before it happened. The news would travel quickly, and I wanted our staff to hear it from me. I messaged Alex, who was in the Hart compound with the team:

> Big attack at baron. Numerous US casualties. NFD [no further details] but will keep you posted. Pse keep an eye on the staff as news breaks.

Simon Gass had a call booked with Prime Minister Johnson at 6:30 pm, to discuss how to approach the Taliban. I jumped on the call and broke the news of the attack, updates coming in by text message as we spoke.

Two British nationals and the child of a British national had been killed. An injured British national had been patched up by the military medics. I met him briefly at the Hart, still in bloodstained clothes, with his wife, a young Afghan woman too shocked to speak. Her brother had died in the attack.

ISKP claimed responsibility. Thirteen US soldiers were killed, and at least 170 Afghan civilians. Some time later, reports surfaced in the media that the suicide bomber had been released from the Parwan prison at Bagram airbase some days before the attack.

There were more reports in the media of tensions between US and UK forces, this time over keeping the Abbey Gate open as the terrorist threat escalated, to allow the UK evacuation to continue. The reality was that by this stage everyone was working to a brutal equation of risks and benefits. If the evacuation routes closed, they would never reopen, leaving behind people who would not get another chance to escape. The military commanders on the ground needed no reminding of the risks to the lives of their soldiers. They did what needed to be done.

The security alerts continued late into the night. There were incessant false alarms and controlled explosions around the airfield. There were reports of sniper fire being directed into the airport from the Abbey Gate direction; of a breach of the perimeter by an assailant on a motor bike; that a suicide bomber had slipped under the wire and was at large on the airfield. The team at the Hart complex went into a defensive lockdown: lights off, people lying on the floor in their body armour.

On one of my journeys between Taipan and the Hart complex, a group of soldiers intercepted several young men climbing over a high wall. It looked like just another breach of the airport's long and poorly reinforced perimeter rather than an attempted attack. But nerves were on edge. There was shouting and pointing of guns as the soldiers seized the intruders.

The all clear came just after midnight. The Hart team got to work among the portakabins and container offices. The small hours: the hardest shift, and for a team already exhausted and on edge. The Hart was very different from the Baron: a dusty compound next to a service road on the airfield, a jumble of broken-down portakabins and container offices behind a checkpoint. Planes roared down the runway the other side of the wall and across a few hundred metres of dirt. At least 500 people had been transferred from the Baron. They sat in the dust, anywhere they could, waiting to be processed.

By now many, perhaps most, of those presenting themselves for evacuation did not meet the criteria. Many were just people who had managed somehow to get to the front of the queue. There were lots of rejections, and bad reactions from Afghans traumatised by the explosions and now so near but so far from the tail ramp leading up to a plane out of Kabul. There were loud protests and physical resistance, dealt with by the military who had the awful job of ejecting people from the makeshift evacuation centre. The translators left, making it next to impossible to communicate. Communications with London were patchy at best, leaving the team to make snap judgements on the fate of individuals and families. And still people arrived in one last desperate effort to get out before the evacuation ended.

By 9:00 pm on Friday 1,500 people had been processed at the Hart complex, with 1,100 manifested onto flights. The team spent the night in the relative safety of Taipan and returned to the Hart complex the next morning. The airport was by now locked down. It was next to impossible to get people in. Time to end this.

An hour before the Hart and Operation Pitting were due to shut down a busload of Anglo-Afghan families showed up. Not clear how. They were processed with minutes to spare before closedown.

In London, people were still trying to work out whether and how to keep a presence in Kabul once the evacuation was over. I kept London updated on what we knew of others' plans. It turned out that a small Turkish team would be staying on at their embassy, led by Ambassador Cihad Erginay. I contacted him and wished him the best of luck. He responded with his usual dry humour: a line of laughing face emojis. The Turkish military withdrawal, meanwhile, was well under way.

Overnight, the UK military closed their operations at the Baron and began the withdrawal.

FRIDAY 27 AUGUST

The saddest of duties. Together with Dan Blanchford, Colonel Max (my defence attaché) and the close protection team I attended the US ramp ceremony, a short, simple ceremony in which the military loaded the coffins of their dead comrades onto a US Air Force C-17.

The American system was in shock. No one had been clear what time the event would take place. We had been told it would be 5:00 am, and had driven across the runway from Taipan to the military north terminal in the dark, meeting Dan in a deserted street. On the way we passed medics wheeling a severely injured patient across the hardstanding, on a trolley under a plastic tent.

It turned out that the timings had changed but the message had not reached us. We drove back to Taipan to get an hour's sleep. At 7:00 am we drove across the runway to the north terminal flight line again: another false start.

The ceremony took place mid-morning, in blazing sunshine. I stood in the shade of the gigantic wing of an American C-17 transport plane, alongside Tom West, Khalilzad's deputy and later successor as US Special Representative for Afghanistan. Soldiers lined the short route to the ramp of the aircraft. Pick-up trucks drew up slowly, one by one, at the flight line. Thirteen coffins draped in the Stars and Stripes were carried to the plane by soldiers: men and women, some of them stone-faced, others visibly struggling with the weight and the emotion of the moment.

There was no conversation, no music, no speeches. Just the unceasing roar of jet engines. Burly, hard-bitten men were close to tears. Some *were* in tears. After the last coffin had been loaded onto the C-17. I shook Ambassador Ross Wilson's hand and muttered some useless words. And then we got back to work.

The Taliban denied responsibility for the attack, implicitly blaming the Americans:

> The Islamic Emirate strongly condemns the bombing of civilians at Kabul airport, which took place in an area where US forces are responsible for security.

The whole 20-year campaign had taken on some awful symmetry, beginning and ending with innocent people's lives being taken away in acts of obscene violence. In that moment, outside the Abbey Gate, died any last hopes and illusions of the 20-year campaign to build a different kind of Afghanistan. It seemed that all that was left was fear, bigotry, violence and chaos.

In the UK evacuation handling centre, an Afghan woman went into labour. The baby was delivered by military medics. The woman had been involved in a car accident earlier that day and was in shock. Her husband was in the UK. A picture taken on a phone showed the grandmother at the Hart complex, holding the child. A handsome, kind face, lined by experience and fatigue, with a half-smile and brown eyes. The pride and hopefulness of a new grandparent somehow broke through her fear and uncertainty for the future.

Back in London the UK media broke the story of the papers left behind at the embassy. Inevitably, the news was accompanied by recriminations and demands that heads must roll. It was a bitter moment, and I knew the team members would be beating themselves up. But there was no time to dwell on what had happened. That would have to wait until after the evacuation was over.

London asked if I would do a media interview as we closed everything down. It was hard to feel enthusiastic about the prospect after some of the things that had been briefed to the media by people in Whitehall in recent days – I just wanted to turn my back on the whole lot of them. The interview got a No from Dominic Raab's SpAds anyway. No reason given, as usual. Eventually we agreed that I would do another short clip for social media as Operation Pitting closed down and the UK personnel left Kabul.

As the day wore on there were intelligence warnings of further ISKP attacks being planned. It was becoming increasingly difficult to continue the evacuation without putting lives at intolerable risk, so once again we reworked the plans, to close down the evacuation on 28 August. The team at the Hart compound would finish processing the people there, working against the clock, and close that part of the operation. We would then consolidate operations at Taipan, but with a smaller team to deal with any last-minute cases as we approached the final, most dangerous hours.

The Foreign Office asked me for an update on our plans to withdraw staff. Who would remain to the end and who would leave, and on which flights? By when would the withdrawal of staff be complete? When was I planning to leave? People in London were getting nervous about the risk of our staff being killed or seriously injured in the final stages of the evacuation.

We had made it this far with no losses, and intended to keep it that way. Neither I nor anyone else wanted to tempt fate further than necessary. The growing terrorist threat meant that we should only keep staff in Kabul for as long as there was a clear operational need for them to be there. I set out the timetable, which was carefully coordinated with the UK and US military. If there was little or no work left to do on the 28th and earlier flights were available, we would put people on them.

Apart from the risk to our staff, I did not want civilians getting under the feet of the military at the point of maximum risk to them. I asked Nigel in London to do what he could to prevent long screwdrivers being inserted by people far from the action and with insufficient knowledge of the situation on the ground: 'It's essential that London does not try to second guess the operational commanders on this.'

Late that evening, Jason confirmed that the team at the Hart complex had completed processing and were now all at Taipan. There were more people to be processed than expected, and the team had worked right down to the very last minute. The Hart operation was closed.

The soldiers were busy clearing Taipan of sensitive equipment, documents, anything that might be of use to the Taliban. Things were starting to look increasingly deconstructed. A large burn pit had been going for some days on some waste ground outside the canteen. Into it went papers, equipment, anything that could not be shipped out or left behind. A detachment of young soldiers was assigned to clear my office. Office equipment was whisked away or trashed unless we were actually using it.

Through the night, work went on to find and evacuate some people and their families at very high risk – Afghan soldiers and others who had worked closely with us and were being hunted down by the Taliban. There were some acts of extraordinary courage and resourcefulness to get those people through the Taliban cordons. A significant number of those people made it onto flights.

Meanwhile, the story playing out in public had a different focus. There were increasingly heated exchanges taking place in the media and on social media over efforts to evacuate the staff and animals of the Nowzad sanctuary for stray dogs and cats. In Kabul we were clear that this was a distraction that we did not intend to get drawn into. I have nothing against dogs or cats – quite the opposite. I sympathise with people under extreme stress watching everything they worked for and loved being destroyed before their eyes. But our priority was to evacuate people.

A report from one of the airfield gate coordinators found its way to me:

> Accurate numbers:
> We received 50 UK Dogs (1 UK person only)
> 1 Japanese
> 13 NATO
> 83 × Fin[n]ish
> 1 × random Canadian.

Saturday 28 August

My early morning scan of the UK newspaper headlines confirmed that in London an ugly game of recrimination and buck-passing was in full flow. It felt cheap and dishonourable that this was going on while people's lives were on the line in Kabul.

We were out of time. But the evacuation was not quite over. From nowhere, a last-minute busload of Afghans turned up. They were processed. And that was it: Operation Pitting was over.

In the late morning, I had a final meeting with some of our senior military and their US counterparts, to tie up loose ends and to say our thank yous. Somehow, the UK military team in Taipan still had the means to make decent coffee – or mint tea, for those who preferred. The atmosphere was relaxed, and we enjoyed a few moments in the sun. But there was no time or space for complacency or self-congratulation. Occasionally, crashing noises in the background reminded us that the soldiers were taking the place apart. The burn pit was running constantly.

Everyone knew that for the military one of the most dangerous parts of the operation was still to come. The last of the military contingent to leave would be taking off in the dead of night from an airport with no security other than the Taliban themselves.

The time came for me to leave Taipan and move across the runway to the military terminal. I did a last check of the office where I had worked and the cell-like room that had been my home for two of the most intense weeks of my life, to make sure that I had missed nothing and that every last scrap of paper had gone on the fire. Some quick goodbyes and good lucks to the soldiers who had been such a joy to work with in such a joyless time. And then we were on our way to a holding area in the military terminal. The rest of the team were already there, chatting or sleeping or staring into space in plastic garden chairs under awnings, amidst a sea of rubbish. A friendly dog snuffled around, evidently part of the despatch team who were putting together the passenger lists.

With less than an hour to departure, it was time for me to do my last media clip. Again, Andy McCoubrey and I worked out what I wanted to say, and jotted down my notes. Ben and James, the military comms team, would do the filming, and had worked out how to get the large data file back to London for editing and uploading to the internet. There was no way we could do any of this on a phone, especially with the rapidly dying mobile network.

We quickly scoped out possible locations. Maybe not alongside the overflowing dumpsters and wrecked vehicles or the increasingly tired-looking terminal buildings. It was a no-brainer: out on the taxiway, near the runway, with a Royal Air Force plane in the background.

Military transport planes are incredibly noisy, even when parked at a distance waiting to be loaded. There were half a dozen or more of them parked up, engines running. The noise was impressive. Ben and James set up the camera on a tripod at the edge of the taxiway, using a special directional microphone to minimise the background noise. It was hard not to squint in the blazing sunshine. Andy kept tight hold of my sheet of notes in case the wind grabbed it and whisked it away across the runway. There were some nervous giggles from the close protection team. We did the clip in one take.

As we were filming, a couple of SUVs roared across the concrete apron. Heavily armed and heavily built US personnel demanded to know who we were and what we were doing. Maybe they put it a bit more assertively than that.

Filming for social media, of course. What else would we be doing on a Saturday afternoon in Kabul airport? Have you met the British Ambassador?

Nice to meet you folks. You take care now.

It was time to go. We picked up our backpacks and got into vehicles, walking the last 100 metres out to our C-17. Dan Blanchford walked out with me. Someone took a photo of us at the back of the plane. The plane quickly filled up: civilians, soldiers, equipment. Dan and the last of the British military would leave later that evening after dark, coordinated with the US military withdrawal timetable. The Americans would be the last to leave.

At 3:29 pm I messaged Fiona to say that we were on the plane. The bright sunlight was blocked out as the ramp closed. The aircraft taxied out to the end of the runway. Body armour on until we were well clear of the risk of ground fire. The pilot opened up the throttles and we were in the air, climbing steeply to clear the city and the surrounding mountains.

It was a subdued flight. Most people slept or silently turned over in their minds what had happened, and the things they had seen and done and been part of. The aircraft noise required earplugs, further discouraging conversation. Three hours later we landed at Minhad airbase. While we had been in the air, military colleagues still in Kabul had messaged me about another possible terrorist attack being planned.

Overnight, all remaining UK military personnel left Kabul airport safely. Only then could anyone exhale. A day later, as the last of the US military were leaving, the C-RAM system intercepted a rocket attack on the airport.

A brief stopover at Minhad gave us the opportunity of a shower, some food and a few hours on a camp bed as evening turned to night. The fierce air conditioning in the Royal Air Force transit facility battled with the intense summer heat outside. Jason was still working, carefully accounting for the last of the embassy's firearms and protective equipment. The close protection team could relax for the first time in weeks. My phone pinged every few seconds. Messages of support; requests for information; requests for evacuation.

SUNDAY 29 AUGUST

Time to move. We walked out across the tarmac in the hot, still night. A delay while the passenger manifest was checked and checked again to be sure that everyone on board was accounted for. And then we were airborne again for the overnight flight to Brize Norton. This time on a Royal Air Force Airbus together with several hundred troops. Most slept the sleep of the exhausted. I did not: too much adrenalin.

We arrived to a grey summer Sunday early morning. I was asked to exit the plane first and alone; the media needed a photograph with which to wrap up the operation and this part of the story. I did as requested, and then asked the embassy staff and Rapid Deployment Team, the last of the civilians to leave Kabul, to join me for a team photo on the steps from the plane.

There was one last job to do. The press office had asked me before we left Minhad to do a final media clip on arrival in Brize Norton, to mark the end of Operation Pitting and to summarise what our people had achieved. I pointed out that I would be wearing the clothes I had worn for the previous three days or more, and would look tired and dishevelled. London agreed that tired and dishevelled was probably the right look in the circumstances. Finding the right words was a bigger problem. London sent me some suggested lines, which I mostly ignored. I paid tribute to the work of the personnel of Operation Pitting and underlined the government's continued commitment to the people of Afghanistan. The first part was easy. The second part was much harder to say with conviction.

Philip Barton, the head of the Foreign Office, had come to Brize Norton to meet us. I introduced the team to him. Before leaving, we borrowed the base commander's office for a quick private word.

And then it was time to go. We found our bags, which had miraculously appeared in the arrivals hall, and said our goodbyes. A fleet of taxis and buses were waiting to take people home or to their barracks. The drivers looked bewildered, not sure what was going on with all these sunburnt soldiers and bedraggled bureaucrats. Suddenly I looked round and realised that the last of our people had left and it was just me.

In the car, I drifted away in the back seat, interrupted by the constant pinging of the phone as more messages came in. Of relief, congratulations, questions and requests. And always, more Afghans asking for help or seeking information about their application for resettlement. Over the year that followed, the messages became fewer and eventually trickled out.

I had forgotten to tell Fiona and my parents that we had landed in the UK. They learned about it from the early morning BBC news.

Epilogue

Diplomacy is not a spectator sport. It is about getting things done. Sometimes it's about stopping bad things happening. Much of the time you are dealing with people who do not agree with you and may not like you or what you represent.

There are two questions that all diplomats always face: what are we trying to achieve? and how are we going to do it? In Afghanistan, in the summer of 2021, these questions were becoming stark. As was the absence of good answers to either of them.

How you answer those questions reflects the context in which you find yourself. Choices that you and others have made, or not made, in the past; what others – friends and foes – are doing; what else is going on in the world. Your options are always shaped by these things. Sometimes they are narrowed to a choice between courses of action with bad outcomes or very bad outcomes. You play the hand you are dealt. That is the situation we reached in Kabul in August 2021.

The allies had gone into Afghanistan 20 years earlier in response to the 9/11 attacks, to suppress the threat from al-Qaeda's virulent strain of transnational terrorism which had struck at the heart of the USA and forced everyone to rethink their assumptions about their own security. The 20-year campaign that followed succeeded in that there were no successful terrorist attacks mounted out of Afghanistan against the USA or its allies. There were some very significant achievements, in particular for women and girls compared to their lot under the Taliban's benighted rule. But after the Taliban had been ejected the project to build a successful state failed, in the end destroying whatever else was achieved.

That failure was starkly visible in the speed and finality with which the Taliban returned to power on 15 August 2021. It took only nine days from the loss of Zaranj, the first provincial capital to be taken by the Taliban, to the fall of Kabul and the collapse of the Islamic Republic of Afghanistan. There was a strange symmetry with the rapid collapse of the Taliban's rule in 2001.

During the 20-year Afghanistan campaign, 457 British service personnel lost their lives. Many more suffered life-changing injuries and damage to their physical and mental health. The same is true of our US and other allies. Countless Afghans lost their lives, their livelihoods and, finally, their hopes of a better life. We owe it to them all to learn from what happened, at such great cost.

The failure of the Afghanistan campaign was not for want of resources. In 2011, at the height of the 'Obama Surge', NATO had more than 130,000 troops in Afghanistan. The UK spent over £30 billion on the military campaign and aid to Afghanistan between 2001 and 2021. US expenditure was on a truly biblical scale: between $1 trillion and $2 trillion over 20 years, more than the entire cumulative GDP of Afghanistan over that period. Yet these immense outlays, made over nearly two decades, had not brought peace or stability or good governance to Afghanistan.[33]

Despite the enormous expenditure of blood and treasure, large parts of the public and some political leaders were no longer convinced that we had enduring interests in Afghanistan or that protecting these required accepting even the relatively modest costs and risks of NATO's Resolute Support Mission – modest, that is, relative to what had preceded it. Therein lies the problem. It is not hard to understand why the politicians and the public had lost patience with the Afghanistan campaign. Afghanistan had become seen by many as a pit which swallowed people, resources and political capital, with diminishing returns.

It was no longer possible to explain clearly to the public why we were in Afghanistan, or to convince the public that the war was winnable. Successive US presidents wanted out of a long war that had lost public support, but they could not find a coherent and safe exit strategy. This was the case also in the UK and in other European allies. As I was preparing to go to Kabul in early 2021, a close relative asked me pointedly: 'Why are we still there, and how are we going to get out?'

The enterprise was tainted by the catastrophe of Iraq. The decision to invade Iraq in early 2003 diverted resources and attention from Afghanistan at exactly the time when the USA and its allies needed to focus attention, resources and thinking capacity on achieving a stable future for Afghanistan. Over time, the failure of a war of choice in Iraq helped undermine the war of necessity in Afghanistan.

President Trump's Doha Agreement in February 2020 was his answer to the question: 'How are we going to get out?' Trump's answer was to walk away. Trump's deal planted the seeds of what happened in August 2021. The agreement made major concessions to the Taliban, requiring none of the Taliban in return. It struck what turned out to be a mortal blow to the republic, and put the USA and its allies under time pressure. It did not make the military withdrawal conditional on the Taliban even engaging seriously in the intra-Afghan negotiations, still less reaching a negotiated political settlement.

The Doha Agreement is a strong contender for the title of worst deal in history if it is understood as a serious attempt to achieve a negotiated settlement. But it was not. Trump's deal was driven by something rather different: the US electoral timetable. It is probably a mistake to understand it as a serious attempt to find a genuine lasting settlement in Afghanistan. It is better understood as the product of a determination to shake Afghanistan off regardless of the cost (to others) and take the political dividend. Understood in that way, at least, it was brazen in its intent.

Biden's decision to press ahead with the withdrawal from Afghanistan was driven by his long-standing scepticism about the purpose, conduct and costs of the war. Biden was in my view right to think that there was no good time to leave, and that in the absence of a coherent exit strategy an open-ended commitment to a military presence would not change that. The circumstances of the beginning of Biden's presidency – the 6 January 2021 insurrection on the Capitol, egged on by Trump regardless of the cost to America's democracy and standing in the world – meant that Biden needed to demonstrate grip and deliver an important, difficult policy goal early in his presidency.

But upping and leaving is only a viable exit strategy if you understand and accept the likely consequences of doing so. We saw those consequences play out in Kabul airport, and in the nightmare into which Afghanistan has descended since.

President Biden's decision to press ahead with the military withdrawal on a tight timetable compounded the problem created by Trump's Doha Agreement. The speed of the US-led military withdrawal in the first half of 2021 visibly demoralised the Afghan military and the Afghan Government. The Doha Agreement committed the USA to refraining from airstrikes against the Taliban. That handed the initiative to the Taliban, who operated under no significant constraints in conducting offensive operations against the republic. In the final weeks of the war the USA intensified airstrikes against the Taliban but, as senior US officials acknowledged, the effect of this was to slow down the Taliban advance, not to reverse it.[34]

Meanwhile the military withdrawal led inevitably to the withdrawal of the contractors on whom Afghanistan's armed forces relied for maintenance of key assets that should have given them an edge over the Taliban, in particular aircraft and helicopters. There was never a realistic prospect that these high-tech Western machines could be kept airworthy by Afghans who lacked the necessary skills to do so, based on advice delivered on Skype.

The underlying problem was that Afghanistan's NATO allies had helped build, train and equip a force capable of fighting alongside NATO, but not one capable of doing so effectively without NATO. Biden and others justified the decision to end the NATO military presence by reference to the enormous resources put into giving Afghans the opportunity to determine their own future and creating the military capabilities to defend their republic. On the wall of my office in Kabul was a large framed document celebrating the 5,000th Afghan army officer to graduate from 'Sandhurst in the Sand', the UK's Afghan National Army Officer Academy just outside Kabul. The purpose of the academy was to create an officer corps to lead a modern army. But in the summer of 2021 the Afghan military capabilities NATO had helped build were cruelly exposed as mostly illusory.

And finally, conducting the NATO withdrawal at speed as the summer 2021 fighting season got under way gave the Taliban the time they needed to capitalise on the withdrawal before winter set in. By early summer, even as the military withdrawal was still taking place, it was already clear that the republic was losing quickly and badly. These were consequences not just of Biden's decision to leave but of Trump's Doha agreement and ultimately of 20 years of flawed strategy and self-deceiving policy.

The consequences of these choices should not have come as a surprise.

The republic's political leaders failed to rise to the challenge, just as they had done for the previous 20 years.

President Ghani seemed to be clinging onto an unfounded hope that President Biden would reverse Trump's decision to withdraw US and NATO forces, or else reverse his own decision to press ahead with the military withdrawal once it became clear that the republic's armed forces were facing the likelihood of defeat. This was not just Ghani's misreading of the Americans but indicative of Ghani's evident lack of the leadership skills needed to lead a country at war. There were times when Ghani seemed to be completely missing the point, which was that the republic was in mortal danger and that its president had not the ghost of a plan to save it.

I doubt that Ghani or his closest civilian advisers ever fully understood the scale and speed of the unfolding military defeat until it was too late to reverse it. Nor were the wider Afghan political caste capable of putting aside personal ambitions, fears and rivalries to do what was necessary to salvage a softer landing than a complete Taliban military victory. These failings ran through Ghani's and other republican leaders' approaches to the political negotiations and the military response. Ghani seemed to be just as concerned with not increasing the strength of his rivals as with heading off military defeat by the Taliban.

Throughout the final months of the republic, one of the more likely scenarios was some sort of intra-élite deal – that is, horse trading between factions, power brokers, and warlords, leading to some sort of power sharing allowing the strongest players to protect their interests. In the final days and hours of the republic, there was a fleeting possibility that something like that might happen. None of us thought this would be a good outcome. But by summer 2021 no good outcome was available. There were only bad outcomes, worse outcomes, and catastrophic outcomes. The outcome we got was catastrophic.

For their part, the Taliban wanted to right the wrong, as they saw it, of their overthrow in 2001. They wanted international engagement and recognition, but they wanted it on their terms. The idea, popular among Western diplomats and policy makers, that the international community could exercise leverage over them proved to be as unfounded as the idea that the Taliban were a reformed movement – the Taliban 2.0. I underline that there was no real evidence to support either of these ideas. Both turned out to be wishful thinking.

Over the years that followed the fall of the republic, the consequences of the Taliban's return to power and the path that took them there played out over iconic issues for the West and the big international donors, in particular girls' education and women's freedoms. One of the first things the Taliban did as they seized power was to tell women to stay at home until arrangements were in place to guarantee their safety. This turned out to be the reversal of 20 years of advances in women's basic rights to work, to receive an education, to make decisions for themselves, even to leave the house without a male chaperone. The arrangements to guarantee women's safety did not materialise. Instead, there came requests to female employees to send male relatives to their place of work to do their jobs. And protests by extraordinarily brave women against what was being done to them and their daughters.

Early on after proclaiming their emirate the Taliban announced that girls would return to school. The position was reversed on the very day that Afghanistan's girls were preparing to do so. The following year, in 2022, women were banned from attending university. Despite the fact that senior Talibs in Doha had long since taken the personal decision to send their own daughters to school, the views of the Taliban supreme leader, Haibatullah Akhundzada, and the conservative clerics around him took precedence. The standing of the most violent and reactionary factions within the Taliban movement was strengthened by what they saw as total military victory over the USA and its puppet administration. In the absence of a consensus to change, the Taliban defaulted to the most uncompromising positions.

The Taliban continued to host senior al-Qaeda figures, including Ayman al-Zawahiri, the Emir of al-Qaeda. In July 2022 a US drone strike killed him as he was standing on the balcony of a villa in the centre of Kabul. The villa was reported to be owned by Sirajuddin Haqqani, a leading terrorist and the Interior Minister of the Emirate which the Taliban proclaimed shortly after they had come to power in August 2021.

The Taliban failed to suppress the threat from ISKP in Afghanistan. In the year following the Taliban takeover, ISKP conducted a steady stream of attacks, with the Hazara community and girls' schools among their targets of choice.

At a more mundane level, on assuming power the Taliban demonstrated their almost complete lack of the skills needed to run a state. Governing a country is very different from mounting an insurgency. International funds dried up, in a country where three quarters of government revenue had previously come from international donors. In 2022, 95 per cent of Afghans did not have enough to eat. Child mortality and severe malnutrition soared. The United Nations estimated that in 2024 more than half the population of Afghanistan would need humanitarian assistance.

None of this should have come as a surprise.

There were valid political and strategic choices behind Biden's decision to focus resources elsewhere. Biden had set this out very clearly in his statements in April and June 2021: the USA and its allies needed to refocus resources and attention on different challenges. In particular, the re-emergence of Great Power rivalry with China and Russia; the systemic challenges of Covid and climate change; and the very pressing domestic issues in the USA that had led to an outgoing president falsely contesting an election result and encouraging a violent insurrection to overturn the will of the voters.

President Biden was and is not wrong, in my view, about these priorities. They are among the major challenges of our time.

But we did not and do not have the option to walk away from Afghanistan at no cost to ourselves. We need a proper reckoning of why the 20-year campaign in Afghanistan ended in the way it did. We need to understand the failures of policy and strategy that were made along the way, and their consequences. We need to work out serious answers to some difficult and troubling questions.

What could we have done differently to produce better outcomes? What should we have done to prepare an Afghan state capable of governing effectively, and an army capable of defending the republic once the USA and its forces withdrew? How should we have avoided both worsening Afghanistan's dependency on the USA and other international donors, and entrenching the corruption and clientelism that eroded the State's legitimacy and effectiveness? As those 20 years neared their end, did Afghanistan's leaders take seriously their responsibility to lead the country? How could we have better incentivised them to do so?

What was the effect on Afghanistan's society and politics of the vast foreign military presence and the operations it conducted? And of the huge resources that we poured into the country?

How to fight a counter-insurgency war without further alienating the population? Should we – could we – have brought the Taliban into a peace settlement earlier, perhaps much earlier? Could we have conducted the military withdrawal differently, making it clear to the Taliban that their only viable path to power was through negotiation?

Should we have managed things differently with Afghanistan's neighbours? In particular with Pakistan, whose leaders, and especially its military, were intent on keeping Afghanistan weak in order to achieve 'strategic depth' against Indian influence in Afghanistan?

How should we have ensured that we were not deceiving ourselves or being deceived by others with a vested interest in the status quo, seeing what we wanted to see at the expense of what we needed to see?

How should we have done all this after years of missed opportunities, during which time a catastrophic war of choice in Iraq was the focus?

Could the military collapse have been averted? In September 2021 both General Milley (Chair of the Joint Chiefs of Staff) and General McKenzie (CENTCOM commander) testified before the Senate Armed Services Committee that they had advised both Trump and Biden to keep several thousand US troops in Afghanistan to bolster the republic. This would undoubtedly have led to renewed Taliban attacks on US forces. There was no appetite to accept the costs and risks of continuing to underwrite policy goals with military force, and the military advice was rejected.[35]

What of the UK? The political debate here focused on our relationship with the USA at a time when the consequences of Brexit were beginning to sink in. The rhetoric of 'Global Britain' was failing to paper over some uncomfortable facts about the UK. The limits of our influence over US thinking were stark. So was our ability to act independently of the USA. The decisions to end the NATO military presence were made in Washington. We in the UK did not agree with the decision to withdraw the NATO forces or with the way it was done; every person I met with experience of Afghanistan was aghast at Trump's dismal deal with the Taliban and then at Biden's botched execution of the withdrawal. But the UK was a junior partner, and we did not have an equal voice in US decision making. The fact that we thought the military withdrawal unwise and badly thought through did not change US policy.

Equally important, no one had managed to convince the Americans that the UK had a better strategy, and no one – not the military, not the diplomats, not the intelligence agencies – had done so for 20 years. Senior retired people criticised the absence of a strategy, invariably neglecting to mention their own role at the time in devising and executing the strategies of the past which had failed to pacify Helmand, eradicate opium, bring about gender equality, or create the conditions for a political settlement.

Fleeting suggestions, made in the heat of the moment as Kabul collapsed and the nightmare unfolded, that the UK should lead a continued military presence despite the withdrawal of US forces were quickly buried, thankfully. Fortunately, we never had to address seriously how or why we would do this – two questions to which there could be no good answers without the Americans.

For the UK, it was uncomfortable for the limits of our influence on US decision making to be exposed so graphically. But this did not tell us anything we did not already know, if we chose to admit it. It was a wake-up call, but not a Suez moment.

It was a difficult moment also in the wider transatlantic relationship, for similar reasons. Talk at the time of a more serious rupture was overblown, and has at the time of writing been comprehensively overtaken by the clarity and unity of response within NATO, as well as the G7 and almost all of the European Union, to Russia's invasion of Ukraine on 24 February 2022.

But that clarity of purpose is being tested hard. We need to build on what has been achieved since February 2022 – to re-invest in the transatlantic security bond.

We need to rebuild a strong consensus that Europe's security and US security are not separable, that we need to address together the same underlying challenges, and that we shall continue to need to do so for many years to come.

One key element of that is how potential adversaries read our actions and intentions. I do not believe that the decision to withdraw forces from Afghanistan was a deciding factor in Putin's decision to attack Ukraine. But I do believe that was a contributory factor in Putin's catastrophic misreading of the West's willingness to defend its interests when faced with difficult choices. In a contest of wills, success can depend on being prepared to demonstrate to an opponent that we can and will do what it takes to prevail, for as long as it takes.

We need to address how potential opponents read our resolve. We are in a new era of Great Power competition. What happened in Afghanistan was not a military defeat for US-led allied forces, nor was it the outcome of great power competition. It was a consequence of changing US defence and foreign policy priorities. It was a failure that stemmed from, and illustrated, a loss of will. And it was seen as such by competitors and adversaries.

We also need to think clearly about how our values relate to our interests, including our security interests, and how we promote and protect our values and interests without one compromising the other. This question is at its most difficult in our approach to countering terrorism and countering insurgency. There were times during the War on Terror when the cure threatened to become more harmful than the disease, calling into question the legal and ethical guardrails on which a democratic society relies to limit the state's power over individuals.

The question is there in a different form over our approach to human development in a war-torn society very different from our own. Over the course of 20 years we invested vast resources in building a functioning Afghan state on the rubble of what the Taliban had in turn built on the legacies of the failed Soviet intervention and the 1989–1992 civil war. Before and after the fall of the republic, we talked of protecting the gains of the previous 20 years, particularly in terms of education and health, and especially for girls and women – the biggest losers from the Taliban's return to power.

That is a moral and a reputational problem for us, not least because of the resources and the priority we gave to improving access to education and health for all Afghans, but particularly for girls and women. We own a part-share in what has happened to them since August 2021. With intense pressure on aid and development budgets, we need to restate the case for human development in poor and war-torn countries being in our own best interests, including our national security interests.

A political choice was made to end the military presence. That is a perfectly legitimate choice for democratically elected leaders to make. But the time-based rather than conditions-based path to the exit handed the Taliban a massive opportunity.

The Doha Agreement helped create a situation where the Taliban were in a stronger position than at any time in the previous 20 years. They exploited it ruthlessly. Meanwhile the allies missed opportunities to bring the Taliban into a negotiation on terms more advantageous to us and to most of the people of Afghanistan. Some of the responsibility for that lies with the Taliban themselves. Much of it lies with us – the USA, its allies, and the republic we supported. Afghanistan's leading politicians themselves failed to agree a united approach to dealing with the Taliban. But if we had taken a different path – making it clear to the Taliban that the NATO military withdrawal was dependent on irrevocable progress towards a negotiated political settlement – that would undoubtedly have meant accepting more risk. We chose not to do that.

The size and posture of the Western military presence and aid flows created a dependency culture. Some Afghans did very well from this: people who knew how to engage with us and tell us what we wanted to hear. Yet the aid flows did not translate into a vibrant economy or the lasting human development that is meant to follow from this. The military capacity in which we had invested so much melted away the moment that direct NATO military support was withdrawn. Although many Afghans fought bravely and tenaciously, the popular uprising against the Taliban in which the republic had belatedly invested its hopes did not materialise.

There were long-standing issues around legitimacy and public support for the Afghan Government and its leaders. This is a story of corruption and predatory behaviour, of weak state institutions, and of compromised political leaders. But that is not the whole story. It is hard to build legitimacy and public support when fighting a counterinsurgency campaign in which civilians are inevitably caught up. It is even harder when your ability to do so depends on massive foreign military forces, some of whom conduct themselves in ways that are alien to the culture in which they are operating.

The Taliban, adept at exploiting the Afghan Government's disconnection from ordinary people's lives, put in place parallel governance systems in areas that they controlled. Their public communications were startlingly effective – far, far better than anything the republic or its backers achieved, at both tactical and strategic levels. These problems did not start under the Ghani Government, but much earlier.

And finally, we failed for 20 years to find a way for the Taliban's natural sympathisers and supporters to participate in a political settlement and building a viable state. We allowed the situation to arise where the Taliban saw a path to military victory, giving power to the hard men, the absolutists and the extremists, and draining influence away from those Taliban leaders who might have been prepared to negotiate a compromise even as the republic was falling, to reflect a wider range of Afghans and their interests. Within the Taliban itself, the fighters and the fundamentalists won. They knew what they wanted, and they played a patient long game. In contrast, we struggled to identify what we wanted, and we struggled to exercise the strategic patience and the willpower to achieve it.

None of what happened in August 2021 should have come as a surprise.

With, at the time of writing, Vladimir Putin's invasion of Ukraine bringing major war to Europe for the first time in generations, seemingly intractable conflicts in the Middle East, the challenge of China, and mounting domestic and economic headwinds competing for attention, it is too easy to think that Afghanistan is yesterday's news and is not our problem any longer. Neither of these ideas is true, and we should not allow ourselves to believe otherwise.

There is, though, a glimmer of light amidst the violence and squalor and wasted opportunity of what happened in Afghanistan. Extraordinary situations bring out extraordinary qualities in people. Through the events recounted in this book I was fortunate to meet some of the most courageous and principled people I have ever known. Afghan women and men who put their lives on the line to defend their and others' right to live freely and in peace. Our own soldiers, development specialists, diplomats and civil servants, who believed in a different sort of Afghanistan and were prepared to put their lives on the line to help Afghans achieve it. And in August 2021 the people who went into Kabul at the bitter end, to do what was right.

Appendix: the Doha Agreement

Agreement for Bringing Peace to Afghanistan
between the Islamic Emirate of Afghanistan which is not recognized by the United States
as a state and is known as the Taliban and the United States of America

February 29, 2020
which corresponds to Rajab 5, 1441 on the Hijri Lunar calendar
and Hoot 10, 1398 on the Hijri Solar calendar

A comprehensive peace agreement is made of four parts:

1. Guarantees and enforcement mechanisms that will prevent the use of the soil of Afghanistan by any group or individual against the security of the United States and its allies.

2. Guarantees, enforcement mechanisms, and announcement of a timeline for the withdrawal of all foreign forces from Afghanistan.

3. After the announcement of guarantees for a complete withdrawal of foreign forces and timeline in the presence of international witnesses, and guarantees and the announcement in the presence of international witnesses that Afghan soil will not be used against the security of the United States and its allies, the Islamic Emirate of Afghanistan which is not recognized by the United States as a state and is known as the Taliban will start intra-Afghan negotiations with Afghan sides on March 10, 2020, which corresponds to Rajab 15, 1441 on the Hijri Lunar calendar and Hoot 20, 1398 on the Hijri Solar calendar.

4. A permanent and comprehensive ceasefire will be an item on the agenda of the intra-Afghan dialogue and negotiations. The participants of intra-Afghan negotiations will discuss the date and modalities of a permanent and comprehensive ceasefire, including joint implementation mechanisms, which will be announced along with the completion and agreement over the future political roadmap of Afghanistan.

The four parts above are interrelated and each will be implemented in accordance with its own agreed timeline and agreed terms. Agreement on the first two parts paves the way for the last two parts.

Following is the text of the agreement for the implementation of parts one and two of the above. Both sides agree that these two parts are interconnected. The obligations of the Islamic Emirate of Afghanistan which is not recognized by the United States as a state and is known as the Taliban in this agreement apply in areas under their control until the formation of the new post-settlement Afghan Islamic government as determined by the intra-Afghan dialogue and negotiations.

PART ONE

The United States is committed to withdraw from Afghanistan all military forces of the United States, its allies, and Coalition partners, including all non-diplomatic civilian personnel, private security contractors, trainers, advisors, and supporting services personnel within fourteen (14) months following announcement of this agreement, and will take the following measures in this regard:

A. The United States, its allies, and the Coalition will take the following measures in the first one hundred thirty-five (135) days:

    1) They will reduce the number of U.S. forces in Afghanistan to eight thousand six hundred (8,600) and proportionally bring reduction in the number of its allies and Coalition forces.

    2) The United States, its allies, and the Coalition will withdraw all their forces from five (5) military bases.

B. With the commitment and action on the obligations of the Islamic Emirate of Afghanistan which is not recognized by the United States as a state and is known as the Taliban in Part Two of this agreement, the United States, its allies, and the Coalition will execute the following:

    1) The United States, its allies, and the Coalition will complete withdrawal of all remaining forces from Afghanistan within the remaining nine and a half (9.5) months.

    2) The United States, its allies, and the Coalition will withdraw all their forces from remaining bases.

C. The United States is committed to start immediately to work with all relevant sides on a plan to expeditiously release combat and political prisoners as a confidence building measure with the coordination and approval of all relevant sides. Up to five thousand (5,000) prisoners of the Islamic Emirate of Afghanistan which is not recognized by the United States as a state and is known as the Taliban and up to one thousand (1,000) prisoners of the other side will be released by March 10, 2020, the first day of intra-Afghan negotiations, which corresponds to Rajab 15, 1441 on the Hijri Lunar calendar and Hoot 20, 1398 on the Hijri Solar calendar. The relevant sides have the goal of releasing all the remaining prisoners over the course of the subsequent three months. The United States commits to completing this goal. The Islamic Emirate of Afghanistan which is not recognized by the United States as a state and is known as the Taliban commits that its released prisoners will be committed to the responsibilities mentioned in this agreement so that they will not pose a threat to the security of the United States and its allies.

D. With the start of intra-Afghan negotiations, the United States will initiate an administrative review of current U.S. sanctions and the rewards list against members of the Islamic Emirate of Afghanistan which is not recognized by the United States as a state and is known as the Taliban with the goal of removing these sanctions by August 27, 2020, which corresponds to Muharram 8, 1442 on the Hijri Lunar calendar and Saunbola 6, 1399 on the Hijri Solar calendar.

E. With the start of intra-Afghan negotiations, the United States will start diplomatic engagement with other members of the United Nations Security Council and Afghanistan to remove members of the Islamic Emirate of Afghanistan which is not recognized by the United States as a state and is known as the Taliban from the sanctions list with the aim of achieving this objective by May 29, 2020, which corresponds to Shawwal 6, 1441 on the Hijri Lunar calendar and Jawza 9, 1399 on the Hijri Solar calendar.

F. The United States and its allies will refrain from the threat or the use of force against the territorial integrity or political independence of Afghanistan or intervening in its domestic affairs.

PART TWO

In conjunction with the announcement of this agreement, the Islamic Emirate of Afghanistan which is not recognized by the United States as a state and is known as the Taliban will take the following steps to prevent any group or individual, including al-Qa'ida, from using the soil of Afghanistan to threaten the security of the United States and its allies:

1. The Islamic Emirate of Afghanistan which is not recognized by the United States as a state and is known as the Taliban will not allow any of its members, other individuals or groups, including al-Qa'ida, to use the soil of Afghanistan to threaten the security of the United States and its allies.

2. The Islamic Emirate of Afghanistan which is not recognized by the United States as a state and is known as the Taliban will send a clear message that those who pose a threat to the security of the United States and its allies have no place in Afghanistan, and will instruct members of the Islamic Emirate of Afghanistan which is not recognized by the United States as a state and is known as the Taliban not to cooperate with groups or individuals threatening the security of the United States and its allies.

3. The Islamic Emirate of Afghanistan which is not recognized by the United States as a state and is known as the Taliban will prevent any group or individual in Afghanistan from threatening the security of the United States and its allies, and will prevent them from recruiting, training, and fundraising and will not host them in accordance with the commitments in this agreement.

4. The Islamic Emirate of Afghanistan which is not recognized by the United States as a state and is known as the Taliban is committed to deal with those seeking asylum or residence in Afghanistan according to international migration law and the commitments of this agreement, so that such persons do not pose a threat to the security of the United States and its allies.

5. The Islamic Emirate of Afghanistan which is not recognized by the United States as a state and is known as the Taliban will not provide visas, passports, travel permits, or other legal documents to those who pose a threat to the security of the United States and its allies to enter Afghanistan.

PART THREE

1. The United States will request the recognition and endorsement of the United Nations Security Council for this agreement.

2. The United States and the Islamic Emirate of Afghanistan which is not recognized by the United States as a state and is known as the Taliban seek positive relations with each other and expect that the relations between the United States and the new post-settlement Afghan Islamic government as determined by the intra-Afghan dialogue and negotiations will be positive.

3. The United States will seek economic cooperation for reconstruction with the new post-settlement Afghan Islamic government as determined by the intra-Afghan dialogue and negotiations, and will not intervene in its internal affairs.

Signed in Doha, Qatar on February 29, 2020, which corresponds to Rajab 5, 1441 on the Hijri Lunar calendar and Hoot 10, 1398 on the Hijri Solar calendar, in duplicate, in Pashto, Dari, and English languages, each text being equally authentic.

Endnotes

1 Seth Jones, *In the Graveyard of Empires: America's War in Afghanistan* (New York: W.W. Norton, 2010), 127. Quoted in Anand Gopal, *No Good Men Among the Living: America, the Taliban, and the War Through Afghan Eyes*, (Picador, 2015), p.107.

2 Remarks by President Biden on the Way Forward in Afghanistan | The White House https://www. whitehouse.gov/briefing-room/speeches-remarks/2021/04/14/remarks-by-president-biden-on-the-way-forward-in-afghanistan/

3 Blinken Proposes New Steps to Peace, Keeps May 1st Pullout Option | TOLOnews 02.pdf (tolonews. com) https://tolonews.com/afghanistan-170509 02.pdf (tolonews.com)

4 Dr M. Naeem on Twitter: 1/2 Until all foreign forces completely withdraw from our homeland, the Islamic Emirate will not participate in any conference that shall make decisions about Afghanistan.' / Twitter https://twitter.com/ieaoffice/status/1382060804162400259

5 Biden Afghanistan Speech: 'Time To End This Forever War': NPR https://www.npr. org/2021/04/14/986955659/biden-to-announce-he-will-end-americas-longest-war-in-afghanistan

6 Biden to withdraw all troops from Afghanistan by September (nbcnews.com) https://www.nbcnews. com/politics/white-house/biden-withdraw-all-troops-afghanistan-september-n1263944

7 NATO – Opinion: Joint press point by NATO Secretary General Jens Stoltenberg, US Secretary of State Antony Blinken and US Secretary of Defense Lloyd J. Austin III., 14-Apr.-2021 https://www. nato.int/cps/en/natohq/opinions_183061.htm

8 Top US general foresees Afghan civil war as security worsens | AP News https://apnews.com/article/ joe-biden-afghanistan-9636261069b03719d569b5cf9fe5e4e5

9 PM: Statement on Afghanistan - GOV.UK (www.gov.uk) http://PM:%20Statement%20on%20 Afghanistan%20-%20GOV.UK%20(www.gov.uk)

10 Remarks by President Biden and President Mohammad Ashraf Ghani of the Islamic Republic of Afghanistan Before Bilateral Meeting | The White House https://www.whitehouse.gov/briefing-room/speeches-remarks/2021/06/25/remarks-by-president-biden-and-president-mohammad-ashraf-ghani-of-the-islamic-republic-of-afghanistan-before-bilateral-meeting/

11 Redacted version, published in *The Times*, 18 October 2021

12 https://www.whitehouse.gov/briefing-room/speeches-remarks/2021/07/02/remarks-by-president-biden-on-the-june-jobs-report/

13 Taliban Fighters Advance After U.S. Closes Main Afghan Base – WSJ https://www.wsj.com/articles/ taliban-fighters-advance-after-u-s-closes-main-afghan-base-11625427044

14 Pakistan Stops Official Contact with Afghan National Security Chief (voanews.com) https://www. voanews.com/a/south-central-asia_pakistan-stops-official-contact-afghan-national-security-chief/6206345.html

15 Afghanistan: All foreign troops must leave by deadline – Taliban – BBC News https://www.bbc.co.uk/news/world-asia-57714808

16 *This Week* Transcript 7-4-21: Jeff Zients, Gov. Jim Justice & Gen. Austin 'Scott' Miller – ABC News https://abcnews.go.com/Politics/week-transcript-21-jeff-zients-gov-jim-justice/story?id=78659208

17 Remarks by President Biden on the Drawdown of U.S. Forces in Afghanistan | The White House https://www.whitehouse.gov/briefing-room/speeches-remarks/2021/07/08/remarks-by-president-biden-on-the-drawdown-of-u-s-forces-in-afghanistan/

18 Taliban Willing to Halt Attacks on Cities — Temporarily (voanews.com) https://www.voanews.com/a/south-central-asia_taliban-willing-halt-attacks-cities-temporarily/6208058.html

19 Published in *The Times*, 18 October 2021

20 Risch Afghanistan Report 2022.pdf (senate.gov) https://www.foreign.senate.gov/imo/media/doc/Risch%20Afghanistan%20Report%202022.pdf

21 Taliban Threaten Turkish Troops with 'Jihad' if They Stay in Afghanistan (voanews.com) https://www.voanews.com/a/south-central-asia_taliban-threaten-turkish-troops-jihad-if-they-stay-afghanistan/6208200.html

22 S_2021_655_E.pdf (securitycouncilreport.org) https://www.securitycouncilreport.org/atf/cf/%7B65BFCF9B-6D27-4E9C-8CD3-CF6E4FF96FF9%7D/S_2021_655_E.pdf

23 Risch Afghanistan Report 2022.pdf (senate.gov) https://www.foreign.senate.gov/imo/media/doc/Risch%20Afghanistan%20Report%202022.pdf

24 Published in *The Times*, 18 October 2021

25 Ghani Announces Afghanistan Security Plan, Promises Improvements in 6 Months (voanews.com) https://www.voanews.com/a/south-central-asia_ghani-announces-afghanistan-security-plan-promises-improvements-6-months/6209063.html#:~:text=Afghan%20President%20Ashraf%20Ghani%20speaks%20at%20the%20extraordinary,lack%20of%20strategy%20in%20the%20last%20three%20months.

26 https://www.theatlantic.com/magazine/archive/2023/10/afghanistan-withdrawal-biden-decision/675116/

27 The AP Interview: Karzai 'invited' Taliban to stop chaos | AP News https://apnews.com/article/afghanistan-police-middle-east-taliban-ashraf-ghani-438230aa716f175cc35d3506d727f8b3

28 Remarks by President Biden on Afghanistan | The White House https://www.whitehouse.gov/briefing-room/speeches-remarks/2021/08/16/remarks-by-president-biden-on-afghanistan/

29 Redacted version published in *The Times*, 18 October 2021

30 https://www.theguardian.com/world/2021/aug/23/uk-scrambles-to-complete-airlift-out-of-kabul-after-warning-about-taliban

31 G7 Leaders Statement on Afghanistan: 24 August 2021 – GOV.UK (www.gov.uk) https://www.gov.uk/government/news/g7-leaders-statement-on-afghanistan-24-august-2021

32 Afghanistan: Taliban warns there will be 'consequences' if Biden delays withdrawal of US troops | World News | Sky News https://news.sky.com/story/afghanistan-taliban-warns-there-will-be-consequences-if-biden-delays-withdrawal-of-us-troops-12388436

33 Afghanistan statistics: UK deaths, casualties, mission costs and refugees - House of Commons Library (parliament.uk). https://commonslibrary.parliament.uk/research-briefings/cbp-9298/ UK doubles aid to Afghanistan - GOV.UK (www.gov.uk). https://www.gov.uk/government/news/uk-doubles-aid-to-afghanistan Afghanistan: What has the conflict cost the US and its allies? - BBC News https://www.bbc.co.uk/news/world-47391821

34 U.S. Airstrikes in Afghanistan Could Be a Sign of What Comes Next - The New York Times (nytimes.com) https://www.nytimes.com/2021/08/03/us/politics/us-airstrikes-afghanistan.html

35 Milley, military leaders contradict Biden on support for complete Afghanistan withdrawal | PBS NewsHour https://www.pbs.org/newshour/show/milley-military-leaders-contradict-biden-on-support-for-complete-afghanistan-withdrawal